Edible and Medicinal Plants of the Rocky Mountains and Neighbouring Territories

by

Terry Willard, Ph.D.

assisted by James McCormick, M.Sc.
photography by Blaine Andrusek

Foreword by Michael Moore

Wild Rose College of Natural Healing, Ltd.
302, 1220 Kensington Rd. N.W.
Calgary, Alberta
T2N 3P5

© 1992 Wild Rose College of Natural Healing, Ltd.

400-1228 Kensington Rd. N.W.
Calgary, Alberta, CANADA
T2N 4P9
Phone: (403) 270-0936
FAX: (403) 283-0799

Photograph Credits: Blaine Andrusek (BA) and Terry Willard (TW).

Illustrations by : Naomi Lewis, Robyn Klein, James McCormick and Rob Renpenning plus digital adaptations from materials in the public domain.

ISBN # 0-9691727-2-9

Printed in Canada

First Edition

        second printing Sept. 93

        third printing Sept. 94

        fourth printing July 95

        fifth printing Oct. 96

Table of Contents

Foreword

by Michael Moore

Michael Moore is Director of the Southwest School of Botanical Medicine in Albuquerque, New Mexico and author of *Medicinal Plants of the Mountain West* and *Medicinal Plants of the Desert & Canyon West*. He is affectionately regarded as "the godfather of American herbalism".

Ah, yes, these are good times. For the last couple of decades some of us have been in our own satrapic enclaves, learning our plants, developing our methodologies, perceiving separate but interlocking approaches to the use of our native and naturalized herbs. Independently, we have arrived at similar conclusions. Most of the older books are junk. Most of the recent books just rehash the older ones and are second-hand junk. North America, and particularly my side of the border (USA), has a medical and pharmaceutical establishment that is off in a high-tech never-never land of "procedures", leaving the lesser discomforts of life in the hands of Over-The-Counter non-prescription drugs, and failing miserably, in helping the rest of us to understand WHY we get sick, HOW we get sick, WHAT gets sick, and, most of all, WHAT WE CAN DO.

Some of us have been working on the presumption that plants are our oldest medicines, they grow around us, and, with some sensible guidelines, can be used for the aforementioned "WHAT WE CAN DO". We have had to build up these guidelines and perspectives nearly from ground level. We have talked to native folks, talked to old ranchers, perused older medical texts, looked in university libraries for old anthropology papers, dusty doctoral theses, check the chem and bio abstracts, rounded up bemused friends to translate a monograph in German, made teleological leaps of presumption that usually work, and gather in, gradually, the sensible guidelines I mentioned above.

But, first things first. You need to get your hands dirty, your feet sore, your forehead scratched by branches. You need to go out in your wildlands, check the plants over different seasons, different years, find out firsthand what can be spared, what cannot. You need to get to KNOW the plants, how much you can kill (yes, kill, for, after all, aren't all animals parasitic on plants?) and what you may need to spare or replant so that they thrive after you leave.

You need to know how to strip the bark, when not to gather the berries, how many stems you can leave with the dried foliage, and where to find the best medicines. **Then**, using older guidelines and trial and error, you figure out how to prepare the plants for medicine or food. It helps to live in a place where some people still live close to the land and can tell you WHY the berries mold or WHEN (according to their grandma) is the best time to dig the roots for different uses. Terry lives in Western Canada, I live in the Southwestern United States and we both have the benefit of Elders.

Then you try the plants yourself, you give them to friends, clients, patients, customers, you build up some empirical knowledge, add it to your intellectual pursuit of useful fragments from the past and the Biosearch abstracts, mix it with that German article, and you end up with a lovely offering for those readers that have brains, common sense, love the land, have a strong back, and feel the need to take things back into their own hands.

Terry and I are a couple of herbalists that have developed our own approaches to evaluation, treatment and training, but we share the same central approach to botanical medicines. Start with the plants... then add the rest. To me, an herbalist needs to be a professional generalist, understanding field botany, knowing wildcrafting, acting as a pharmacist, knowing appropriate chemistry, knowing the body and its physiology, and understanding the idea of differential therapeutics so that herbs can be used when they are indicated, and other methods used when they are not indicated. If the herbalist is ALSO a teacher, and knows the importance of training students as generalists, then that community is fortunate indeed. Terry Willard is such an herbalist.

I have written several similar books for my part of the continent, using the same type of knowledge-gathering scenario I mentioned above. To know enough about my own plants to write as an intelligent herbalist for the intelligent generalist user, building up knowledge, piece by piece, until I feel I can morally offer my information for the use of others... well, it's just hard work. As I look through this book, I find the stuff I want to know. I find the hand of an experienced old pro, who knows the plants personally, has had dirty hands and a sore back, gotten sore eyes from searching the abstracts, understands the chemistry, took some of the plants until he threw up, drank cups of lousy coffee while listening to old folks tell their stories, put it all together, offering it up for our use. Thanks to Terry Willard, I don't have to live a couple of decades in the North Country to learn the plants the way I want to. Now I have this book.

Thanks.

Acknowledgements

This project has been in and out of many boxes and dusty old binders. The manuscript was thought about from time to time but mostly neglected over the last 19 odd years. I'm sure I won't remember many of the people that have contributed or supported me during the writing of this book. All I can do is apologise.

First I should thank Stephen Herrero, who started me on this project. Even though he probably didn't know it, his guidance helped forge the direction of my professional life. Yes ... a bear expert started me on the path toward being a herbalist. After I got my B.Sc., I decided to go out and pitch a tipi and learn the plants. I guess I'd better thank all of the wardens and forestry bureaucrats that let me live on public land back in the mid '70s!

After spending a summer alone I joined up with other tipi dwellers to "winter" up on the North Burnt Timber Creek. That was one of the best winters of my life. During that time I worked on the initial stages of the present manuscript, blending data I collected during the previous summer with further book research. A heartfelt thanks to all the people of our camp, and to the visitors that spiced up our lives. Special thanks has to go to Dick Persons for his guidance in wilderness living, Jean Persons for her great cooking, friendly smiles and, of course, her wisdom. I couldn't forget Scott Smith, for the best trout I ever ate and a friendship that helped me grow. Mary Kelly deserves a thank-you for her reading and quiet support. And to Kathryn Chapman, the Lady that came in and out of my life several times during this era, thanks for putting up with all the papers scattered over our tipi that winter.

In the following years I met up many people who influenced this book in one way or another. Thanks to Buffalo Child, Bear Walker and other Native Folks and Old Timers who gave me a tale here and story there. Some of these anecdotes were traded over afternoon tea, others came from patients over many years. And some wise souls showed me that Velveta cheese in a white bread sandwich won't kill a person. Assuming the conversation is good enough.

In more recent times, I have to thank Blaine Andrusek for blessing this book with such beautiful photographs and for co-teaching so many great herb walks, not to mention sharing some exceptional campfires. Other people who contributed to this book through their herb walks are Jo White, Morgan Wells and Michael Moore. Michael Moore deserves a special mention, of course, as contributor of the Foreword. Thanks also goes out to Robyn Klein for coming up with some eleventh-hour, much-needed line drawings and information on *Astragalus*.

As with my previous five books, this manuscript would never have made it to the printers without the help of James McCormick. He picked up the weatherbeaten typed copy from a back shelf, looked it over and bugged me continuously for half a decade to finish the writing. To back me up, he also spent many hours editing, designing and wrestling with the computers.

To all of you, my sincere thanks. It always seems to take the kind of support you have given to bring a project like this to fruition.

Species List in Botanical Order

Sphagnum moss *Sphagnum spp.*
Club Moss *Lycopodium sp.*
Horsetail *Equisetum sp.*
Juniper berries *Juniperus spp.*
Red Cedar, Western *Thuja plicata*
Fir *Abies sp.*
Larch, Tamarack *Larix americana, L. laricana, L. lyallii.*
Spruce *Picea spp.*
Lodgepole Pine *Pinus contorta*
Cattail *Typha latifolia*
Sweet Grass *Hierochloe odorata*
Onions *Allium cernuum* and related species.
Camas *Camassia quamash*
Glacier Lily *Erythronium grandiflorum*
Yellowbells *Fritillaria pudica*
Tiger Lily / Wood Lily *Lilium montanum,L. philadelphicum*
Solomon's Seal, False *Smilacina stellata and S. racemosa*
Twisted Stalk, Liverberry *Streptopus amplexifolius*
False Hellebore *Veratrum viride*
Yucca *Yucca spp.*
Venus'-slipper *Calypso bulbosa*
Lady's-slipper *Cypripedium spp.*
Balsam Poplar *Populus balsamifera*
Aspen, Quaking *Populus tremuloides*
Willows *Salix spp.*
Alders *Alnus crispa & A. incana*
Paper Birch *Betula papyrifera*
Stinging Nettle *Urtica urens & gracilis*
Sorrel, Mountain *Oxyria digyna*
Bistort *Polygonum spp.*
Dock & Sorrels *Rumex sp.*
Lamb's Quarters *Chenopodium album*
Strawberry Blite *Chenopodium capitatum*
Pigweed *Amaranthus retroflexus & spp.*
Spring Beauty *Claytonia spp.*
Bitter Root *Lewisia pygmaea*
Purslane *Portulaca oleracea*
Moss Campion *Silene acaulis*
Chickweeds *Stellaria spp., Cerastium sp.*
Lily, Yellow Pond *Nuphar variegatum*
Water Lily *Nymphaea spp.*
Baneberry *Actaea rubra*
Crocus, Prairie *Anemone patens*
Columbine *Aquilegia flavescens*
Marsh Marigold *Caltha leptosepala, C. palustris.*
Clematis *Clematis verticillaris*
Larkspurs *Delphinium bicolor, D. glaucum & related species*
Meadow Rue *Thalictrum sp.*
Barberry, Oregon Grape *Berberis repens*
Shepherd's Purse *Capsella bursa-pastoris*
Sundew *Drosera rotundifolia*
Stonecrop *Sedum spp.*
Alum root *Heuchera spp.*
Currant, Gooseberry *Ribes spp.*
Saskatoon, June-berry, Serviceberries *Amelanchier alnifolia*
Hawthorn *Crataegus spp.*
Strawberry *Fragaria glauca*
Ocean Spray *Holodiscus discolor*
Silverweed *Potentilla anserina* and related species
Cinquefoil, Shrubby *Potentilla fruticosa*
Chokecherry, Pin Cherry *Prunus pensylvanica & virginiana*
Wild Rose *Rosa acicularis*

Raspberry and related species *Rubus spp.*
Mountain Ash *Sorbus aucuparia*
Hardhack *Spiraea douglassii*
Meadowsweet, White *Spiraea lucida*
Licorice *Glycyrrhiza lepidota*
Milk Vetch *Astragalus americanus*
Sweet vetch / Bear Root *Hedysarum boreale var. mackenzie*
Alfalfa *Medicago sativa*
Red Clover *Trifolium spp.*
Cranesbill Geranium, Sticky Purple Geranium *Geranium viscosissimum*
Flax *Linum sp.*
Crowberry *Empetrum nigrum*
Sumac, Smooth *Rhus glabra*
Snow Brush, Red Root *Ceanothus velutinus*
Buckthorn *Rhamnus alnifolia*
Cascara Sagrada *Rhamnus purshiana*
Mallow, Common *Malva neglecta & related spp.*
Pansy - Violet *Viola tricolor & V. adunca*
Prickly Pear cactus & Pin Cushion cactus *Mamillaria & Opuntia spp.*
Green Ash *Fraxinus pensylvanica*
Buffalo Berry *Shepherdia canadensis and argentea*
Fireweed *Epilobium angustifolium*
Evening Primrose *Oenothera spp.*
Sarsaparilla, Wild *Aralia nudicaulis*
Devil's Club *Oplopanax horridum (a.k.a. Echinopanax horridum)*
Cow Parsnip *Heracleum lanatum*
Lovage, Canby's, Osha *Ligusticum canbyi, L. porteri, L. scorticum*
Biscuit Root *Lomatium dissectum (Tritenatum)* (a.k.a. Leptotaenia multiflora)
Sweet Cicely, Sweet Root *Osmorhiza occidentalis*
Yampa, Squaw Root *Perideridia gairdneri*
Bunchberry *Cornus canadensis*
Pacific Dogwood *Cornus nuttali*
Red Osier Dogwood *Cornus stolonifera*
Wintergreen, Bracted *Pyrola sp.*
Arbutus *Arbutus menziesii*
Bearberry *Arctostaphylos uva-ursi*
Salal *Gaultheria shallon*
Labrador Tea *Ledum groenlandicum*
Heaths, Blueberry, Bilberry, Huckleberry, Cranberry, *Vaccinium spp.*
Shooting Star *Dodecatheon spp.*
Indian hemp, Spreading dogbane, Canadian hemp *Apocynum androsaemifolium, A. cannabinum*
Buckbean *Menyanthes trifoliata*
Periwinkle *Vinca minor*
Milkweed *Asclepias spp.*
Wild Mint *Mentha arvensis*
Horsemint *Monarda fistulosa*
Self Heal, Woundwort (Common), Heal All *Prunella vulgaris*
Skullcap *Scutellaria galericulata*
Indian Paintbrush *Castilleja spp.*
Lousewort *Pedicularis lanata, P. artica, P. canadensis*
Mullein *Verbascum blattaria, V. thapsus*
Plantain, Common *Plantago major & related spp.*
Bedstraw, Northern *Galium boreale*
Cleaver, *Galium aparine*
Honeysuckle, Bracted *Lonicera involucrata*
Elderberry, Black *Sambucus melanocarpa*
Snowberry *Symphoricarpos albus*
Cranberry, High Bush *Viburnum edule, opulus & trilobum & spp.*
Valerian *Valeriana septentrionalis (and related species)*
Bluebell, Harebell *Campanula rotundifolia*
Yarrow *Achillea millefolium*
Pearly Everlasting *Anaphalis margaritacea*
Burdock *Arctium minus & spp.*
Arnica *Arnica spp.*
Wormwood *Artemisia spp.*
Balsam Root *Balsamorhiza sagittata*

Ox-eye daisy *Chrysanthemum leucanthemum*
Chicory *Cichorium intybus*
Thistle *Cirsium spp.*
Echinacea, Cone Flowers *Echinacea spp.*
Fleabane *Erigeron sp. (25 species)*
Gaillardia, Brown Eyed Susan *Gaillardia aristata*
Gumweed *Grindelia integrifolia, G. squarrosa*
Sunflower, *Helianthus spp.*
Rush Skeleton Weed *Lygodesmia juncea*
Pineapple Weed, False Chamomile *Matricaria matricaioides*
Coltsfoot *Petasites spp. (a.k.a. Tussilago spp.)*
Prairie Cone Flower *Ratibida columnifera*
Goldenrod *Solidago spp.*
Ragwort & Groundsel *Senecio vulgaris* and related species
Dandelion *Taraxacum officinale*
Salsify *Tragopogon porrifolius*

Other Useful Plants

Arrowhead, *Sagittaria latifolia*
Broom Rape *Orobanche fasciculata*
Monkey Flower *Mimulus guttatus*
Orach *Atriplex sp.*
Pipsissewa *Chimaphila umbellata*
Speedwell *Veronica spp.*
Rock Rose *Oenothera caespitosa*
Bear Grass *Xerophyllum tenax*
Puccoon *Lithospermum sp.*
Hazelnut *Corylus sp.*

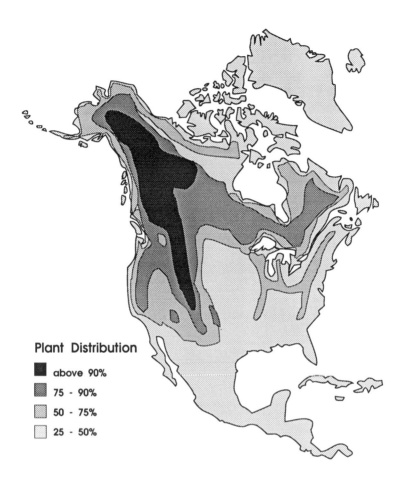

Plant Distribution

- ■ above 90%
- ▦ 75 - 90%
- ▨ 50 - 75%
- ☐ 25 - 50%

At least a quarter of the plants mentioned in this book can be found through-out North America. The map above shows where you are most likely to find the species in *Edible and Medicinal Plants of the Rocky Mountains*. Plant distri-bution in local environments can range from rare to abundant, depending on microclimatic conditions. Obviously, distribution in arctic, desert and moun-tain regions is strongly affected by the location of ice and rock.

Introduction

Close to twenty years ago, this book was born. In 1973, I was going to university and taking a special studies course under the direction of Dr. Steve Herrero, a world-renowned expert on bears. My topic for study was the useful plants of Alberta. Before long, I realized the information I wanted was scattered all over the place. It would take considerable effort to pull it together. Since I was gathering the information for my own use, Steve suggested I write it down and turn it into a book to share with other interested people. Here we are, nineteen years later. Honest, Steve. I didn't think it would take this long!

The original manuscript was typed, stored, re-typed, edited, lost and variously delayed. Publishers were found and unfound. Computer systems gobbled the text and just as quickly spat out more versions. As the years passed, my interest switched from the academic to the practical. My experience as a herbalist recast virtually all the knowledge I uncovered. My research expanded to include the most useful plants from Alaska to California and east into the Great Plains. The major emphasis of the manuscript however continued to be the mountain and prairie plants in the areas where I often travel.

This book, more than anything else, is a treasure trove of useful information for my own use. As a practising herbalist, my appreciation for the "tools of the trade" was only enhanced when I found special plants growing in my own "backyard". The last decade has seen tremendous changes in the public attitude towards herbology (also known as herbalism). Working in two clinics (one in Calgary, one in Vancouver), I've also noticed a shift in perspective from the national government, herbal manufacturers, the pharmaceutical industry and even medical doctors.

With pressure on our health care system from all sides, preventive natural health methods start to make much more sense. Growing respect for the culture of Native Americans, has placed herbalism in a new light. The skills of Asian practitioners from India and the Orient have also influenced public opinion. The ecological perspective has gone from "fringe" philosophy to practical lifestyle for thousands of people. I hope this book can make a small contribution to the broader changes in attitude in our society. Knowing more about these plants will increase their value in our eyes and encourage efforts to preserve the planet they grow on.

The plant uses recorded in the following pages are drawn from historical records and should not be applied in lieu of medical or professional advice. We have much to learn about medicine from the indigenous peoples and the herbalists. I have tried to present these records in a unbiased fashion.

I have drawn heavily from ethnobotanical information for most of the Amerindian plants uses though a lot of detail was transmitted to me personally by the native peoples of Alberta and British Columbia. Please note that I've used the Canadian term – Blackfoot – for the Amerindian confederacy which straddles both sides of the Canada-U.S. border, instead of the name "Blackfeet" by which they are known on the American side of the border. Pronunciation of the Latin names can be confirmed by consulting the phonetic guide in any English dictionary.

Even though the major focus of the book is on the Northern Rocky Mountains, a large number of species are found along the whole mountain chain. Roughly 20% of the plants mentioned in this book are found throughout North America, even in the vacant lots of our biggest cities. There are 154 separate plant entries in this book (some containing multiple species). All can be found within easy driving distance from my home in the foothills outside of Calgary, Alberta. The map which precedes this Introduction clearly shows the breadth of distribution of the plants in this book. Even so, I did not attempt to cover **all** the edible and medicinal plants of the region. Priority was given to those most often encountered, those most important as medicines, plus a few rare, but important, species. I have included many "weeds", common non-native plants and some "escapees" from household gardens. As a clinical herbalist, I know many species are missing but I wanted keep the field guide within manageable size.

People who own textbooks published by the Wild Rose College of Natural Healing will notice some information repeated in this book. Few people need the details about plants which are important to the herbalist but the basic facts make this field guide more useful and more interesting.

I hope this book is your companion in many parts of the Rocky Mountains, mountains which are surely amongst the most beautiful on Earth. If your reading stirs your desire to know more about the world we live in and to keep it a healthy place for plants and humans, then my fondest wishes will have come true.

I. Edible Plants

Eating wild plants may strike some people as a risky business at best. Pause for a moment, though, and consider the fact that all of our cultivated plants were originally wild. A myriad of changes and advances separate the "cultivar" from its wild relative. Food yield has been increased, taste improved and texture enhanced in many plants.

But compare the taste of wild strawberries to domestic strawberries. The cultivated varieties are large, appealing to the eye, and are designed to "ship better", but what they have gained in these respects, they have certainly lost in flavour.

Wild plants have an added benefit. They are closely adapted to the place where you, and they, live. They are adapted to the same sunny summers and cold winters which we humans experience. Largely free from the dangerous chemicals used in growing commercial plants, adding these local plants to your diet can be very beneficial to your health. Our ancestors and the indigenous people of this fine land used their diet as a very practical part of their everyday medicine. As an example, if your stomach was a "little off", more bitter food (herbs) was added to the diet for a while.

Local wild plants can be freshly picked, often only minutes before eating. The deterioration rate of green leafy vegetables is very rapid. When vegetables are obtained from the local market they have already lost a sizeable proportion of vitamin and food value. Some plants lose as much as one third of their food value in the first hour after picking.

We are using sound economic sense when we don't overlook this part of the ecological food chain. Instead of weeding out and burning chickweed, lamb's quarters, pigweed and dandelions, we should use these foods to enhance our meals or for medicinal benefit. Not only are they enjoyable and healthy to eat but we avoid wasting our natural resources.

Beyond the economics, there is great adventure and sport in trying to forage one's own wild food and to create a delicious meal. Eating wild plants is fun, healthy, economical and the result is delicious. For perhaps a few minutes, we can get a real sense of where we fit into the world around us.

Food Preparation

When collecting wild plants for any purpose, we should always keep in mind the ecological implications. Picking a few leaves off a plant for a salad doesn't hurt the plant much. Digging up the root kills the plant. Taking all the seeds stops the propagation of that plant. Stripping bark off a branch destroys that branch. In some delicate ecological areas (such as alpine meadows) it can take many years for some plants to become established. It is unfortunate to see such plants destroyed in ten minutes by hungry (but not desperate) visitors to the area.

When picking plants, choose to collect where the overall population of plants won't be affected greatly (unless in dire emergencies). Some plants are quite rare. Others are too beautiful to pick unless urgent need arises. Finally, you should be aware that many wild plants are protected in certain areas by laws restricting or prohibiting picking. In general, fruits and seeds may legally be taken.

Tools

Collecting roots with fingers and a jack knife can get quite frustrating if rocky soil is encountered. The Indians used to make digging sticks to help dig roots. To make a traditional digging stick, select a hardwood such as red osier dogwood, saskatoon, or chokecherry. Cut a stave about 3 feet long and an inch in diameter. This stave is then skinned of the bark, hardened in a fire, and scraped into a chisel shape by rubbing on a rock.

To harden the stave it takes only 5-6 scorchings in a fire. Several more scorchings are needed to completely drive the sap out. Scorching doesn't mean charring! A bit of practice is necessary to find the balance.

When using a digging stick, it is much easier to make the root come to you rather than digging down to the root. Push the stick down alongside the plant until it is slightly below the root. The root is then flipped to the surface by prying. This process moves a lot of dirt as well. A knife, ax, even a shovel, will work.

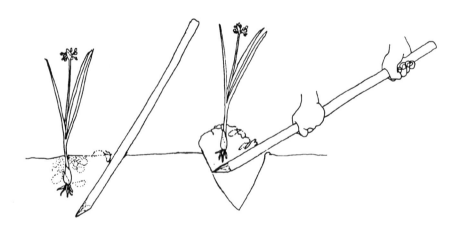

Roots

Roots, once dug up, can be processed many ways. One of the principal Indian uses was for flour. The root is dried in a well-ventilated place on a warm day. It is then ground into a coarse flour. Grinding is easy. Place the root on a flat rock, sometimes called a metate (pronounced may-taught-ay), then grind the vegetable material with a second rock.

Roots can also be roasted, baked or boiled. If the root is bitter, boiling is a good way to remove the bitterness. Boil the root in several changes of water and/or wring and mash the root through a bag. These processes take away much of the root's nutrient value, however, and should only be undertaken when necessary.

The most effective way to cook roots (and many other foods), is to use a steam pit. To make a steam pit, first line a pit with flat, dry stones and build a fire in it. After an hour or so scrape away the coals and line the pit with wet grass. Place the food on the wet grass and quickly cover with more with wet grass. Add more water and put a flat stone, tarp, hide or any other cover over the grass. The pit is then completely sealed with dirt and left for several hours. The end result is a very nutritious and flavourful meal.

Greens

The stems and leaves of wild plants can be used in the same way as domestic greens. The leaves and stems are good chopped up into salads or cooked into stews. If the leaves are bitter they can be leached in several changes of water. Another more effective way is to blanch the leaves. Simply reduce the amount of light the leaves receive while growing by covering them with a bag, sand or straw.

Steaming greens is also a good cooking method. Put the greens in a basket or steamer and steam cook them. Stir frying, wok style, is a delicious way to eat vegetables.

Seeds

To make seeds palatable, one first has to remove the chaff. Beat the seeds and toss them in the air to let the wind blow away the lighter chaff. Work over a blanket to prevent losing seeds. Although this technique may seem primitive, one can remove the chaff from a considerable amount of seed in a short time.

Seeds are usually tastier if ground into flour or cracked and made into a meal (like mush). It is sometimes easier to grind the seeds if a little water is added first. It soaks in and softens the seeds, which can then be ground to a dry paste.

Berries

Berries bring an immediate processing method to mind. The hand simply passes the berries from plant to mouth. And pies, jams and jellies seem like a perfectly natural resting place for good berries. Berries are also good dried. They store well when made into dried cakes. The berries are lightly cooked and then pressed into cakes and dried in the shade. These cakes will keep a long time and can be broken up into stews and pudding. See the pages on saskatoons for a more detailed description of how the Indians dried berries.

Bark

Young strips of bark can be harvested with care and eaten like greens. Bark should be eaten fresh and can be kept that way for a while by soaking in water. Bark can also be dried and ground into flour.

Young Shoots

Many young shoots can be eaten. For example, raspberry canes, when peeled, are very delicious.

Storage

Plants can be dried for future use. Roots should be mashed, formed into cakes, and dried in the shade. Greens, like lettuce, can be dried in the shade on a hot day by keeping each piece well ventilated. Many dried leaves are tasty when added to soup and stews, much as people commonly add parsley and bay leaves.

Seeds can be stored in their natural state if in a dry environment or they can be lightly parched. Putting the seeds in a frying pan and lightly heating them is the standard parching technique. Take care to avoid burning them. Fruits and berries can be also dried in the sun or shade.

Experiment with drying plants the way the squirrels do it. Simply put the item on the branches of an evergreen conifer about 3 - 5 feet off the ground. This keeps them in the shade but well ventilated. Of course the squirrels sometimes claim the right to steal the food (thinking it theirs). But in return, if you are hungry some day, you might find their stored winter food in the same manner.

Storage Pits

Dried plants can be safely stored in a pit for future use. Make a pit approximately 2 feet deep and line it with dry grass. It is best to make the pit in a cave, or in a shaded, dry place. Place the food in the pit and cover it with wormwood sage (*Artemisia spp.*) and juniper boughs. Cover with about 6 inches of dry dirt. This should safely preserve the food for several years with little fear of being bothered by rodents or insects if the pit keeps dry. Other more modern ways of storing wild plants include freezing, canning, pickling and storage in a root cellar.

II. Herbology

North American Indian Medicine

Most of the books dealing with American Indian medicine emphasize its shamanistic aspect. A shaman is a medicine man, witch doctor or healer. While rituals played an important part in Indian curing procedure, there was also extensive use of what has been called rational therapy. In this rational therapy, indigenous botanical drugs played an extraordinary part.

At the time Europeans discovered North America, Indian herbal medicine was probably at par with European herbology, with the exception of birth control. The Indians used several methods of birth control that were very effective. Some of these botanicals have guided present medical research in the area.

Indian treatment of external injuries, where the origin of the ailment was perfectly obvious, was usually rational and effective. In cases of persistent internal diseases, where the cause was not obvious, the usual Indian custom was to attribute the disease to supernatural agents.

If ordinary medicine did not quickly bring relief, they resorted to shamanistic methods, such as incantations, charms, prayers, dances, shaking of rattles, and beating of drums. The effect of this would have a strong psychological and maybe even psychic effect on the patient. In Indian terms, it would raise the energy of Good Medicine in the area so bad spirits could not live there.

Most of these internal diseases were attributed to animals or spirit intrusion. If a hunter didn't treat an animal body properly after killing it, or didn't observe proper taboos, the spirit of this animal would enter his body.

It is often suggested that Indian medicine is pure superstition. Dr. R. Bergman, a psychiatric doctor who has been assigned to oversee a Medicine Man School funded by the National Institute of Mental Health, a United States federal agency, has changed his opinion on superstition. He says, "*I usually answer that question by pointing out the proper definition of the word superstition is — my knowledge, your belief, his superstition. Superstition is a word which conveys a lot of things without conveying a whole lot of information.*"

It should be emphasized that for a Indian medicine man to reach the higher levels of the art, the education would take many years and extend for a lifetime. It is reasonable to say that the level of dedication required is equivalent to undertaking a modern Ph.D. or an M.D. Even though the Amerindian system is quite different, it is logically consistent. By that we mean that it begins with some primary assumptions about the way the world works and then expands upon those first principles in a logical manner. In the case of North American Indian medicine, it is an oral tradition, passed from generation to generation.

The most important elements of medicine power are:

1. Vision Quest, usually undertaken at puberty and sometimes repeated later in life. A vision quest involved self-denial, with no food, water or shelter, continuing til the person had what they considered a suitable vision.

2. A reliance on Vision, was also a very important. To pursue the path of life directed by one's personal visions and dreams.

3. A personal song, allowed one to attune oneself to the primal sound of the cosmic vibration of the Great Spirit.

4. Partnership with the spirit world. It was sometimes necessary to make contact with the Grandfathers and Grandmothers who have changed planes of existence.

5. Non-linear time sense, was necessary in order to deal with the spirit world.

6. Omnipresence, to know that the Great Spirit may be found every-where and in everything.

7. Passion for the Earth Mother, and an awareness of one's place in the web of life, and one's responsibility toward all plants and animals.

8. A total commitment to one's belief, that permeates every aspect of one's life to enable one to truly walk in balance.

Even though the dogma varied from tribe to tribe and Nation to Nation, the personal way was most important. The tribe's rituals were always considered secondary to the guidance a medicine person received from their personal vision. In the Navajo school for medicine men, at Rough Rock, Arizona, after 3-4 years of full time study, a medicine person only learns two or three ceremonies. Traditionally, medicine men knew many ceremonies. The important ceremonies take five to nine nights to perform, with a difficulty and elaborate-ness approaching that of open heart surgery.

These ceremonies often demand that the entire extended family be present. The attendance of the patients most distant social connections are also de-sired. Many of these people are employed in important roles during the cer-emony. The singer medicine-man is required to do a letter-perfect performance of up to one hundred hours of ritual chanting. The feat could be compared to a perfect recitation of the New Testament from memory. In addition, the medi-cine man has to produce many sand drawings, recite myths and manage a very large group of people.

It must be remembered that a Indian medicine man was as much a mental/spiritual councillor as they were a person that healed wounds. The medicine man tradition is not dead today. In fact, a revival is in process. The revival involves as many non-natives as it does natives. Some of the new Medicine Tradition is evolving into slightly different forms with the addition of traditional elements from around the world.

The American Indian uses the term *medicine* to embrace much more than the cure of disease and the healing of injuries. Medicine, in the Indian sense, connected most things that were good.

Besides the botanicals that might or might not be used in a healing, there are three major components: the medicine pipe, the sweat lodge and a person's medicine bundle. To these were added masks, rattles and other implements.

The version of Native American medicine which I am outlining here is part of prairie and foothill Indian tradition as practiced in the region covered by this book. Please note that other areas of North America have completely different systems of medicine. There was no one homogenous system of "medical belief".

The Pipe

The medicine pipe was used to open ceremonies, to initiate deal-making, for healing or to start the healing process itself. First the pipe was cleansed in ritualistic smoke. The botanicals used for this were usually one of three sacred plants: sweetgrass, artemisia sage, or juniper. Depending on the circumstances one of these would be chosen, burned as an incense, with the smoke being used to wash the pipe. The pipe would then be filled with a smoking mixture.

The first smoke would be offered to the heavens, the next to the spirits of the four directions. Prayers accompany all of this ceremony in asking for aid of the spirits in the healing process. The pipe was always passed onto the next person (usually part of a circle) in a sunwise (clockise) direction. When passing the pipe, it would be rotated in a small sunwise circle, with the stem of the pipe offered to the next person.

The pipes were made of carved stone (often red stone - hematite) with pipe stems decorated with a person's own power symbols.

Sweat lodge

The sweat lodge is a small domed structure made out of bent willow branches, covered with hides, tarps or blankets. Inside the structure, the floor is usually covered with juniper and/or sage with a pit in the center. Sweat lodge ceremonies were used to heal physical ailments, to start vision quests, and as an important preparation for most major ceremonies. Ceremonies differ from location to location, with sweat lodge leaders in control of the details.

The dome is usually dark. After the person or group enters, hot rocks are passed in to be placed in the pit. These stones are heated up in a big fire to the east of the sweat lodge. Before the sweat sessions are started, there is a ceremony of bringing in single rocks. The first rock is brought in with the first steam being sent to the heavens, the next four rocks are again for the spirits of the four directions, thus starting the sweat. The sweat is a series of four sessions. For each session, a group of rocks are brought in, the door is closed, and water is poured on the hot rocks.

As the steam accumulates, the temperature inside the sweat lodge becomes very hot. With each session the heat gets even more intense. An eagle feather fan is often used to increase the intensity of the heat. Songs and chants are often sung in the sweat lodge. These can be group songs, but are most often individual songs for each person. As the heat increases, the person usually escapes into their song more. By the third or fourth session, if you don't escape into your song (almost escaping your body) it is felt you will not make it to the end of the session due to the extreme heat. To be able to escape into one's song was in itself considered good medicine.

Often diaphoretic teas such as yarrow or geranium are drunk to stimulate sweating before starting the sweats. Inside the lodge, herbs such as wormwood sage are often rubbed on the body, stimulating sweat and detoxifying the body.

It is easy to see that the sweat lodge can have medicinal qualities and the modern tradition of saunas, steamrooms and hot tubs is a reflection of this ancient ritual. The tradition of sweating (in saunas) was very common to the European healing tradition at the time of the European discovery of North America and is still used heavily in the Scandinavian countries and in naturopathic medicine. The medicinal quality of the herbs used could also increase the healing potential. The greatest healing quality that the Indians attributed to the sweat lodge was to cleanse out the spirit, forcing evil spirits to leave the body. Speaking from personal experience, a person certainly does feel more enlivened, fresher and cleansed after a sweat lodge ceremony.

The Medicine Bundle

One of the most dramatic parts of the training of a Native American healer was the experiential aspect. A Medicine Person takes their healing energies from the power of a totem or ally. If you wanted to obtain a personal totem or ally for your medicine bundle, you have to experience the power of the animal, (plant or mineral) to obtain a wisdom or power over and through it, for use in healing energy.

Lets say you want to obtain the very powerful totem of the eagle. This would mean, after four days of fasting and purification sweats, you would go up into the hills and dig a pit. Over this pit you would put some branches, tethering a hare upon them. With a eagle bone whistle and chanting, you would call an eagle to you. This could take many hours or days. When the eagle swoops down to pick up the hare, you would have to reach up and grab its razor sharp talons, pull it down into the pit and wring its neck to kill it. Great speed must be used in order to avoid injury. To do this would take extreme concentration and an oneness with the eagle spirit. The eagle would be hypnotized by you. Thus you obtain one of many articles in your medicine bundle. As can be imagined, many do not make it through the educational system of a medicine man. They quit or die.

After obtaining an article or the medicine bundle, a medicine person could call on the spirit to aid in the healing process, sometimes to conquer the evil spirit that was causing the problem.

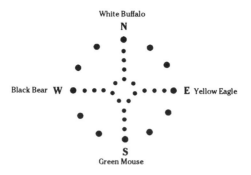

The Medicine Wheel

In some Indian traditions, the information of the medicine ways was transferred in an oral tradition with the aid of a group of stones placed in a circle and called the Medicine Wheel. Each direction (east, north, west and south) represented an animal, colour and attribute.

The medicine wheel represents the philosophy behind the medicine way. It represents our planet, how we perceive ourselves and how others perceive us. It indicates how we can share in our group perception and thus heal each other.

Each person may perceive the world differently; with the industriousness of a mouse, the sneakiness of a weasel, the cunning of a fox, or the wisdom of an owl. By sharing in this council, the group would be stronger and healthier. This represents the tribe, the nation, or even one's individual person (body, soul and spirit). In this tradition, it is felt that the universe is a mirror of the person and each person is a mirror to every other person.

In the medicine circle the light comes in from the illumination of the east, which represents the far-sightedness of the yellow eagle. The south represents the innocence and industriousness of the green mouse. The introspection of the great black bear takes up the position of the west. The north is left to the wisdom of the white buffalo. These are but four perceptions with many varying perceptions in between. Each perception has subperceptions inside itself. The white buffalo of wisdom also needs to understand the yellow farsightness of wisdom, the green innocence of wisdom as well as the black introspection of wisdom.

Native American Medicine in Perspective

The evolution of the medicine person can be represented by the stages of the Medicine Wheel they have conquered. People often wear the name representing their personal energies (e.g., Green Buffalochild), with great people becoming chiefs or the nation's powerful medicine men — as stubborn as Sitting Bull.

An example of a particular type of Indian medicine way can be found in H. Storm's *Seven Arrows*.[1] As can be seen, the uses of the word medicine varied. One meaning involved power — this dance has "great medicine" — meaning great power. It might be the Bull Dance, to help in a buffalo hunt, or an Eagle Dance, to help them see far and to gain illumination.

It should be noted at this point that not all medicine men were or are sincere — just as is the case in modern Western society. They were not always above trickery in making their patients think that they were released from these animal/spirit intrusions. This approach might have positive psychological effects but it should also be remembered that a shaman usually demanded payment in advance, and that the trickery was not always in the patient's interest.

When a medicine man decided that an evil spirit had entered the body of a patient, he would try to scare it out. Through the shaking of rattles, by dancing, by wearing masks, and by chanting for hours or even days, the shaman was eventually sure that the evil spirit had left the body. Another method was to suck the spirit out. This was done by sucking on a hollow stick or bone inserted into the wound or into an incision made by the medicine man. This usually resulted in the recovery of some foreign object.

Sucking or extraction obviously helped in some cases, (e.g. if the person had a sliver) but in other cases the medicine man was not above sleight-of-hand tricks. For example, a medicine man might suck an eagle claw from a sick man — this was the spirit inside the patient — even though the patient had not been anywhere near an eagle before his sickness.

There were different types of medicine men. For example, in the Ojibwa tribes there were four ranks:

1. **Priest and highest rank**, to which membership was gained by initiations.

2. **Dawning Men** : practitioners of medicinal magic, hunting medicine and love powers.

3. **Seers and prophets**, revealers of hidden truths, possessors of the gift of clairvoyance.

4. **Herbalists**, who knew about mysterious properties of a variety of plants, herbs, roots and berries. The powers were revealed upon the payment of a fee.

The herbalists were often women. It was not unusual for a person to be in more than one rank. Often those of the priest rank also were herbalists. In some tribes, one person would have the medicine for some ailments while another person had the medicine for others. The specific information was passed on to a new generation after a payment was given to the previous owner of the knowledge. The knowledge of the natural world could offer a Native American both social and financial benefits.

There are four basic components of cure set up in the Indian tradition. These four components are similar to allopathic (orthodox, Western medicine) traditions, as well as most healing traditions throughout the cultures of the world. They include:

1. **The naming process:** By giving a name or cause to the ailment the patient is often put at ease. One of the most frightening things in human experience is the Unknown. Naming lets the patient know that the practitioner has come across their situation before and recognizes it. Of course the names in Native American lore are not those of allopaths (e.g. cancer of the prostate,) it is more like "a spirit of the bear is biting your behind".

2. **The personal characteristics of the healer:** The charisma of the healer/doctor is very important. The patient has to feel that the practitioner is caring, convincing and genuine.

3. **The patient's expectations:** It is common practice for doctor/healers all over the world to use much the same method of raising their patient's expectations. Physical stimulus like rattles, amulets, stethoscopes and diplomas are common ways to increase patient expectation. It can be commonly observed that the farther a patient has to travel to see a healer, the greater the chances of cure.

4. **The doctor/healer's training:** All sincere healers go through a training period that takes several years of rigorous work. The insincere usually drop out in the process.

We tend to think of things done in a medical center as scientific whereas something done in a tipi is magical. But the methodology seems to be very similar. Many of the herbs that the Indians use in their healing processes have been shown to have active pharmaceutical actions, with biochemical rationale. The old Indian who had a backache never looked at bearberry leaves and said,

"That plant has arbutin in it. That arbutin will undergo hydrolysis in my body and change to hydroquinone beta-glycoside in my kidneys to act as a local antibiotic, thus relieving the inflammation in my kidney, to stop the pain in my back." He just knew that a certain type of pain in the back could be overcome by the strong spirit in bearberry (*Arctostaphylos uva-ursi*).

The Indian medical tradition was mostly oral, with several societies within the tribe responsible for different remedies. This helped build up a mystique about the healer, much as medical terminology does today. Plants transferred in an oral tradition had many stories attached to them. The knowledge of the herbs came from the ancestors. This usually meant powerful medicine people had a specific plant(s) as their ally or totem. By fully understanding the spirit of the plant they could tell how it could heal the body. This information, once learned and tested, was passed on to future generations. This is not very different from herbalists in Europe up to the present day. Even though a scientific rationale has been assigned to many of these plants, and synthetic and more economical drugs have been created as copies of the botanical, much of the original information for botanical use comes from folklore.

Though only one of several advanced herbologies on the planet, Native American medicine has special significance for all North Americans. This tradition can potentially re-establish the "roots" of Western herbalism on the continent. It's heartening to see this medical tradition undergoing a renaissance.

European Herbal Philosophy

Plant medicines have a very long history in Europe. Many clinics in Europe still use ancient techniques of healing. The spas and "bads" of Europe are often located in spots where the Romans first took a healthful dip.

In turn, the early European settlers also brought much of this herbal tradition to North America. They quickly adapted their medicine and augmented it with information gained from the Native American peoples.

The rationale for using botanicals in medicine stems from the philosophy of vital energy. This philosophy believes that the body is surrounded by a vital force, an intelligent energy that endeavours to maintain the function of the human body. Any obstruction of this vital force would predictably cause poor health. Botanicals, having their own vital energy, would be employed to assist the body in removing the obstruction.

To systematically describe the vital energies of botanicals, herbalists constructed a system of major attributes. Plants were often put in herbal families according to these attributes. Most herbs would also have many minor or secondary attributes. It was common to find a botanical described as a stimulant, diaphoretic, relaxant and tonic. The stimulant effect is the major attribute while the others are secondary. The various categories of herbs are reviewed in more detail in the Appendices.

Alternative Perspectives in Medical Theory

Healing methods around the world take many approaches. The Western medical philosophy we are most familiar with (ie., modern M.D.'s and allopathy) has generally taken a mechanical-scientific view towards health. If you have a broken arm, it can be splinted. Missing a chemical in a biochemical pathway? A pharmaceutical can replace it or provide a suitable substitute. If a bacteria or virus is present in your body, a powerful biochemical (antibiotic) can often be found to destroy it or subdue it. The success of Western medical professionals speaks for itself. By focusing on the physical level of health, modern Western medicine has provided everything from artificial hearts to trauma care.

Around the world, the history of medicine has many examples of sophisticated, ancient and alternative means of organizing medical care. These systems start with theories of life energy and relate it to the physical forms of human beings and diseases they have. Medicine (in European herbology, American Indian medicine, East Indian medicine and Chinese medicine) is seen as conscious manipulation of energy for healing the human body.

The energy in the human body is known by many names – the life force, chi (qi), ki, prana and also 'vital energy'. Vital energy is the term used in the Western tradition. The purpose of non-allopathic medicine to keep this energy flowing correctly through the body. If the flow is improper, it needs to be returned to its natural path. The herbalist feels that disease is caused by stagnant or incorrectly directed energy related to some energy blockage. The herbalist's role is not so much to attack a disease but to maintain the natural flow of vital energy. The energy itself will rid the body of disease. Herbal substances not only affect a person on a biochemical level, they also function on a vital energy level. In the vitalist medical tradition, herbs are seen as conveyors of life energy. That energy will, in turn, support human life energy.

I have dealt with this subject in much more detail in *Helping Yourself With Natural Remedies*, *The Textbook of Modern Herbology* and the *Textbook of Advanced Herbology*.

III. Collecting and Drying Medicinal Herbs

There are no hard and fast rules for collecting herbs. For every rule, there are exceptions. Consider the following suggestions as general guidelines. Implement them with an open mind and don't be afraid to learn from your own experience.

The guidelines for edible plants are clear – pick what you'd want to eat. If the plant is a garnish or nutrient, it can be dried and stored. If the plant is meant for salads, or meant to be eaten raw, then pick in moist or cool conditions if possible.

When collecting medicinal herbs, it is seldom necessary to pick the entire plant since the active principles are usually concentrated in specific plant parts. Medicinal qualities of a particular part will also vary with the season. Keep the variations in mind when gathering medicinal herbs. As a general rule, wild varieties are more potent than cultivated medicinal herbs. Nonetheless, potency will vary from season to season and from place to place.

When circumstances render it impractical or impossible to choose the ideal plant materials, use other plant parts (unless they are specified as dangerous) or use out-of-season and cultivated herbs.

Some herbs are better fresh, others dried. Herbalists and herbal gatherers must adapt to specific conditions. Those conditions will determine the wisest or most practical choice. Ecological consciousness is important when picking wild herbs. Do not pick an entire herb population from one area. Pick here and there. Do not pull the entire plant unless the roots are required. Remember also that in much of the country there are laws protecting some wildflowers and other plants (e.g. Lady's-slipper orchid).

General Gathering Rules

The medicinal qualities of herbs are affected by the weather, the time, the place, and the method of picking.

Weather

It is best to collect medicinal herbs in dry weather. Medicinal constituents are usually diminished by rain (and affected by soaking the plant in water). Wet herbs are likely to spoil more quickly. In dry periods, herbs contain more oily and resinous particles (which encourages better storage).

Time of Day

The best time of the day to collect herbs is in the early morning, after the dew has evaporated, or in the evening, before the dew begins to form. When the sun is high and hot, the leaves tend to droop, releasing some of their medicinal qualities into the atmosphere.

Locality

It is best to collect wild herbs from high spots, dry soil and where the air is fresh and clean. Avoid picking herbs in stagnant water or downhill from human occupation (where groundwater contamination is possible). Picking herbs by a road is not a good idea. Some people feel that you should pick herbs an extra 10 feet (3 m) away from the road for every car that travels that road per hour – up to 70 - 80 feet (20 - 24m), beyond which there shouldn't be a problem. You might also want to consider oil wells, refineries or other industrial complexes as contaminating sources. Wind direction is also a consideration.

Appearance

The size and shape of plant materials can be important to the herbalist but often in a way that is opposite to what one might think. The condition in which the herb grew will be reflected in the strength of the herb. Often an old, but small, root is valued more highly than a large root. A tough struggle during life is thought to produce a stronger herb. The herb is said to have a strong "personality". The concentration of particular chemicals can vary dramatically between patches of particular plants. Experience will increase your ability to detect herbal value. In the field, taste, texture and appearance are the gatherer's analytical categories.

Roots

Annuals - The roots of annuals are seldom collected. When they are, the root should be collected shortly before the flowering period because the medicinal principles will tend to gravitate toward the sexual parts as they develop. The plant will soon deteriorate after the seeds are produced, and then the roots die.

Biennials - These roots are best harvested in the autumn of the first year or in the spring of the second. The roots are storage organs and accumulate plant constituents during the summer months. In the second year, most of the root's contents has migrated into the above-ground parts. The root now becomes woody, hollow and more or less worthless as a herbal medicine.

Perennial - The roots and rhizomes are picked simultaneously and are best selected in the fall after the sap has returned to the root, or in the spring before it has risen. Root bark should be removed soon after picking (if not needed or if it is the active part). The bark is easier to remove at this time and allows the root to dry more quickly. Most wild perennials are better medicines after two years of growth. They get richer in quality as they mature. This isn't always the case, however.

Tubers

Tubers should be collected in or just after the flowering season. They should not be damaged during collection since their medicinal qualities may be greatly reduced if the tuber surfaces are gashed.

Bulbs

Gather after the leaves of the plant begin to wither.

Leaves

Young leaves and basal leaves are generally considered the best. Leaves can be collected throughout the season but are best selected before flowering and after fruiting. The active principles tend to migrate from the leaves into the flowers and fruit and then back into the leaves after the fruit has matured. Some prefer to pick leaves from sterile stems (stems that do not have any flowers or fruit on them).

Make sure you do not entirely strip any branch or plant of its leaves. This will probably kill it. Select some here and a few there and you will soon have all you need.

"Herbage"

(Aerial or top parts of the plants.) It is best to pick herbage while the flower buds are forming before the flowers open. When the flowers open, the medicinal qualities of the plant begin to move into the flowers and into seed production.

Flowers

The commencement of the flowering period is the optimum time for picking flowers. Flowers rapidly deteriorate after this time.

Fruits and Seeds

These plant parts should be picked just before or at the time of ripeness. They will ripen off the plant and will not deteriorate (over-ripen). They should be picked before they are ready to fall off.

Bark

The sap flow is most active in the spring, just before the buds open, and in the fall, just after or even as the leaves are falling. The bark is most saturated with the medicinal qualities at these times.

When collecting bark, remember that if a strip is taken 360 degrees circumferentially from the trunk, the entire tree will die. It is best to remove it in little patches; better yet, take it from the smaller side branches.

Buds

Buds are to be gathered when formed and before they start to open.

Drying

Proper drying is crucial in retaining the active ingredients of the herb for long periods. When properly dried, a herb will usually retain its original colour. Plants that become mouldy, musty smelling, much lighter or browner from too much heat, have lost some of their medicinal qualities in the drying process.

Plants may be dried in three ways:

1) Outdoors
2) Indoors
3) Artificially

Outdoor Drying

The plant material should be spread thinly on a drying screen. The drying screen can be rust-free steel mesh, (e.g., a new window screen), stretched cheese cloth or fibre mesh screen. The drying screen should be mounted to ensure good air circulation. Screens can be placed on the edges of chairs, sawhorses, or by suspending it from strings. I have also found it useful to cover the area with mosquito netting to keep insects away.

Drying must be done in a well ventilated, shady place. Food can be dried in the sun, but medicinal herbs cannot. One should turn the herbs a few times, checking to see if they are ready. The herbs will probably take two to four days to dry properly.

Indoor Drying

Indoor drying must be done in a dust-free, well ventilated room. The herb can be dried as if outdoors, on a drying screen. Some people prefer to dry leafy foliage in bunches. The bunches should be tied together and hung with the flower-heads down or more properly, the roots up. Keep the herbs out of direct sunlight (even light shining through a window).

Artificial Heat

Though it's hard to control heat in an oven, this quick-drying process is best. The heat should be kept under 40 degrees C. (100 degrees F.). Commercial oven dryers have fans that aid ventilation. Mistakes in controlling temperature may destroy the plant's medicinal qualities.

If you are drying several different herbs together, make sure they are properly labelled. After they are dried, store them in an air-tight, lightproof container. I have found that if you take a gallon mayonnaise jar and paint the outside a dark colour, it makes a nice airtight container for herbs.

IV. Poisonous Plants

"Eating something poisonous" is often the biggest worry of novices when they begin searching for wild edible plants. There are not many deadly plants in our area, but there are a few. This is enough reason to be very cautious. A larger number of plants in the West will make you quite ill if you eat them. "They won't kill you but you'll surely wish you were dead!"

The best rule I know is: **if you don't know what the plant is, and whether it is edible or not, don't eat it.** Some survival manuals tell you to eat only a little bit of an unknown plant and wait about 8 to 12 hours. If it hasn't affected you at that point, it must be safe to eat. **Bad idea.** Some very poisonous plants, lethal in fact, don't create any noticeable effect on the human body for at least 24 hours. Until you build up a knowledge of edible plants, stick with the few that you do know. Another old "chestnut" suggests watching what animals eat to judge safety and edibility. This is definitely not true. Different components of a plant react differently in different species of animals. The larkspurs (*Delphinium spp.*) poison cattle, are harmless for sheep but are toxic for humans.

If you find yourself in a situation where you don't have food and you don't know any of the plants, simply don't eat. Hunger is partly psychological and the discomfort is not worth the risk of consuming food which could immobilize you. Water is far more important for human survival than food in an emergency wilderness situation. Few places in the Rockies will place an ordinary hiker or camper beyond walking distance from a easily identifiable food source.

The following list of poisonous species should be frequently consulted when searching for wild plants. Many will be poisonous only in special situations and in large quantities. In fact, you will sometimes find a plant in both the poisonous and edible sections of this book. Use these plants only as directed. Know which plants one should not eat and pass this information on to others.

Pass it on. No more baneberry in the salads!

Euphorbia spp. (Spurges) - This weedy plant has a white sap that can cause skin irritation and blisters. If spurges are eaten in large quantities, they can cause severe poisoning. In small quantities, they cause photo-sensitivity.

Ranunculus spp. (Buttercups) - Buttercups contain a juice that can cause skin blisters. This same juice is said to have a "narcotic" effect on livestock if eaten in large quantities. These plants are rendered completely harmless to humans by drying and boiling.

Toxicodendron spp. (Poison Ivy, Oak, Sumac) - These famous poisonous plants are well known for causing severe dermatitis. The leaves contain a juice which has the active constituent. Some people can be poisoned by these plants without even touching them. Burning poison ivy is not a good idea: the juice is carried on the ashes and can cause poisoning over a wide area.

Rheum spp. (Rhubarb) - The leaves of rhubarb are poisonous even though the stems of the leaves are quite good to eat.

Chenopodium spp. (Lamb's quarters, Strawberry blite) - Although these plants are edible, large quantities eaten raw can be toxic. When cooked, they are quite harmless.

Actaea spp. (Baneberry) - It is a good general rule to stay away from any plant with the name "bane" in it – bane means "poisonous". The berries and roots of this plant are very poisonous. Children are especially susceptible because they are curious and will eat the brightly coloured berries. As few as six berries have killed children. A single berry can cause acute stomachache, cramps, headache, increased pulse and circulation and circulation failure. A strong emetic such as *Lobelia inflata* or powdered mustard should be taken as soon as possible if the berries are ingested. Baneberry also appears in the edible/medicinal section (for external use only).

Heaths (Dwarf laurel, Labrador tea, rhododendron) - These plants are all reported toxic in large quantities although I have consumed considerable amounts of Labrador tea without effect. A volatile oil present in Labrador tea can cause muscle cramps. Labrador tea was smoked by the Indians for its mild euphoric effect. Dwarf laurel, however, is very toxic.

Asclepias spp. (Milkweed) - If milkweed is eaten in large quantities it will cause profound depression and in some cases even death. Once again, this plant appears in the edible/medicinal section.

Datura stramonium (Jimsonweed) - This highly poisonous plant has gained much fame in ritual Indian use. As little as 4 to 5 grams has been known to cause death in children. A strong emetic should immediately administered if this plant is ingested.

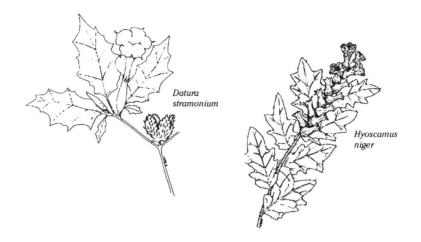

Datura
stramonium

Hyoscamus
niger

Hyoscyamus niger (Black Henbane) - This deadly poisonous plant should never been eaten. The symptoms are headache, nausea, rapid pulse, convulsions, then death. Neither drying nor boiling destroys the poisonous effects. A strong emetic of mustard followed by large amounts of warm water should be taken. Stimulants such as coffee will also help. Artificial respiration will be needed in acute cases.

Solanum nigrum (Black nightshade) - Small amounts of this plant can be poisonous. It causes stomach pains, paralysis, diarrhea, vomiting and dilated pupils. The berries and leaves are the most poisonous parts.

Lycopersicon spp. (Tomatoes) - The leaves of tomato plants are quite toxic.

Castilleja spp. (Indian paintbrush) - Indian paintbrush readily absorbs selenium. If large amounts of selenium happen to be in the soil, the plant can become poisonous. I have eaten large quantities of this plant several times and have never felt any ill effects in the Canadian Rockies but the same plant ingested in Colorado has been known to be toxic.

Legume Family (Peas) - It is a good rule to never eat any of the plants in the pea family unless you are absolutely certain about its edible status. Legumes are hard to identify at first, and many are poisonous, such as:

> *Astragalus* (milk vetch)
> *Oxytropis* (Loco weed)
> *Lathyrus* (vetch pea)
> *Lupinus* (lupines)
> *Vicia* (vetch)

Leafy spurge
Euphorbia sp.

Buttercup
Ranunculus sp.

Yellow Locoweed
Oxytropis sp.

Poison Ivy
Toxicodendron sp.

Milk Vetch
Astragalus sp.

Purple
Laurel
*Kalmia
sp.*

Red Baneberry
Actaea sp.

Lupine
Lupinus sp.

Water Hemlock
Cicuta sp.

Death Camas
Zigadenus sp.

Poisonous Plants

Elderberry
Sambucus sp.

Western Anemone
Anemone sp.

Buffalo Bean
Thermopsis sp.

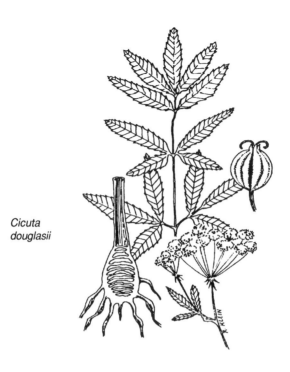

Cicuta douglasii

Cicuta spp. (Water-hemlock) - Most people have heard about this poisonous plant. A piece the size of a marble has been known to cause death. An emetic and cathartic should be administered immediately if there is even a suspicion of ingesting this plant.

Sambucus spp. (Red elderberry) - The black elderberry is completely harmless, but the red elderberry has a poisonous stem and leaves. Ingestion is unlikely to kill a human, but it can cause extended sickness.

Thermopsis spp. (Buffalo bean) - More poisonings are reported each year from this plant than any other in the area. Coming up early in the season, it has enticed many young children to eat it and become very sick. It can cause death.

Zigadenus spp. (Death camus) - As the name of this plant suggests, it is lethal for humans. Death camas looks quite similar to onion and it has often been mistaken for wild onions. When picking wild onions break them open. If they don't smell like onions, leave them alone. Some of the species in this genus are less poisonous than others but it is best to avoid the whole genus.

Delphinium sp. (Larkspur) - As mentioned in the edible plant section of this book, *Delphinium* species can be poisonous in large quantities. The most poisonous part is the seed. The symptoms are upset stomach, nervous condition and depression. Take a strong emetic and cathartic if symptoms occur.

Anemone narcissiflora - This plant can cause skin irritation and has effects similar to *Delphinium*.

Triglochin maritima (Arrow grass) - This plant contains hydrocyanic acid in both fresh and dried forms. On ingestion of this plant, the respiratory system will fail to function properly. Large doses are fatal.

Despium spp. (Fairy Bells) - The berries are toxic if eaten in large quantities.

The following plants can cause skin irritation in some people:

> Cow Parsnip root and sometimes leaves (rare)
> *Chrysanthemum spp.* whole plant
> *Anthemis spp.* (Dog Fennel), leaves
> *Phacelia spp.* (Scorpion weed), leaves

The following plants can be toxic if eaten in large quantities:

> Monkshood *Aconitum sp.*
> Stinkweed *Thlaspi arvense*
> Marsh Marigold *Caltha sp.*
> Devil's Club *Oplopanax horridum*
> Ragwort *Senecio sp.*

This list does not include every poisonous plant that grows in our area, but it covers all the major ones that have caused problems in the past. For more information, consult *Poisonous Plants of United States and Canada* by Kingsbury or the *AMA Handbook of Poisonous and Injurious Plants*.

V. Edible and Medicinal Plants

Sphagnum moss   *Sphagnum spp.*

Identification: Looking like tassels, the head of sphagnum forms in rosettes, which are pale green to bright red in colour. This moss grows up to 10 - 20 cm in height, but the peat layers have been found to be over 30 m in thickness. New sphagnum grows on old ones.

Distribution & Habitat: Forms peat bogs throughout the mountainous and north lands.

Preparation & Uses: As a bandage, there is no better. It was used during both World Wars as an esteemed bandaging material. England produced as many as one million dressing a month from sphagnum. One ounce of sphagnum can hold one pound of blood (much better than cotton). Sphagnum dressings have also been used for eczema, psoriasis, hemorrhoids, acne and other forms of skin problems, even insect bites. Recently, commercial menstrual pads containing sphagnum have been marketed in North America.

Sphagnum was used by Amerindians for wounds, menstrual pads and as padding in cradle boards (both for its absorptive ability and its antiseptic nature).

Club Moss   *Lycopodium sp.*

Identification: This plant is not really a moss but a spore-bearing vascular evergreen herb, that looks moss-like. It spreads by prostrate stems and produces adventitious roots. The spores resemble a sulphur-yellow powder.

Distribution & Habitat: Found in coniferous woods and rocky places. The geographic range extends from Alaska to California. Many species are circumpolar.

Preparation & Uses: The spores appear as a yellow powder, often called "vegetable sulphur". It can be sprinkled on skin sores, eczema, herpes, diaper rashes and the like. The spores are highly flammable, used to create explosions in the theatre. Maria Treben, a European herbalist, used pillows stuffed with the whole plants, applied to aching areas.

L. clavatum was used as a tea by Amerindians for pain after childbirth, fevers and weakness. A related species is being researched in China for Alzheimer's disease.

Caution: Some club mosses contain poisonous alkaloids, particularly *L. selago*, so they should not be used internally.

Lycopodium is commonly used by homeopaths.

Sphagnum Moss
Sphagnum sp.

Horsetail
Equisetum sp.

Horsetail
Equisetum sp.

Club Moss
Lycopodium sp.

Horsetail   *Equisetum sp.*

Equisetum = L. Horse-hair (a name in Pliny for a horsetail)

Identification: Horsetails are perennial plants with jointed, branched, creeping root stocks. The aerial stems are jointed with scale-like leaves at the nodes, which are encased in a toothed sheath. The internodes are hollow. The branches are whorled from the nodes, when present. The plant reproduces from spore-bearing, terminal cones. There are eight species within the area, four with annual stems and four with perennial stems.

Distribution & Habitat: Horsetails are common in a wide distribution, from lowlands to the high alpine. They are found in moist and shallow aquatic habitats.

Preparation & Uses: The tough outer tissue of *Equisetum* can be peeled away and the sweet inner pulp eaten raw. The young heads of this common plant can be boiled like asparagus, but it is advisable to boil them for about 20 minutes with a change of water (if large amounts are being eaten), due to their toxic effect. Boiling will take away many of the nutrients and health giving properties of the plant. Kirk states that no human poisoning has been reported. After *Equisetum* is boiled, it can be mixed with flour or dipped in an egg and crumb mixture, then fried. Horsetail roots are somewhat tuberous and can be eaten raw in the early spring or boiled later in the season.

Some Indians and early settlers used the stems of horsetail as a stimulating tea, but its most prominent property is as a diuretic and for treatment for dropsical disorders. Both Brown and Johnston list *Equisetum* as a horse medicine used by the Indians. The Blackfoot Indians called *E. hyemale* (*hyemale* = L. "of winter") *Sa-po-tan-a-kio-toi-yis* and they used it mainly as a diuretic. It was also used to help heal wounds, applied in the form of a poultice. Horsetail has also been used by Indian women as a tea to expel afterbirth and for gonorrhea. Quileule Salish Indians boiled the stocks with willow leaves to treat irregular menstruation in young women. *E. arvense* roots were infused to soothe the gums of children who were teething, often mixed with an infusion of the tips of witch hazel. Horsetail is used today by many herbalists for eye and skin treatments, because of its high silica content. Tablets of *Equisetum* silica are used for catarrhal conditions, such as pus-like discharges from the ear, nose, and throat. It is also used for glandular discharges, skin disorders, and offensive perspiration, especially of the feet.

Horsetail strengthens the heart and lungs and is a good tonic when the whole system is run down. There are few better plants for soothing the discomfort caused by difficulty in urination. It also is good for internal bleeding of all kinds and is known to strengthen connective tissue.

As a tea, use 1 teaspoon per cup of water, boil for 45 minutes in a covered container, cool and take in mouthfuls, four times a day. The Nevada Indians dried *E. arvense* (*arvense* = L. "of the field, of `ploughed' fields") burned it, and used the ashes for sores in the mouth. The silica acid content is said to stabilize scar tissue in the lungs.

The juice of this plant, especially the sterile stems, is good for anemia which may have resulted from internal bleeding from such illnesses as stomach ulcers. It acts by promoting coagulation of the blood. Tea made from this herb is also good for excessive menstrual flow and for leucorrhea, when it is used as a douche.

Externally, the tea makes a good wash for wounds, sores, skin problems and mouth and gum inflammations. The Blackfoot applied pieces of the root to rashes under the arm and in the groin. Fertile powdered stems were given to horses in their water, to perk them up. The same powder was also put in moccasins to avoid foot cramps when travelling long distances. As an infusion, steep 2 tsp. dried plant in ½ cup water and take one cup per day.

As a decoction take 1 heaping teaspoon to ½ cup water and boil one minute. Steep for one minute, strain and take 1 to 1 ½ cups a day, in mouthfuls. For external use, boil and steep longer.

Most of the silica is deposited in the epidermis. *E. hyemal* has so much silica that it has been sold as a polish for metal and for cleaning pots and pans.

Caution: "Excessive" dosages (over ½ a pound) lead to symptoms of poisoning. Some authors define "excessive" as high as 20% of body weight. There are several chemicals in this plant that have slightly toxic effects – typically the destruction of thiamine (a B vitamin). Consumption of B vitamins will speedily reverse major side effects.

Juniper berries   *Juniperus spp.*

Juniperus = yoo-ni-pe-rus, from its classical Latin name.

Identification: The various species of juniper grow as shrubs and small trees. They have leaves that are scale-like or awl-shaped and are arranged opposite or whorled on the branches. The pollen and seed cones can be borne together on the same plant or on different plants. The seed cones are berry-like and are greenish the first year and bluish when ripe the second. They contain 1 to 4 seeds.

Distribution & Habitat: These plants grow throughout North America except on the prairies.

Preparation & Uses: The so called juniper "berries" are in fact fleshy cones which take two years to ripen. They are green in the first year and turn purple during the second year. All of the species of juniper have edible berries (*J. deppeana* and *J. horizontalis* are the tastiest). The purple-bluish berries taste the best in the fall of the second year or spring of the third year when they are sweet. They can be used to flavour stew or meat. Some Indians dried them for winter use, forming them into cakes. Their primary food use is as a seasoning. Six juniper berries per pound of meat is excellent with moose, venison or rabbit and poultry. The berries have also been roasted and ground, for use as a coffee substitute.

Juniperus communis

Juniperus horizontalis

Juniperus horizontalis

Juniperus communis

The berries of juniper give gin its distinctive and well-known flavour. The berries can also be made into a mush, then dried in cakes. Again, the purple berries are the ones to eat. I've often eaten them raw and enjoyed them. Some people find them distasteful.

Juniper is well known by herbalists as an excellent diuretic, cleansing out the kidney and bladder. It is especially effective for dissolving stones. The oil of juniper can be irritating to the kidneys if they are weak. Juniper is usually used with a demulcent such as marshmallow root to avoid this. The berries were used by herbalists in the Middle Ages to help them avoid getting contagious diseases. Herbalists who treated people during the Black Death usually kept a few berries in their mouths to avoid infection. It works by forming an antiseptic barrier. A strong tea of the berries was used as a disinfectant for needles and bandages. The berries are known to stimulate the production of hydrochloric acid in the stomach. Juniper berries have also been used to expel intestinal gas.

The Cree called juniper *Ka-Ka-Kau-mini* and made a poultice for wounds out of the inner bark. *J. horizontalis* is called *sik-si-nou-koo* (black round objects) by the Blackfoot. Many Indian tribes believed that if a woman took a daily tea made with five juniper berries, she would not become pregnant.

A liniment was made by the Blackfoot to remedy backaches by infusing juniper root and poplar leaves. They also used an infusion of the root as a general tonic. Dena'ina Athabasca drank juniper berry tea for sore throats, colds and tuberculosis. The Inipiat used a berries-and-twigs tea for respiratory problems. An "incense" of the needles has often been burned to cleanse a house, driving infectious disease out. Juniper oil extract has been used as an external application for stiff joints, but should be diluted with other oils (e.g. olive or almond oil) because it can cause blisters.

The Blackfoot used juniper to floor their sweat lodges and to floor the Sun Dance lodge.

Some proud Indian horse owners would bath their horses in water in which the root had been soaked. This would make the horsehair shine. A decoction of juniper branches is an anti-dandruff rinse.

Black beads can be made from the berries of juniper. After collecting a fair quantity of berries, you string them on a small sliver of wood and let them dry. After they have dried, pour grease on the fire and smoke the dried berries in the thick smoke, which turns the berries black. The beads are then polished and strung and can be interspersed with wolf willow beads.

Red Cedar, Western   *Thuja plicata*

Thuja = thoo-ya, from the Greek name for juniper or Theophrastus' name for a resinous fragrant wooded tree, *plicata* = pli-kah-ta, the appearance of the shoots, "pleated, folded lengthwise".

Identification: Fairly common in parts of the area, this large tree often gets to heights of 45-65 m. It has a large diameter at the bottom (up to 2.5 m) tapering rather fast. The bark on older trees is thin, reddish brown, shallowly grooved and coming apart in loose shreds. The leaves are small and scale-like, bright green, formed in flat lacy sprays. The cones form in clusters at the end of the branches.

Distribution & Habitat: This tree can be found in moist areas along the Pacific from California to Alaska, east to Idaho and Montana, from sea level to 7,000 feet in elevation.

Preparation & Uses: The Western red cedar was only used occasionally for medicinal purposes. The Nez Perce Indians made a tea of the boughs to relieve coughs and colds. The bitter tea tastes much better if some sweetener is added. The leaves were used in a tea to combat diarrhea. Moore states that it is a phagocyte stimulator, especially macrophage activity. It is also mildly diuretic.

The buds of the cedar can be chewed for toothaches. An infusion of bark and twigs is good for kidney problems. A steam from a decoction was inhaled by expectant mothers to induce labour or to relieve hard pressure of the abdomen. The oil has been used externally for warts, fungus infection and piles. It is being used in some clinics to treat herpes simplex.

The Western red cedar is much prized for construction. The soft wood is easy to work and is resistant to rot and insect decay. It was used by the Nez Perce, Flathead and Kutenai Indians to construct shelters, canoes, rafts and cradle boards. The fine roots or shredded bark can be used to make baskets and containers. If the bark is boiled with sifted wood ash, the fibers become softer, separate more easily and are more easily worked.

Caution: the oil of the leaves is toxic, causing low blood pressure and convulsion. Deaths have been reported.

Fir   *Abies sp.*

Abies = ǎ-bee-ayz, from its classical name, L. for "Rising One" (tall tree).

Identification: Two very similar fir species in the Rocky Mountains are balsam fir (*Abies balsamea*) and alpine fir (*Abies lasiocarpa*). *A. lasiocarpa* is the one mostly found in the southern mountains, hybridizing with *A. balsamea* in the northern mountains. Firs can be distinguished from spruce easily by their flat needles, which are not as prickly as those of the spruce. An easy way to remember this is: "flat-needled-friendly fir" - the "f" in flat and friendly stands for fir; whereas, spruce have square needles - the "s" stands for square-spiky-spruce.

Distribution & Habitat: They extend from lower altitudes into the subalpine stands. Usually, they grow in moist woods, and are intermixed with spruce, poplar and lodgepole pine.

Preparation & Uses: Balsam fir (*Abies balsamea*) was an important plant used by the Indians for medicinal purposes. Lewis and Clark kept it as part of their medicine kit, calling it *Balsam traumalick*. The tar or pitch was given for colds, coughs, asthma and consumption, both as an infusion and raw. An ointment was used for piles and root canals. The Nevada Indians used the soft resins from the bark of *A. concolor* to cure tuberculosis (1 tsp. daily). The boiled needles were found valuable for pulmonary troubles and resin from the bark was often added to a brew. A wash for venereal disease was made with juniper berries and the resin of *Pinus monophylla*. For stitches in the side or backache it was smeared onto toast and bound to the side while warm. Penobscot Indians smeared the resin over burns, sores and cuts. Other Indians smeared it over their chest or back to relieve pain in the heart or chest.

The twigs can be steeped for a laxative, while the liquid balsam from the trunk is good for colds and other pulmonary troubles. The inner bark was steeped and drunk for chest pains. A decoction of the bark of balsam fir was used as a diaphoretic and taken internally for gonorrhoea and sore chest. It was also applied externally for sores and cuts. The roots were held in the mouth as a remedy for mouth sores. The Chippewa Indians made a decoction of the root by sprinkling the root and water on hot stones using the steam to soothe rheumatic joints (especially the knees). It has been listed as a stimulant, diuretic, laxative and diaphoretic. It is also useful as a glue and the resin is often used in lieu of Balm of Gilead (see Balsam Poplar).

Balsam fir has been listed in the U.S. Pharmacopeia from 1820-1916 and the U.S. National Formulary since 1926.

The Blackfoot Indians used alpine fir (*Abies lasiocarpa*) quite extensively. Fragments of cones left behind by chipmunks and squirrels were pulverized into a powder, then mixed with back fat or marrow. This was cooled until solid and served as a delicacy at social events. It was also an aid to digestion.

Alpine Fir
Abies lasiocarpa

Western
Red Cedar
*Thuja
plicata*

BA

Fir
*Abies
balsamifera*

BA

Larch
Larix sp.

BA

A smudge (smoky fire) of alpine fir needles was used for many purposes. During thunderstorms, it was burned as incense or offerings to the thunder gods, so they would not strike the camp with lightning. This smudge was also used as a fumigant for swollen faces caused by venereal diseases. Headache and fainting were also treated this way, as were sick horses.

The resin of alpine fir was brewed as an emetic to "clean out the insides," and used in a poultice for fever and chest colds. An infusion of needles was given to people who were coughing up blood, a sign of tuberculosis.

The resin was often chewed for pleasure and to cure bad breath. An infusion of needles was sometimes mixed with grease and applied as a hair tonic. The needles were used as a perfume, by packing them into moccasins or hanging a bundle around a horse's neck.

Larch, Tamarack   *Larix americana, L. laricana, L. lyallii.*

Larix = lă-riks, from it classical Latin name (Dioscorides' name for a larch), *laricana* = L."larch-like".

Identification: These deciduous conifers have needle-like leaves that form in clusters of 10-40. They are pale green and turn yellow in the fall before dropping off. The wood is very heavy and hard with rough bark. The tree is 10 - 50 m tall. The erect cones are spruce-like.

Distribution & Habitat: Larch usually grows in swamps, bogs and damp forest areas with some species found along the alpine tree line. It is found along the Rocky Mountains and north-west as far as the Yukon River in Alaska.

Preparation & Uses: The bark was made into poultices and used for chronic eczema, psoriasis, bruises, wounds and ulcers. The gum from the bark has been chewed for indigestion and is considered good for an enlarged, hardened liver. Its astringent qualities have been employed to combat bleeding of the lungs, stomach, bowels and profuse menstruation. The bark and needles have been used as an astringent for diarrhea but at the same time have been found to be laxative in cases of constipation. The gum and bark are also recorded as being useful both internally and externally, for rheumatic problems. Kloss indicates uses for bronchitis and asthma, and as a poultice for insect bites. *Larix americana* was listed by the Canadian Pharmaceutical Journal as a medicinally used plant in 1868.

The Ojibwa used the dried leaves as an inhalant and fumigator. The roots were used to sew canoes, the strong root fibers for weaving bags.

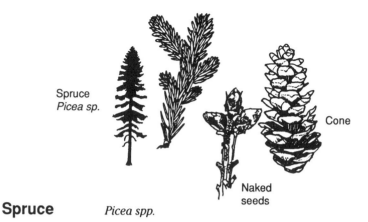

Spruce
Picea sp.

Cone

Naked seeds

Spruce   *Picea spp.*

Picea = pi-kee-a, from L. *pix* "pitch" (the resin).

Identification: There are several species of spruce in the area, two of which are found throughout the mountains. *Picea engelmannii* (Engelmann Spruce) is 25-30 m tall and it is usually found in the subalpine where it merges with *Picea glauca* (white spruce) at about 5,000 to 6,000 ft. above sea level. White spruce is found at lower elevations and in more northerly locations. There is a very wide integration of hybrids between these two species. The third spruce, *Picea mariana* (Black Spruce) is found more to the north. Spruce can be distinguished from fir by its square needles and their prickly feeling.

Distribution & Habitat: Spruces are quite common throughout the area.

Preparation & Uses: The gum of spruce has been used as a healing agent for many years. The gum can be applied to cuts and wounds and used as plaster for setting bones. The young shoots of some spruce can be boiled and taken warm for colds and catarrh, producing sweat if taken hot. The vapour has been inhaled for bronchitis. The needles and shoots are used in a calming bath. The gum can be applied to the skin to protect against sunburn.

A beer of spruce root, which tastes similar to root beer, can occasionally be found in health food stores and is delicious. We can also find spruce still being used as an ingredient in some "natural" root beers.

I spotted an interesting old recipe for spruce beer in the *The Druggists' Recipe Book* (1871) by Henry Beasley:

> 10 gallons of water
> 6 pounds of sugar
> 4 oz. spruce oil
> 2-4 tbsp. of yeast
> Ferment. Then bottle.

I haven't tried the recipe but it sounds fun. Many old recipes require a bit of experimentation but can add delightfully to your larder. The roots were also used for weaving baskets.

Lodgepole Pine
Pinus contorta

Lodgepole Pine   *Pinus contorta*

Pinus = pee-nus, from the Latin name for pine, *contorta* = kon-tor-ta, twisted, referring to young shoots of the California variety.

Identification: *Pinus contorta* is an evergreen coniferous tree, reaching a height of 25 m. The needles are in bundles of two, the cones are 2-5 cm long and each scale is armed with a minute, recurved prickle. The trunk is usually straight and narrow, with a clean scaly bark.

Distribution & Habitat: Lodgepole pine is the most common tree species of middle and lower altitudes on the eastern slopes of the Rocky Mountains. It grows in dense stands that can be hard to hike through.

Preparation & Uses: As an emergency food, the pine needle can be made into a tea, which is high in vitamin C and beta-carotene (vitamin A). Chewing on the needles, however, would provide more nutrients. The seed of lodgepole pine is high in fat and protein, although it tastes rather like turpentine. In the spring the young needles are soft, tender and quite edible. Indians often ate the inner bark of pine as a spring tonic.

The inner bark pulp is also used as a poultice to draw out infections. The gum can be put on any cut, scrape or sore to promote healing. Some Indians would chew the bud to treat sore throat. The buds can also be decocted and used as an aid for tuberculosis and stomach ailments.

The turpentine pitch is slightly irritating and antiseptic, giving it a diuretic, expectorant and rubefacient quality. It can also be used as a carminative for flatulence and as a vermifuge. Too much of the pitch or even needle can be

Engelmann Spruce
Picea engelmannii

Spruce Buds
Picea sp.

Pine
Pinus sp.

Lodgepole
Pine
*Pinus
contorta*

Cattail
*Typha
latifolia*

irritating to weakened kidneys. This was employed by some Indians as a method of birth control. They made a strong infusion of the needle. This could be very dangerous and so should not be taken during pregnancy.

Inhaling "steam" of the pitch helps loosen up lungs and has been used for many respiratory problems. The Missouri Indians inhaled the smoke of burning twigs to relieve head colds.

I consider the most important use of the lodgepole pine to be the construction of tipis. As it is a tall, straight tree it has traditionally been used for the poles of Indian lodges or tipis, thus its common name. The poles were traded over great distances.

Cattail *Typha latifolia*

Typha = tee-fa, from Gr. "of the bog"; *latifolia* = lah-tee-fo-lee-a, "broad-leaved".

Identification: Cattails are tall marsh (aquatic) herbs, growing up to 3 m and have a coarse creeping rootstock. The flowers are very small, on conspicuous mace-like flower-spikes. The leaves are long, linear, upright, flat and sheathed. The seeds are borne in minute achenes on slender stalks that are scattered in fluffy masses in late summer.

Distribution & Habitat: This plant is very common in marshes and shallow water throughout the area.

Preparation & Uses: This plant has so many diverse uses that it is hard to know where to begin. Two of the best descriptions of this plant I've heard are Schofield's "One-stop Shopping center" or "Supermarket of the swamp".

Among the edible uses, the young shoots can be pulled loose from the rootstock. The outer leaves peeled away, and the tender core can be used for salads or cooked. When the shoot gets a little older, it is best to boil it.

The young flower stalk is a much-favoured item. Remove the sheath and cook it any way desired. If boiled about 20 minutes, they can be eaten like – and taste like – corn on the cob. Nibble the flowers off the tough inner stalk.

When the pollen is being produced, the flowers can be scraped off and used alone, or as a thickening and flavouring agent. The pollen also makes a nice flour that can be used to make bread, biscuits, pancakes and such, but is best sifted if possible. Mix the pollen with equal parts of whole wheat flour. The pollen stores well dried, for about one year.

A friend of mine even made bannock from the down, using equal parts down and flour. I thought it would taste like cotton batten, but it was surprisingly good.

The roots can be boiled, roasted or dried and ground into meal for flour. The flowers can be dried for future use either in the hot sun, or in a preheated oven. Store in a closed container.

Here is a famous recipe:

Cattail Flapjacks

2 cups cattail pollen (or flowers)	½ cup evaporated milk
1 teaspoon salt	1-½ cups water
2 cups wholewheat flour	1 tablespoon syrup
4 teaspoons baking powder	bacon drippings or oil
2 eggs	

Beat eggs, add milk, water and syrup. Mix and add dry ingredients, beating well until mixture is creamy. Add bacon drippings. Fry in a hot greased skillet over a campfire. Makes about 20 flapjacks.

The roots of cattail are edible at any time, though they become bitter late in the season. The best tasting roots are those which are going to form new shoots in the spring. The new buds are very tender. The outer peel should be discarded. My favourite way of cooking the roots is to bake them in a fireless pit (see Camas for pit method). The ripe seed can also be utilized as a meal or pressed into an oil.

Cattail
*Typha
latifolia*

The down from the mature seeds makes a perfect tinder. Its good insulation qualities lead to its use as stuffing for mattresses or pillows. The Indians often stuffed the down into cradle boards as padding for a child. The down was used by some Amerindians for dressing burns and scalds, and to prevent chafing. It was also used for infant diaper rash much as we use talcum powder. The down was often employed as a menstrual pad, especially right after childbirth. The ashes of burned spikes were sprinkled on infants' navels to stop bleeding.

The roots were pounded into a jelly-like poultice to be applied on wounds, sores, carbuncles, boils, burns and scalds. The flower heads are a bit astringent and can be eaten to stop diarrhea. The root can be infused in milk to alleviate dysentery and diarrhea. The root of narrowleaf cattail (*T. angustifolia*) has been used as a tea for kidney stones. The sticky juice is said, in Tom Brown's *Field Guide to Wilderness Survival*, to be good to rub on the gums as a novocain substitute for dental extraction.

The pulp of cattail can be converted to make rayon. Torches can be made out of the stalk, especially with the aid of coal oil or wax mixtures. The long mature leaves and stalks can be easily woven into mats, chairs, bags and many other useful items.

Sweet Grass   *Hierochloe odorata*

Hierochloe = L. "Holy Grass", *odorata* = L. "fragrant, scented".

Blackfoot - *siputus-simal* (fragrant smell)

Identification: Sweet Grass is a perennial, sweet-smelling grass, with flat leaf blades. The smooth culms are 30 - 60 cm tall. The spikelets are shining, yellowish brown, or purplish. The whole plant is fragrant when dried.

Distribution & Habitat: Sweet Grass has a circumpolar distribution. It likes low meadows and occasional dampness. It is also found along lake shores and is most commonly seen in early spring. Sweet Grass sometimes persists as a weed in recently broken ground.

Preparation & Uses: In late summer, sweet grass was gathered by the Blackfoot. They would take a handful of it and braid it to use as incense. I often put some of this sweet smelling grass on coals, or on the airtight stove in my tipi. This freshens up the air, leaving a pleasant odour.

Amongst the Blackfoot, virtually every holy article was cleaned in the smoke of sweet grass before use. Medicine men made a ritual of burning this grass twice a day. Sweet Grass was sometimes chewed by prairie Indians during a prolonged fast to give them extended endurance.

This herb had many ritualistic uses, e.g., to cleanse women in smoke after they had given birth. It was often given to help in expulsion of afterbirth and to stop vaginal bleeding. The tea was also used by men to treat venereal infections.

It was used as a treatment for sore throats. The stems were soaked in water and used to treat chapping and wind burn. This was sometimes combined with bear grease. This infusion was also used as an eyewash.

A hair tonic was made of sweet grass water with the addition of gelatin from boiled hooves. It was also mixed with red ochre, which the Blackfoot used to decorate their clothing and bodies.

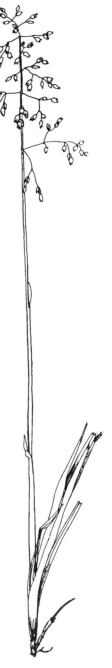

Sweet Grass
Hierochloe odorata

43

Cattail
Typha latifolia
Note cloud of pollen.

BA

Young
Cattail
shoot &
roots
*Typha
latifolia*

BA

Sweet Grass
Hierochloe odorata

BA

Pink-flowered Onion
Allium sp.

BA

Prairie Onion
Allium sp.

BA

Nodding Onion
Allium cernuum

BA

Onion, Nodding   *Allium cernuum*

Allium = ă-lee-um, from Greek name for garlic, *cernuum* = L. "drooping, curving forwards".

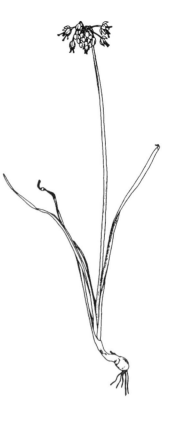

Identification: This perennial plant grows 10-50 cm tall, with an umbel of nodding pink or white flowers. The basal leaves are flat or channeled and fleshy. The root is very similar to the cultivated green onion. Nodding onion has a distinct onion odour which distinguishes it from the poisonous plant it closely resembles, death camas. If you're going to eat the plant, make sure of its odour.

Distribution & Habitat: Nodding onion is found in diverse habitats ranging from subalpine meadow, to parkland, prairie, open slopes, thickets and rock slides.

Preparation & Uses: This easy-to-find onion is a good choice in salads and in all onion or garlic dishes. The bulb can be easily stored for winter use. The Blackfoot did this and called them *Pis-satse'-miakim.* The taste is between onion and garlic. The tops are as good as the bulbs, but are a little stronger than normal green onions. They are delicious in stews and soups.

Backpacker onion soup is quite a favourite with some people. You take three cups of water, three beef bouillon cubes, about one cup chopped onion (whole plant). Heat to boil and simmer for a few minutes. Season with salt, pepper, soy sauce and adding anything else that tickles your culinary fancy.

Onions are listed as stimulant, carminative, antiseptic, diuretic and expectorant.

The juice of wild onions can be boiled down until it is thick and can be used as a treatment for colds and throat irritations. Honey can be added to this mixture.

Onions are natural antiseptics, warding off bacteria and fungi. Try putting crushed garlic or onion under a glass with some bacteria or fungi – the latter will die. The Dakota and Winnebago Indians applied the crushed bulb of this genus to relieve pain of insect stings and to act as a repellent.

I have often chewed garlic cloves to get rid of colds and flu. This is not always socially acceptable when mixing with people. A way to get around this is to suck on some cloves (the type your mother puts in the ham), after you have eaten the raw garlic. This will sweeten you breath and make it quite pleasant.

Both onion and garlic can be used for stopping fermentation in the intestines, so if you have gas problems when eating various foods, maybe spicing them up with onion and garlic will help. Garlic and onion are supposed to restore sexual potency which has been impaired by mental stress or illness.

All of the *Allium* species have been shown to lower "bad" LDL cholesterol and overall cholesterol. These herbs are antibacterial, antiviral and antifungal.

The Blackfoot Indians often took an infusion of the bulb to stop vomiting and to enable the patient to retain his food. Mixing *Allium spp.* with *Monarda* in an infusion, by contrast, produces vomiting when consumed.

Nursing women would often eat onions to transfer the medicinal effect to their child. When a Blackfoot Indian had a swollen penis with severe constipation, a drink made from an infusion of the bulb was taken. Snuff was made from the dried bulb to open the sinuses. Crushed onion can be put on burns to soothe them and stop blisters from forming.

Caution: One should take care when collecting this plant and not confuse it with death camas (*Zigadenus spp.*) It often grows in the same areas and is similar in appearance. The easiest way to tell the difference is that nodding onion smells like onions, whereas death camas does not. A mistake could prove fatal if the wrong species is eaten.

Camas   *Camassia quamash*

Camassia = Ka-ma-see-a, an Amerindian quamash or camas, bulbous sweet herbs.

Identification: This perennial has a scale-like stem arising from a bulb (10 - 30 mm wide) blackish on the outside and white on the inside. This lily-like plant has a cluster of bright blue flowers in a raceme. The grass-like leaves grow as tall as the flower stalk.

Distribution & Habitat: Camas grows in moist meadows that become dry in late spring in British Columbia, Alberta, Montana, Wyoming and Utah.

Preparation & Uses: The taste of the root can be summed up in the name camas, which comes from a Chinook Indian's corruption of a Nootka Indian word *chamas*, meaning sweet. This plant was sometimes so abundant and dense that some early travellers to this area mistook it for distant lakes. Its prominence can still be seen as several village names in Idaho, Montana, Washington, Utah and the Camas valley of Oregon. The original name for Victoria on Vancouver Island B.C. was Camosun or gathering place of camas. This root was so prized by the natives that several wars were fought over it. Not surprisingly, it is also surrounded with many taboos.

The Prairie Indians believed that if the roots where undercooked or overcooked, death would come to the relatives of the roaster. This fear was so widespread, that many people would only trade the roots rather than eating them themselves, for fear of roasting them improperly. During the roasting of the roots the men were not allowed near the pit except to bring in firewood. If the men came too close, famine or at least bad luck would overcome all. These taboos were very widely believed by many tribes.

There are many stories about the origin of the sacred camas root. Most of them have a key character, Coyote, and either Elk or Moose. The Flathead Indian version is as follows:

> Coyote and his five sons went travelling one day to visit Elk, who also had five sons. When they arrived at Elk's lodge they found no one home and nothing to eat. They were quite angry and put out because they were very hungry. Shortly Elk arrived and after greeting his guests leaned over and picked up a stick and started digging at his backside with it. Out came camas roots. Coyote was very disturbed. He felt it was impolite to serve one's guest dung and so he loudly complained. Elk said "that is not dung but delicious camas root. I often carry them that way when I travel". Coyote tried them and found them quite tasty. He and his sons ate their fill.

> When Coyote departed, he asked Elk to visit him some day. The next day Elk showed up. Coyote went over and picked up a stick to dig at his own backside, only to cause a wound. Elk said that only he could do it so he took the stick and produced another feast of camas from his backside. As a form of friendship, Elk spread material from his backside all around the area to form camas roots.

> To this day, camas roots appear a little bit like elk or moose dung when they are first dug up, and after they are roasted.

The proper time to collect the roots is usually June, or to be a bit more specific, when at least the lower raceme flower begins to fade. They taste better, however, after the flowers have all dried out. Only the women used to gather the roots. Gathering roots often became a contest among the young women, as gathering many roots raised one's status, thereby assuring a marriage to a great brave. There are accounts of one woman gathering as many as sixty 1½ bushel sacks.

The roots were cooked for two to four days in earth ovens. A fire was built in a pit lined with rocks. After these were hot enough the ashes were removed and the rocks covered with a little dirt and vegetation (usually skunk cabbage, balsamroot leaves, and willow). The camas roots (sometimes mixed with Alectoria lichen) were then placed in the pit, sometimes in alternate layers with hot rocks, depending on the quantities. The pit was then covered with more vegetation and dirt. Often a fire was built on top of this. The roots were kept moist by placing a willow bark tube into the camas root oven and pouring water into it. When the roots are cooked they are dark brown and quite moist and soft, retaining their original shape. Those that were not immediately eaten in a great feast were dried for about a week and stored for the future, sometimes mixed with berries or meat.

Because of their sweetness, camas roots became very prized trade items. Camas roots contain no starches but only an indigestible sugar which changes to a fructose sugar after the root is cooked. The sugar represents as much as 43% of the dry weight. The roots were sometimes boiled down into a syrup, but more often cooked in pits.

Too large a quantity of camas roots is both emetic and purgative. Some people find the plant a bit too mucilaginous.

Caution: Don't mix this plant up with the poisonous camas, *Zigadenus gramineus* (Death Camas), which can grow in similar habitat and is of similar appearance, but has white or yellowish flowers.

Glacier Lily   *Erythronium grandiflorum*

Erythronium = e-rith-ron-ee-um, from *erythronion*, the Greek name of the plant or L. "red" (flower colours), *grandiflorum* = grǎnd-i-flŏrum, "large flowered".

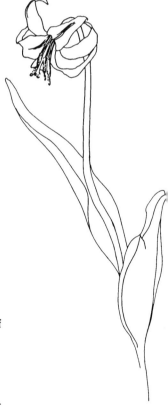

Synonyms: Dog tooth violet, snow lily, fawn lily.

Identification: Glacier lily is a perennial herb, 20-30 cm high. It has a large, nodding yellow flower. The flowers are usually solitary, but occasionally there are up to three on a plant. The pair of basal leaves are oval-lanceolate. The roots are bulb-like.

Distribution & Habitat: This flower is so anxious to come out in the spring and show its beauty, one often sees it in snow beds or along alpine brooks.

Preparation & Uses: This plant is fairly rare and should only be eaten in emergencies. The bulbs of this plant, which may be boiled and/or dried for storage, are quite nutritious. The leaves and fresh green seed pods make good greens (some find them a bit laxative).

The seed pods can be eaten raw or cooked. Eating the seed pod will not destroy the plant, especially if you spread the seeds around first.

Another species, *E. americanus*, is listed medicinally as an emetic, emollient, and antiscorbutic when fresh. The fresh root has been simmered in milk, or the fresh bruised leaves applied as a soothing poultice for hard-to-heal ulcers. I have not tried it, but it is likely the *E. grandiflorum* has some of these qualities as well. Iroquois women ate raw leaves as a form of birth control. A water extract has been shown to have activity against both Gram-positive and Gram-negative bacteria.

Yellowbells   *Fritillaria pudica*

Fritillaria = fri-ti-lah-ree-a, L. *fritillus* "dice box" referring to the shape of the flowers; *pudica* = pu-dee-ka, L. "retiring, modest, bashful" referring to the drooping flower which hides its reproductive parts.

Identification: This plant has a single, terminal yellow bell hanging downwards, 1.5 - 2 cm long. The plant stands 10 - 30 cm tall, with narrowly oblong to lanceolate leaves. The flower blooms very early in the season and turns brick red to purple. The corm is about 2.5 cm in diameter.

Distribution & Habitat: This plant is found from Alberta south to New Mexico and California in open grassland up to high alpine regions. It is rare throughout most of its range.

Preparation & Uses: The bulbous rootstalks are quite tasty and edible raw or lightly cooked. They are usually collected in early May in the lowlands, until July in the alpine areas. The fruit pods are also eaten as a pot herb and are especially good with salt, pepper and butter.

Tiger Lily   *Lilium montanum, L. philadelphicum*

Lilium = lee-lee-um, from the classical Latin name (used by Virgil), *montanum* = L. "of the mountains", *philadelphicum* = L. "of Philadephia".

Synonyms: Western Wood Lily

Identification: These lilies grow 20-60 cm tall, forming a thick-scaled bulb. There are 1 to 3 large flowers which have similar sepals and petals. The flowers are red and orange-red with purplish-black spots at the base of the interior. The leaves are linear and alternate with the exception of the uppermost which are whorled.

Distribution & Habitat: These plants are found throughout North America on the prairies, in open woods and moist subalpine meadows.

Preparation & Uses:

> I took a day to search for God
> And found him not.
> But where the scarlet lily flamed
> I saw his footprint in the sod.
>
> Bliss Carmen

Tiger Lily
Lilium montanum

The bulb of this plant is edible if cooked like potatoes or can be used to thicken soup. The roots are starchy and slightly sweet. The flower is probably the most delicious salad herb you could ever eat. Amerindians used the root in the form of a tea for coughs, consumption, fever, stomach disorders and to expel placenta. It was used externally for wounds, sores, bruises and swellings. As a poultice it can be applied to spider bites.

There is an old legend from Asia about this plant. A Korean hermit befriended a wounded tiger by removing an arrow from its body. The tiger asked the hermit to use his magic to perpetuate their friendship after the tiger died. The hermit agreed and when the tiger died, his body became a tiger lily. Eventually the hermit drowned and his body was washed away. The tiger lily spread everywhere looking for its friend.

Glacier Lily
Erythronium grandiflorum

Tiger Lily
Lilium montanum

False Solomon's Seal
Smilacina sp.

False Solomon's Seal
in berry stage
Smilacina sp.

Solomon's Seal, False   *Smilacina stellata* and *S. racemosa*

Smilacina = smee-la-keen-a, from Gr. *Smilax* (ancient Greek name); *stellata* = ste-lah-ta, star-like (the flower); *racemosa* = ra̬-kay-mō-sa, flowers in racemes.

Synonyms: Solomon-plume, wild lily-of-the-valley, wild spikenard, treacleberry, star-flowered solomon's seal.

Identification: False Solomon's Seal is a perennial herb, 10–40 cm tall, with creeping rhizomes and small cream-coloured flowers. There are 6 perianth parts and stamens. The annual stem bears few or many leaves which are sessile and broad. The fruits are spherical berries that are green with bright red stripes, turning black when ripe.

Distribution & Habitat: False Solomon's seal is found in moist places, often in thickets associated with willow or alders.

Preparation & Uses: This plant has a starchy rootstock that may be eaten. It should be cooked overnight in lye. The Ojibwa Indians used white ashes from their fire pits instead of lye. This removes the bitterness. The roots are then boiled and rinsed several times to remove the lye. The rootstock is also said to make a good pickle. Porslid lists this plant as non-edible. It is not listed as poisonous either to livestock or humans though it tends to be a purgative.

The young leaves and shoots can be used like asparagus and are good pot herbs. The berries are edible raw, but purgative if eaten in quantity. Anyone with loose bowels should not eat them. Cooking these bitter-sweet berries removes much of the purgative element and also makes them more palatable.

Moore lists *S. racemosa* roots as an effective demulcent and expectorant for inflammatory stages of lung infection, sore throats and to soften up mucus in the bronchials. He also adds it is good for frontal headaches associated with indigestion.

False Solomon Seal
Smilacina sp.

The Blackfoot used to powder the root and apply it to wounds. The Nevada Indians used the roots as a poultice for boils, sprains or swellings. The pulp of the root was sometimes used for earaches, as an infusion for eye inflammations and for regulating menstrual disorders. The Nevada Indians also used a tea of the leaves as a form of birth control (drinking one cup daily). Other Indians used the root to close up wounds by laying bruised roots on the wound for a couple of days. The roots, made into a decoction, are said to relieve sunburn. Inhaling the smoke of roots was used to treat "insanity" and to quiet crying children.

S. stellata roots were made into infusions to regulate menstrual disorders and as a form of birth control (conception is said to be prevented by drinking tea of the leaves regularly). The berries are high in vitamin C and help to stop scurvy and rickets.

Twisted Stalk, Liverberry   *Streptopus amplexifolius*

Strepto = L. "twisted", *amplexifolius* = L. "embracing the leaves".

Synonyms: Cucumber root, white mandarins, scootberries.

Identification: Twisted stalk stands 30-100 cm high with whitish-green flowers along the stem. The leaves are alternate and lanceolate, with conspicuously parallel veins. The fruits are red berries, which are elliptical to spherical in shape.

Distribution & Habitat: This herb occurs locally in moist woods and thickets.

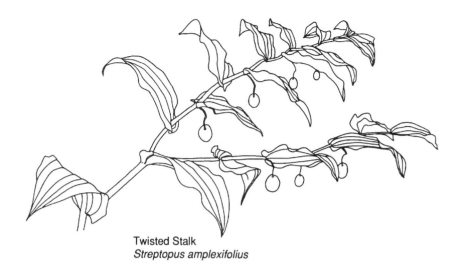

Twisted Stalk
Streptopus amplexifolius

Preparation & Uses: The red, juicy berries may be eaten raw or cooked in soups and stews. One of its common names is "scootberry" so if one has loose bowels, it is wise to avoid twisted stalk. The laxative effect seems to be only mild. Another common name is liverberry and one would presume it has some effect on the liver but I have been unable to find any clinical or historical reference to it. When eaten raw the new spring shoots have a cucumber-like taste and in summer, a watermelon-flavoured fruit.

False Hellebore   *Veratrum viride*

Veratrum = vay-rah-trum, from it classical Latin name, *viride* = vi-ri-dee, "fresh-green, youthful".

Identification: False hellebore is a tall, coarse herb, standing 1 - 2 m tall. The stout, unbranched erect stem rises from a thickened rootstock. The leaves are somewhat hairy, alternate, elliptical 10 - 20 cm long, sessile (or nearly so) and strong veined. The flowers are yellowish-green, grouped in terminal clusters 15 - 70 cm long.

Distribution & Habitat: False hellebore is found in moist areas from low wooded areas to high mountain meadows. It is found throughout the area.

Preparation & Uses: This plant has poisonous and medicinal applications which were used by both pioneers and Indians. Because of the poisonous properties, it should only be used externally. Leave the internal applications alone! I only list the following uses for interest's sake. It has been used as an analgesic, for epilepsy and convulsions, as a heart sedative, and for pneumonia and tonsillitis.

Twisted Stalk
Streptoptus amplexifolius

BA

Twisted Stalk
in berry stage
Streptoptus amplexifolius

TW

False Hellebore
Veratrum viride

TW

Many groups of Indians used the powdered root on wounds, often mixed with some form of grease (preferably raccoon or wildcat). The root can be sliced thinly, boiled in vinegar and applied externally for shingles or herpes. A tea from the decoction was used by pioneers to rid themselves of head lice. A comb was dipped in the liquid and applied to the affected hair.

Internally false hellebore is claimed to be one of the best remedies for reducing the pulse and lowering the arterial blood pressure. In severe cases of hypertension it has been combined with *Rauwolfia*, with side effects of nausea and vomiting. It has been used as an expectorant, to promote appetite, as a diaphoretic, for indigestion, a treatment for asthma, rheumatism and gout. Although dangerous, due to its poisonous properties, the root was chewed for toothaches. False hellebore was also used for abnormal menstruation and said to cure nymphomania. A related species, *V. californicum*, was used internally by the Nevada Indians as a form of birth control. One tablespoonful of the decoction was taken three times a day for three weeks to cause permanent sterility, often being taken by both men and women. It was also used by these people to cure venereal disease. The Nevada also used a variety of the plant as a poultice for snake bites. The Quinaults of Western Washington used to take small doses of decocted whole plant for rheumatism, regarding large doses as poisonous.

The major alkaloid (protoveratrine) works on the vagus nerve and as a vasomotor depressant. Besides affecting blood pressure, this property makes false hellebore a strong nervine. The herb was especially employed in spasmodic coughs of an asthmatic nature and for strong pain relief. This plant was in the USP 1820 - 1942 and the NF 1942 - 1960 as a cardiac depressant, for hypertension and as a sedative. The plant is employed by homeopaths.

The Flathead Indians used the root as a decongestant, calling it "sneeze-root". It was taken as a snuff.

Due to its toxic effect the internal dosage was always very small, 1 - 3 drops of fluid extract, 10 - 30 drops of tincture or 1 - 2 grains of powder.

Toxicity is indicated by nausea, vomiting, slow pulse (which later becomes rapid and irregular), prostration, perspiration, pallor with shallow and sometimes strained breathing. Toxicity reduces with maturity of the plant. The antidote, if vomiting occurs, is a few glasses of water with tannic acid (or very strong black tea). If vomiting does not occur, it should be induced and/or the stomach should be pumped. The patient should be kept in a prone position, not even sitting to vomit.

The toxic effects of this plant have been employed by farmers who have soaked corn in decoction of the roots before planting. This is effective in keeping birds away from what they must consider contaminated grain. The powdered roots have been used as an insecticide.

Yucca   *Yucca spp.*

Yucca = yoo-ka, from the Carib name for cassava (*Mamhol esculinte*), originally thought to be of this genus.

Identification: This coarse plant grows from 50 to 120 cm tall and has long spike-like leaves which are often stiff. This appearance has led to the common name "Spanish Bayonets". The large flowers are greenish- white. The fruit is spongy and dry.

Distribution & Habitat: These plants grow in arid, desert areas from southern Alberta into the United States.

Preparation & Uses: The flowers are edible. Immature seed pods are quite nice when steamed. The root is used in the form of a tea to treat arthritis and gonorrhea. The whole plant is useful for arthritis and I have successfully employed it in my clinic for years. As a hair tonic, it is said to be good for dandruff and to stop baldness. A water extract has shown anti-cancer properties against B1 melanoma in mice. An infusion has shown some use for urethral and prostate inflammation. The fruit was used by some southern Indians to induce vomiting.

Venus'-slipper   *Calypso bulbosa*

bulbosa = L. "swollen , having bulbs, bulbous".

Identification: This small orchid rises from a bulbous corm to a height of 5-15 cm. It is one of our most beautiful orchids, with a mauve and white flower. The solitary leaf is basal and round-ovate.

Distribution & Habitat: This plant's geographical distribution is nearly circumpolar, growing in coniferous forest associated with *Cornus canadensis* (bunchberry) and *Equisetum pratense* (horsetail). It grows from low to medium altitudes, disappearing at the upper limits of the lodgepole pine. It is said to be rare but tends to be locally abundant in spring and early summer.

Preparation & Uses: The rather small bulb-corms are quite tasty. They are starchy and nutty-flavoured and I have had several meals with them added to a salad. They are good raw, roasted or boiled. The whole herb is edible. If they are locally abundant, cropping 10-20% of the stand should not affect the population if it is off the beaten track. Remember, some areas have laws against picking this plant.

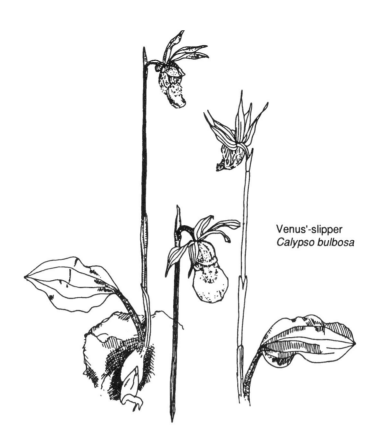

Venus'-slipper
Calypso bulbosa

Lady's-slipper   *Cypripedium spp.*

Cypripedium = kip-ree-pee-dee-um, from the Greek *kypris* (a name for Venus) and *pediton* (a slipper or foot) referring to the shape of the flower.

Synonyms: Nerve root, Two lips, Indian Moccasins.

Identification: This orchid is 15-25 cm high with very beautiful flowers which vary in colour according to species. The leaves are alternate and sheath the stems. The roots are thick, creeping and fibrous.

Distribution & Habitat: These rare plants are found in moist, wooded areas. These plants are fast becoming an endangered species, due mainly to people picking them. Unless in an emergency it would be a shame to destroy this plant. It is cultivated for herbal use and is available in health food stores.

A Lady's-slipper Legend

There was once a little daughter of an Indian Chieftain. One day, while she was playing far away from her camp, she met a rabbit. The rabbit was crying. It had hurt its feet and couldn't go home. The little girl begged the rabbit to

Yucca
Yucca sp.

Venus'-slipper
Calypso bulbosa

Lady's-slipper
Cypripedium sp.

stop crying and gave it her moccasins so it could travel home without further damaging its feet.

It was growing late and the child decided to return to her camp. It was not long before her feet were torn and bleeding. She collapsed in exhaustion along the wooded pathway and fell asleep. Before long a songbird flew by and seeing her bleeding feet, begged the Great Spirit to help the poor little maiden. On awakening, she found a beautiful pair of moccasins hanging on two slender stems. She slipped these moccasins on her bleeding feet and was able to make her way home.

If you don't believe this story, look inside a yellow lady's-slipper orchid sometime and you'll see the reddish purple spots of blood and some lines made by the little maiden's bleeding feet.

Preparation & Uses: The root of this herb is nature's tranquilizer, calming and easing one's mind. It has been used with good results in reflex functional disorders or chorea, hysteria, nervous headache, insomnia, low fevers, nervous unrest, nutrition of the nerve centers, hypochondria and nervous depression accompanying stomach disorders.

For depression, it is best combined with chamomile (*Anthemis nobilis*). If combined with skullcap (*Scutellaria sp.*, *scutellaria* = L. dish [the depression of the fruiting calyx]), it is effective for hysteria, headaches, and other nervous disorders.

To make a good infusion, pour 1 pint boiling water over 5 tablespoons of the root and steep for 1 hour.

According to Dr. Nowell, the lady's-slipper root is almost a pure nervine. It is excellent in relieving pain and inducing sleep. Lab studies indicate that it decreases pain, quietens nerves and promotes sleep. Drink a strong decoction hot.

Strong Decoction: 4 oz. lady's-slipper root
1 quart distilled water
8 oz. glycerine

Soak the root in cold water for 2 hours. Bring to a boil and simmer for 15 minutes, then strain, and remove liquid to a clean vessel. Reduce to 3/4 pint by slow boiling. Remove from the heat and add glycerine while it is still hot, mix thoroughly, cool, bottle and store it in a cool place.

The Menomini Indians considered Lady's-slipper root useful for female disorders, for inducing dreams and for its supernatural properties. The Meskwaki Indians used it as a major part of a love potion.

Lady's-slipper root was officially recognized in U.S.P 1863-1916, N.F. 1916-36.

Because Lady's-slipper is non-poisonous and perfectly safe, it may be taken in larger doses when necessary. Lady's-slipper has caused contact dermatitis in some sensitive people.

Balsam Poplar   *Populus balsamifera*

balsamifera = bal-sa-mi-fe-ra, L. for "yielding or producing a fragrant resin".

Identification: Balsam poplar is a deciduous tree which grows up to 25 m tall. It has a broad crown and, when mature, a dark furrowed bark. The twigs are light grey, and have sticky buds. The leaves are ovate, yellow green or pale brown beneath and dark green above.

Distribution & Habitat: Balsam poplar is locally abundant in the foothills and on the edge of the mountains. It hybridizes with other poplars and is often found in association with aspens.

Preparation & Uses: The Cree called balsam poplar *Metoos* and shredded the bark, obtaining a liquid extract used for coughs. They also noted that its wood burns better than other species while still green.

The Blackfoot called it *As-si-tsix-in*. They used the inner bark in smoking mixtures and as emergency horse food. The Blackfoot used to take the sap and rub it over their body when stalking horses to disguise the human scent. It has been reported that some Indians used the resinous bud to cure snow-blindness. It didn't always work and the application was extremely painful.

I consider Balm of Gilead to be one of our area's more important herbs. It is made from the bark or winter buds of *P. balsamifera* and several other poplar species. Dr. John R. Christopher lists this oily resin as a major cathartic. The bark is a cathartic, tonic, stimulant, diuretic, alterative and expectorant. The buds have the same properties in addition to acting as a nephritic, demulcent, emollient, vulnerary, counterirritant, antirheumatic and nutritive.

Balsam Poplar
(Spring)
Populus balsamifera

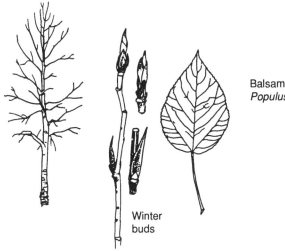

Balsam Poplar
Populus balsamifera

Winter buds

It is very soothing and healing to dry and inflamed parts, both internally and externally. As a soothing expectorant, Balm of Gilead is very effective in bronchitis.

Made into a compounded ointment or oil, it is extremely good for any skin disease. Balm of Gilead is also effective in cleansing the blood and eliminating the cause of scurvy.

The fragrant resinous matter that covers the buds of this and other balsams is easily separated in boiling water. It is soluble in alcohol and oils but not in cool water. As is the case with most cathartics, if the expelling action comes about too fast, griping pains may be felt. If this occurs, add ginger root to the mixture.

Many testimonials could be given for this herb, Here is a personal one:

> I was at a party where some cheese was brought to appease our hunger. Being quite hungry I took out my hunting knife, which was very sharp at the time, and started to cut some cheese. Instead of putting the cheese on the table, I held it in my hand and speedily cut through the cheese and deeply into my index finger. In great pain, I put the cut finger in my mouth. Holding the cut together with my tongue, I ran outside. Fortunately I was by the Elbow river where there were lots of cottonwood poplars. I got a friend to pick some winter buds off a tree. I squeezed the resin out of the buds and put it on my finger. The pain went away almost immediately.

Poplar winter buds
Populus balsamifera

Aspen
*Populus
tremuloides*

For a dry cough or sore throat, take ½ teaspoon of the oil or ointment, mix with honey and lemon juice, and drink it. The oleo-resin can be used internally or externally, but only small amounts should be used internally. Externally, it is soothing to any skin irritation, cuts, bruises, rashes and pimples.

I have found it to be a very good massage oil – soothing and smelling like a fresh spring day. Use almond or cocoa butter oil as the base, if you prefer, because they are a little less oily.

To prepare Balm of Gilead, take:

1 part *P. balsamifera* bud
2 parts olive or other pure oil

Place in a jar and put the jar in a pot of water (like a double boiler) and heat, keeping the water just below the boiling point, steeping the buds for about 1 hour. Strain and cool. After cooling I put about 400 I.U. of Vitamin E per 8 oz. of oil to keep it from going rancid.

Populus balsamifera was also used by many Indians to make their pipe stems. Some Indians believed that there was natural fire in the wood and if properly treated, they could bring the fire out. This legend probably led to the tree being used in the board and drill of friction firemaking equipment.

Aspen, Quaking   *Populus tremuloides*

Populus = Pōp-u-lus, Latin name for poplar - *arbor populi* - "tree of the people"; *tremuloides* = trem-ew-loy-dees, L. for "aspen-like" (ie. like *Populus tremulus*); *tremulus* = L. for "trembling, shaking".

Identification: Quaking aspen looks similar to balsam poplar, with which it often hybridizes. It reaches a height of 30 m and has smooth, light green or greyish bark that becomes furrowed with age. The petioles are slender (from which it gets it name), with orbicular to broadly ovate, finely serrated to nearly entire leaves.

Distribution & Habitat: Generally found in parkland, it inhabits moist and sunny locations from Alaska south to the cooler locations of Mexico.

How Aspens came to tremble (a Blackfoot story)

All of the plants and animals respected Napi (the Blackfoot man/god/clownster) very much. Whenever he went through the woods all of the trees would bow down to him, partly out of fear and partly out of respect. One day the aspens got together and decided that Napi wasn't all that important, so they agreed that they would not bow down for him, next time he was around. True to their word, the next day when Napi came walking by they just stood there indignantly. Well of course Napi didn't like this. In a tantrum he started throwing lightning bolts at them, almost scaring the leaves right off their branches. To this very day the aspens are so scared that every time they hear someone walking in the woods, they tremble their leaves in fear that it might be Napi.

The petioles of aspen leaves are quite thin. Together with the fact that the under sides are greyish-silver and the upper are bright green, it means that the slightest wind make them appear to tremble.

Preparation & Uses: The inner bark was eaten as a spring tonic and an emergency food by the Indians.

The tonic effect of the leaf and especially the inner bark has been well established. Aspen bark is often preferred by herbalists over Peruvian bark or quinine. The tonic effect is useful for stomach pain, liver problems, convalescence and for relaxing headaches, but its greatest effects are on the urinary/genital system. The inner bark has been used to strengthen weakened female organs (especially during excessive menstrual bleeding), for prostatitis, vaginal and renal areas as well as being used for a variety of venereal diseases. It is a diuretic that is often combined with *Arctostaphylos uva-ursi* (bearberry). A tincture of the bark (containing aspirin-like salicin and populin) has been used for fevers, rheumatism, arthritis, colds, worms, urinary infection and diarrhea. A salve made from the leaf can be used for irritated nostrils.

Willow   *Salix spp.*

Salix = Sā-liks, from the classical Latin name for willows.

Identification: There are many species of *Salix* in the area, making it a complex and diverse genus. Willows grow as shrubs and occasionally small trees. Their flowers and fruits are borne as catkins. The leaves are usually narrow.

Distribution & Habitat: Willows are typically found in wet places such as river banks, marshes and swampy areas.

Preparation & Uses: The young shoots and leaves of willow can be eaten raw. The inner bark of willow can also be eaten raw, but is better if it is dried and then ground into flour.

The inner bark of willow contains a chemical called salicin or methyl salicylate which is similar to aspirin and useful as a substitute. The leaves have an astringent quality that is effective when placed on cuts and wounds. The tea of the bark excretes in the urine as salicylic acid and can therefore be used for irritability of the urinary tract.

The Blackfoot Indians used willow in many ways. An infusion of the root was used for venereal disease, bruises, throat constriction, internal bleeding,

Willow
Salix sp.

bloodshot eyes and mixed with kidney fat for head sores. The root was chewed and spat into horse's eyes if they were bloodshot or cloudy. The roots were also dried, crushed, then soaked in water and grease as a dandruff tonic.

Willow branches are very flexible, which makes them useful for many household or camp needs, such as handles, woven items and back rests. The bark can be woven into a cord. Nice little whistles can be made by loosening the bark, carving holes and blowing through it.

Alder   *Alnus crispa & A. incana*

Alnus = Latin name for alder; *crispa* = L. for "with a waved or curled margin"; *incana* = "quite grey, hoary-white".

Identification: Alder grows as a shrub and small tree, with reddish or greyish brown bark. The leaves are simple, ovate to obovate with dentate or serrate margins, and are 2 - 8 cm long. The flowers are borne on cone-like catkins appearing similar to birch, to which it is closely related.

Distribution & Habitat: There are ten species in North America, ranging throughout most of the area, except the Great Plains. Alders are most frequently found beside streams or in other moist places.

Willow
Salix sp.

Willow
Salix sp.

Alder
Alnus sp.

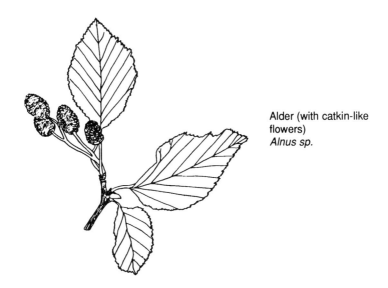

Alder (with catkin-like
flowers)
Alnus sp.

Preparation & Uses: The inner bark and young buds are edible though they aren't delicacies.

A decoction of the bark was ingested by the Kutenai Indians to regulate menstrual flow. The Blackfoot felt this tea was useful in cases of tuberculosis of the lymph glands (especially of the neck). The bark was used, much as Cascara (though milder), for constipation, jaundice and diarrhea. The bark must be aged (for at least a few days) as the green bark will cause vomiting and griping. The decoction is often left to sit for 2 - 3 days until the yellow colour has changed to black. The inner bark can be used as a poultice to reduce swelling, to treat wounds and skin ulcers. The root of the alder was boiled and drunk by the Ojibwa and the Menomini Indians as an astringent because of its very high tannin content. It's astringent effect was sought out when blood was seen in a person's stools. Juice of the fresh scraped bark is said to relieve itching from a rash. A fresh infusion is quite effective on poison ivy.

A decoction of the leaves is useful on burns and inflamed wounds. The fresh leaves were often put in moccasins or shoes to relieve tired and aching feet by reducing swelling and cooling them. One old Indian lady told me she used to place alder leaves under her husband's hat whenever he got too grumpy from drinking the night before. She was convinced it was the best cure for hangovers and it could possibly even cure alcoholism. The dew-moistened leaves were used to banish fleas since, while damp, the leaves will attract them. While still damp, dump the leaves outside. In Lapland, bags full of heated alder leaves were used to cover people as a cure for rheumatism.

Smooth Alder (*Alnus serrulata*), found in the eastern U.S.A., was used for malaria and syphilis in the 1800's.

Alder is one of the great dye plants. It gives us red, gold, olive green, brown and black colours that do not need a mordant. As a fuel, alder doesn't throw sparks or leave much ash. In arid areas, it is used to locate the presence of water.

Paper Birch   *Betula papyrifera*

Betula = bet-ew-la, from the classical Latin name - Pitch - the name in Pliny, bitumen is distilled from the bark, *papyrifera* = pă-pi-ri-fe-ra, paper bearing, referring to the papery bark. Birch comes from Sanskrit *bhurga*, meaning tree whose bark is used for writing.

Identification: Depending on where it grows, paper birch varies greatly in size. In the north it only grows to about 3 m, whereas in ideal conditions it can reach heights of 15 m. The bark is usually whitish or silvery-grey and can be peeled off in thin sheets. The leaves are ovate and irregularly-toothed. Taxonomically it is a complex species that hybridises with other species.

Distribution & Habitat: Paper Birch is usually found in moist ecological situations.

Preparation & Uses: The inner red bark of paper birch is rich in vitamins and minerals; a good addition to soups and stews. The sap of most birches can be made into a syrup quite similar to maple syrup. One should be very careful during sap extraction. It is difficult to stop the sap after tapping and this could kill the tree. I knew one "old timer" that had a huge stand of birch on his property and found the syrup to be the land's best resource. He guarded it jealously.

To tap a tree for syrup, make a two - inch - deep hole on the sunny side of the tree. This hole should be angled upward slightly. Insert some form of tap that can hold a bucket. This should be done in the early spring, before leaves fully come out. A tree can produce ½ - 10 gallons of sap daily, so the container needs to be checked often. Sphagnum moss makes a good plug to seal up the tree. It stops the flow and creates an antiseptic barrier for the tree. It takes 80 - 100 gallons of sap to produce 1 gallon of syrup. You boil it constantly, until it is thick enough. It takes approximately 12 hours and lots of fuel to convert 25 gallons of sap into 1 quart of syrup. If you don't want to go through all the trouble of making the syrup, a great beer or vinegar can be made from the sap.

Young birch leaves and catkins can be added to salad dressing to give an interesting taste. They can also be used as a seasoning for meat or vegetables if cooked along with them.

Straight birch sap was often used as a spring tonic by pioneers. It was also used as a gargle for cankers, sore throat and used as an external wash for skin eruptions. The populin (a methyl salicylate, similar to aspirin) is analgesic. In fact the scent of wintergreen often comes from birch (*Betula lenta*) trees. Both as essence oil and internal dose, birch has been used for headaches, rheumatism and other "aspirin-amenable" problems.

The leaves of birch are diuretic and were used for kidney problems as well as kidney stones.

One of the useful things about paper birch is that it makes a very good paper. Just peel the bark off to the size and thickness desired. Do not do this on the main trunk of a live tree as the tree above the peel will die. (Dead trees or branches are better used.) The bark can be shaped if it is heated, (usually by hot rocks) making it surprising pliable.

Several types of bark utensils can also be made. Horace Kephart has many designs in his *Camping and Woodcraft* book. This book is very enjoyable reading and is a must for anyone doing a lot of outdoor living.

It is even possible to make a birch bark kettle boil water. This is surprising because birch bark is also prized tinder. The water in the kettle quickly absorbs the heat before it has a chance to burn the bark, as long as no flames reach above the water level. All that is necessary is a waterproof box made from birch bark.

Stinging Nettle *Urtica urens & gracilis*

Urtica = ur-tik-a, L. "sting" (the Latin name), *urens* = L. "stinging, burning", *gracilis* = "slender, graceful".

Identification: Stinging nettle is an erect annual herb, 20–40 cm high, with stinging hairs on the stems and leaves. The flowers are green-white and droop in clusters from the stalk. The leaves are opposite, ovate to broadly elliptical, 3 to 5 nerved and toothed.

Distribution & Habitat: *Urtica urens* is an introduced weed that is widely distributed throughout the region.

Preparation & Uses: The first thing that must be considered with nettles are their stinging effect. The little hairs or bristles covering some plants are hollow, and act as "hypodermic needles" that contain formic acid (others feel it is a histamine compound). The penetration of these bristles can be prevented by wearing leather gloves or by carefully picking the stalks with your thumb and two fingers, turning the hairs aside. Other plants can be used to protect the hands while picking nettles. Fortunately, the stinging effect is not usually bad. Surprisingly, the antidote for the sting is also found in nettles. Use nettles as a tea wash or dock (*Rumex spp.*) or mullein. The stinging effect is completely destroyed by cooking.

Nettle is popular all over the world as a pot herb. The best parts of the plant are the tender shoots or pink underground stem parts. Nettle is a little bland-tasting, so mix it with other foods or seasonings, such as vinegar and butter. The roots of nettles are good roasted. Nettles are high in vitamins A, C and D (a rare vitamin in plants). It also contains iron, sodium, potassium, phosphorus, calcium, silica and albuminoids.

A good wine or beer can reportedly be made from nettles with the addition of dandelion flowers, lemon juice, ginger root, brown sugar and yeast.

White Birch
Betula sp.

Nettles
Urtica sp.

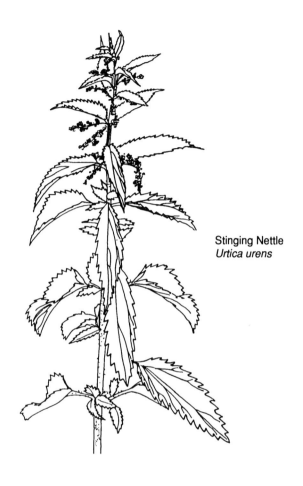

Stinging Nettle
Urtica urens

Medicinally, nettles are listed as diuretic, astringent, tonic, pectoral antispasmodic (specific for the respiratory system), galactagogue and hemostatic. Boiling water is a solvent. The most important herbal application for nettle is to stop internal bleeding. It is probably the best known treatment for treating someone spitting up blood due to hemorrhage of the lungs and stomach and blood passing from the urinary organs. Some people report that the decoction is good, while others say that the fresh juice squeezed from the leaves is better. The dose is one tablespoon of the juice every hour.

The decoction of root and/or leaves will expel phlegm from the lungs and stomach, it is also valuable in treating diarrhea, dysentery, piles, neuralgia, gravel and inflammation of the kidneys. As a diuretic it should not be used for extended periods of time as it can irritate the kidney. This is particularly true of older leaves that contain cystoliths that irritate the kidney.

A spring tonic made from nettle tea was often employed by settlers. The decoction can be used for treating excess menstrual flow. The fresh juice of the plant is reported to promote the flow of milk in nursing mothers. The seeds have been used to treat coughs and shortness of breath. In a freeze-dried form, I often use nettle to help people prevent food sensitivities. It is known to bind up Immunoglobulin G, responsible for many food sensitivities.

Externally, the pounded root and/or bruised leaves of nettle are excellent in stopping bleeding. The fresh leaves should not be left on too long as they will cause blistering. A decoction is often used to treat rheumatic pain and stiff joints.

The Indians were reported to use stinging nettles as a counter-irritant for pain associated with rheumatic problems. They would strike the painful area with nettles, and after a short period the stinging would stop and the rheumatic pain would disappear. The fumes from stinging nettle were inhaled in the sweat lodges of the Nevada Indians to treat flu and pneumonia. Washington state's Salish Indians used nettles to relax a woman's muscles during childbirth. Nettle tea was most often used but sometimes the tips of young plants were chewed during childbirth.

The decoction is usually taken in 2-4 fl. oz. doses.

The old stalks (which have no sting left) are quite strong and can be woven into a twine and have even been made into fine cloth.

Sorrel, Mountain   *Oxyria digyna*

Oxyria = oks-ee-rae-a, from Greek name of
sorrel, from L. *oxys* "acid" (the taste),
digyna = L. "two-carpelled or two ovaries".

Synonyms: Scurvy grass, sour grass.

Identification: This low perennial herb
grows 5-30 cm high and bears small reddish
or green flowers in a dense raceme. The
kidney-shaped leaves are alternate to basal
on long petioles. The rootstalk is short.

Distribution & Habitat: Mountain sorrel is a
circumpolar plant. It is found in the arctic,
high alpine meadows and cool rocky
slopes. It is usually found in moist places at
high altitudes where there is good snow
cover in winter.

Preparation & Uses: The leaves and stems
of this plant have a pleasant, sour taste
when eaten raw and also taste very good
when boiled. Although older leaves can be
eaten, the younger ones taste like spinach
with vinegar, due to the oxalic acid in them.

Indians often let the plant sit in water for a
while to ferment. This makes a kind of
sauerkraut that can be stored for winter
use. The Pacific Coast Indians boiled this herb with various berries. Another
tribe dried it in the sun for travelling.

It has a very high vitamin C content and therefore acts as a good preventative
for scurvy. This herb has also been used as an infusion for itches and ringworm.

Caution: large amounts could cause oxalate poisoning.

Bistort   *Polygonum spp.*

Polygonum = po-li-go-num, from Greek *polys* (many) and *gony* (a knee/joint)
referring to jointed stems.

Synonyms: Knotweed

Identification: Bistorts belong to a genus of annual and perennial herbs. They
grow 20-70 cm high, with raceme, spike-like and dense heads of pink or white
flowers. The basal leaves have long petioles and are lanceolate, while the
stem leaves have no petiole, and are thinner, lanceolate.

Distribution & Habitat: Bistort is found in moist cool places. It can usually be seen in moist alpine tundra, mountain meadows and stream banks.

Preparation & Uses: Many of the species (e.g. *P. aviculare*) have seeds that may be used whole, or ground into flour. Some have peppery leaves which make a good seasoning. *P. bistortoides* and *P. viviparum* can be cooked and used as a substitute for nuts and raisins, having an almond flavour. None of the plants in this genus are poisonous.

The root of bistort can be used as an astringent, diuretic, antiseptic and alterative. It is one of the strongest astringent herbs and is excellent for gargling, injections (vaginal and anal), infection, for cholera, diarrhea, dysentery and leucorrhea. A good wash for a sore mouth or gums can be made from a decoction of the roots. Combined with equal parts of red raspberry leaves, it will cleanse internal cankers. It also makes a good wash for the nose. It is useful for the treatment of smallpox, measles, pimples, jaundice, ruptures, insect stings, snake bites and worms. Combined with plantain, bistort root will stop bleeding of cuts or wounds when applied directly to the injury, making a great first aid remedy. Used as a douche, it decreases or regulates menstrual flow. The powdered root, without the plantain has also had good effects.

To make the decoction, take 2 teaspoons of the rootstock in 1 cup of boiling water and boil for 5-10 minutes.

Dock and Sorrels   *Rumex spp.*

Rumex = ru-meks, from the Latin name for *Rumex acetosa*.

Identification: These coarse, perennial herbs, usually have thick roots. They can stand from 10 cm to 2 m tall, depending on species. The leaves are alternate, with the lower ones often being large, oblong to broadly lanceolate, varying between species. The flowers are small, greenish with a red-tinged edge, found in compound inflorescence; calyx has 6 sepals, found in two whorls of 3.

Distribution & Habitat: Docks are found throughout North America, many being introduced. They are usually found in waste land, many preferring saline or moist areas.

Preparation & Uses: The leaves and petioles of docks are quite tart and can be used as rhubarb substitutes. The tartness is due to oxalates and like rhubarb leaves could be toxic in large amounts. If the tartness is too strong, boil the herb first, with a change of water. No human toxicity has ever been reported, but some livestock problems have been recorded. Because of the tartness, the leaves are often used as a spinach (and vinegar) substitute, both raw and cooked. As an ingredient in salads they are great. It means you don't need any salad dressing as dock conveniently brings its own "vinegar" with it! I prefer the curled dock (*Rumex crispa*) which does not need a change of water when

Dock
Rumex sp.

Lamb's Quarters
Chenopodium album

cooked like spinach. I try to use as little water as possible and it gives it a better taste, not at all watery. The leaves have more vitamin C than oranges and more vitamin A (Beta-carotene) than carrots. It is also very high in calcium, iron, potassium and a minor scattering of some B vitamins.

As a relative of buckwheat, the seeds can be used as a flour.

Sheep sorrel (*R. acetosella*) was a common European herb. The fresh leaves are considered a cooling diuretic and a good poultice for sebaceous cysts and even skin cancer and tumors. Leaf teas were used for fever, scurvy and inflammation. The roots can be used for diarrhea and excessive menstruation.

Yellow or Curly Dock (*Rumex crispa*) root is a famous blood cleanser, used for liver problems, swollen lymphatic glands, skin sores, warts and rheumatism. Varying doses can both cause and relieve diarrhea. Its use for the liver is particularly appropriate in cases of poor digestion of fatty foods (such as dairy products and meats). The root has often been used to treat jaundice and post-hepatitis flare-ups. The root tea has been used for ringworm and other fungi.

The docks were heavily used by Amerindians for the same general ailments listed above. Many Amerindian tribes used the roots to produce a yellow dye.

Lamb's Quarters   *Chenopodium album*

Chenopodium = kay-nō-pō-dee-um, from Greek *chen* (goose) and *podion* (foot) referring to the shape of the leaves, *album* = L. "dead-white".

Identification: Lamb's quarters is a stout many-branched annual 30-100 cm high, varying in appearance. The dense compound flower clusters are more or less white with a bluish tinge. The leaves are green above and densely mealy beneath. The leaf shape varies from ovate, rhombic to lanceolate, with the larger leaves being irregularly-toothed. The branches often turn reddish late in the season. The dense seeds are black.

Distribution & Habitat: This introduced weed is found in gardens, along roadsides and on waste areas.

Preparation & Uses: Lamb's quarters gets its name from its mealy leaves (and its love of manure). In England, Lamb's quarters was called midden myles, and there was a saying "Boil myles in water and chop them into butter and you will have a good dish." Lamb's quarters is also called pigweed. The herb is good eaten as a salad or as a pot herb, prepared like spinach. This plant contains large amounts of beta-carotene and vitamin C. It also contains quite high levels of oxalic acid so large quantities should not be eaten. If first ground into a meal, the seeds are quite good in bread. The meal or flour resembles buckwheat in colour and taste and is considered equally nutritious. The seeds are also good eaten raw. With 70,000 seeds per plant collecting them is not that hard!

Lamb's quarters is good for relieving heat from too much sun, or for a headache. Just bruise the leaves and apply this as a poultice to the forehead. The leaves have been used this way, applied to wounds and eye inflammations. It was also used as a folk remedy for vertigo.

The entire plant can be boiled and used as a crude green dye.

Strawberry Blite   *Chenopodium capitatum*

Chenopodium = L. "goose-foot" (the shape of the leaves), *capitatum* = L. growing in a head, head-like (inflorescence).

Identification: This succulent, annual herb has bright red flowers which form a spherical clustered head. These heads are supposed to look like blighted strawberries. The plant grows from 20-40 cm high with alternate, somewhat succulent, dark green leaves. The fruit of strawberry blite is bright red, berry-like and juicy.

Distribution & Habitat: It is a weed and usually found in clearings, burned areas, roadsides and along trails. It prefers slightly wet places.

Preparation & Uses: The leaves and the tender shoots of this plant are said to make a good pot herb soup. The fruits are said to be sweet, rather insipid and seedy, but good raw or cooked. Kephart stated that it was sometimes cultivated, indicating how widely the plant has been used in some areas in the past.

It has been used externally in decoctions for ulcers of the throat and mouth. It has also been used as an injection for leucorrhea and for hemorrhages of the bowels.

The bright juice was squeezed from the fruit and made into Indian war paint.

Pigweed   *Amaranthus retroflexus & spp.*

Amaranthus = am-a-ran-thus, from Greek *amarantos* (unfading) referring to the long lasting flower, *retroflexus* = L. "directed backwards and downwards".

Identification: This is an erect, sometimes branching annual herb, with a red taproot, that grows 30 cm to 100 cm high. The leaves are ovate to lanceolate and the flowers inconspicuous in narrow clusters.

Distribution & Habitat: This common weed can be found in waste land, gardens, along roadsides and on disturbed soil throughout the area.

Preparation & Uses: The dried seeds were used by the Indians, eaten whole, or ground into meal, and made into cakes and breads (often mixed with cornmeal). This plant is under investigation as a food crop. The young shoots are fairly tasty if eaten as a pot herb right after picking them.

BA

Strawberry Blite
Chenopodium capitatum

Pigweed
Amaranthus retroflexus

BA

BA

Spring Beauty
Claytonia sp.

Pigweed
Amaranthus sp.

Medicinally, the herb is a mild astringent for the mucous membranes. It is used as a poultice to reduce swelling, as a tea for its cleansing properties and to treat dysentery, diarrhea, excessive menstruation, ulcers and intestinal hemorrhaging. A douche can be made for vaginal discharge or the tea can be used as a wash for vaginal itching.

The normal dosage is a strong infusion, drunk every few hours throughout the day. The leaves contain a saponin and were used as a soap for washing clothes.

Spring Beauty   *Claytonia spp.*

Claytonia = clay-to-nee-a, from John Clayton, a 17th century botanist.

Identification: These low perennial herbs have white or pinkish flowers in loose terminal racemes. There are 2 sepals, 5 petals and 5 stamens, with a 3-cleft style. There are usually one or two basal leaves with oblong-lanceolate blades. The two stem leaves are opposite, stalkless and broadly lanceolate. Just above the root, the stem forms a large spherical fleshy corm. There are 3-6 seeds in 3 valved capsules.

Distribution & Habitat: *C. lanceolata* is common above the timber line, in moist mats of herbs. It flowers early and dies back soon after. *Claytonia megarhiza* is quite rare and is found in moist shady places on high mountains.

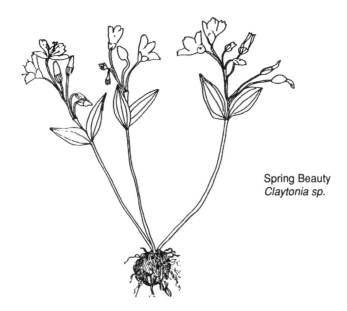

Spring Beauty
Claytonia sp.

Preparation & Uses: Blackfoot Indians used the corm at the base of the stem in different foods. This small root can be eaten raw, boiled or roasted. It can also improve the taste of stew. It is said that many white men, on first eating this root, find it distasteful, but I have found it fairly good to eat.

The roots are quite high in starch and have little flavour raw. When cooked they taste like potatoes (as long as they are peeled before cooking). When the peel is left on, they taste a little more earthy (the peel comes off quite easily after cooking). The root should be boiled or baked for 30 minutes. This plant is not always plentiful so if it is not locally abundant it seems a shame to use the corms extensively except in cases of emergencies.

The rosette leaves can be eaten raw, or cooked, but they have little flavour. They are good mixed in a salad.

The whole plant of *C. perfoliata* was used by the Nevada Indians as a poultice for rheumatic pain. The plant was soaked overnight, mashed and applied. It functioned as a counterirritant. Kodiak Indians believed it would rain if the plant was picked.

Montia spp.

Montia = mon-tee-a, after L. Monti, an 18th century Italian botany professor.

These plants are similar to *Claytonia spp.* without the corms. The stems, leaves and roots can be eaten. It falls into the same genus as Miner's lettuce but the "true" Miner's lettuce (*M. perfoliata*) does not grow in this area. A suitable alterative does. Siberian miner's lettuce (*M. sibirican*) is quite good.

The Songish of Washington used the leaves of these plants as a poultice for headache. The Shoshone used them for rheumatic pain and as a counterirritant.

Bitter Root   *Lewisia pygmaea*

Lewisia = loo-is-ee-a, after Lewis (1774-1809) of the Lewis & Clark expedition (1806-7); *pyamaea* = pig-may-ah, dwarf.

Identification: This perennial herb is usually rare but it can be locally abundant. The flower is pink to rose-red with 6-9 petals. The leaves are mostly basal and spatulate to linear, spreading flat on the ground. The fleshy tap root is long and buried deep in the soil. There are usually 10-20 seeds in a capsule near the base.

Distribution & Habitat: It is found high in the mountains, on alpine slopes, near the timberline in Alberta and Montana.

Preparation & Uses: The Blackfoot called this plant *ax-six-sixi*. Some Indians prized these roots so much that they were said to have traded a bag of them for a horse. It must have had important medicinal uses, but I have only found two. The Thompson Indians ate the root in the belief it would cure insanity. An infusion of this plant was sometimes mixed with *Lomatium dissectum*, *Valeriana sp.*, *Yucca sp.*, and administered through a horse's mouth or nostril for colic or distemper by the Blackfoot Indians.

It was usually dug up for eating in the spring because it was easily found at this time of year. A second reason for spring harvesting was the bitter outer rind peeled off easily then. These roots, when boiled, exude a mucilage substance. The core should be boiled about 20 minutes with one changing of water to help decrease the bitterness. It is soft and tastes good but has a strong background bitterness that makes you suspect it is good for you. The first white man to discover the bitter root was one of the members of the Lewis & Clarke expedition. Lewis gave the flower its botanical name and after several years sent the herbarium specimen back to England, where it was noticed that it still contained a little life. It was planted and it started to grow. In honour of Lewis it was given its scientific name.

You won't be able to find this plant easily because it has been overharvested for many years. Consequently, I suggest you don't dig it up.

Purslane   *Portulaca oleracea*

Portulaca = por-tew-lah-ka, from it classical Latin name "milk-carrier", a name in Pliny, *oleracea* = o-le-rah-kee-a, meaning "vegetable-like", referring to it edible state.

Identification: This is a mat-forming annual weed, with prostrate stems, that are usually purplish-red. The yellow flowers are sessile and in small terminal clusters, opening only in the sunshine. The leaves are wedge-shaped to ovate.

Distribution & Habitat: This is a persistent weed in gardens, wastelands and disturbed soils throughout the area.

Preparation & Uses: The entire above-ground portion of this well-known weed can be eaten, although the young shoots and leaves are the best. Purslane is actually cultivated in some countries. The young leaves and shoots are good in salads. It is best to mix purslane with other plants because it has a sour taste. This plant germinates continually throughout the summer so it is always abundant. You can keep a patch alive by picking the young tender shoots as needed. New shoots will soon appear.

As a cooking herb, treat it similarly to spinach. Change the water once if the sour taste is not desired (though it is not unpleasant). This plant is a bit mucilaginous and therefore excellent when added to soup as a green and thickener. The shoots can also be baked with bread crumbs and beaten eggs or added to meatloaf. The Indians often dried purslane in the sun, storing it for adding to soup in the winter. The seeds can be ground into a meal or flour, then baked or cooked as a mush.

Purslane is rich in vitamins and minerals, especially iron (much-needed by vegetarians). It is also high in oxalic acid, omega-3 essential fatty acids and albuminoids.

Medicinally, purslane has been used in the form of an infusion for stomach-aches, excess menstrual flow and high blood pressure. The seed was used for removing worms in children and as a palliative for hemorrhoids. The juice of purslane can be added to equal parts of honey and used as a cough syrup. It is especially useful for dry coughs. This plant was adopted by Amerindians who used it as a poultice for burns, tea for headaches and juice for cataracts.

Moss Campion *Silene acaulis*

Silene = si-lay-nee, from a related Greek plant (Theophrastus' name for Viscaria, another catchfly), *acaulis* = a-kaw-lis, meaning stemless.

Identification: This low, perennial, cushion plant, forms dense mats which sometimes attain a diameter of up to 1 m. The solitary flowers are purplish pink or rarely, white. Short, flat leaves cover the stems, with old leaves persisting on the stem base.

Distribution & Habitat: This plant is fairly common in alpine meadows where it grows very slowly. It lives in a very delicate situation. Moss campion is also found growing on rock slides and in turfy places on open slopes, above the timberline.

Preparation & Uses: The young *Silene* shoot, not over 5 cm long, makes a good pot herb. The entire aboveground plant can also be eaten. It should be boiled until tender.

As this plant grows very slowly and is found in delicate alpine areas, it should only be used in an extreme emergency. A related species, *S. virginica* has been listed for ridding the body of worms.

Moss Campion
Silene acaulis

Chickweed   *Stellaria spp.*

Stellaria = L. from "star" (the appearance of stitchwort flowers).

Identification: Chickweeds are slender herbs 5-30 cm tall and are found growing in tufts or mats. The flowers are small. The leaves are blue-green, linear and stiff with lower leaves turning brownish with maturity. The seeds are borne in shiny black capsules.

Distribution & Habitat: This common low-lying herb is found in mats along road sides, paths and open meadows from the foothills to the alpine meadows.

Preparation & Uses: As a salad herb, chickweed is excellent. The young shoots are best, as the older ones toughen and become strong-tasting, although they are good blanched.

As a pot herb it is cooked like spinach. It is best boiled in a small amount of water for about 20-30 minutes, salting it if desired. It is good with vinegar or butter. Chickweed is quite small and in mature plants only the youngest leaves are good. This makes it tedious to collect a usable quantity.

Chickweed is an excellent healing herb. It is a good treatment for pulmonary complaints, any form of internal or external inflammation of membrane and skin, and weakness of the stomach and bowels. For inflamed or ruptured appendix, give a strong enema while drinking the tea and a apply hot fomentation over the infected area. It is soothing for external wounds, skin diseases, inflamed surfaces and burns. Bruised leaves in coconut or other oil make a good ointment for skin irritation.

The roots can be used medicinally, like dandelion, as a tonic, laxative and diuretic. The dose is three heaping tablespoons to one quart water; boil down to one pint. Take a wineglass full every three hours.

Chickweed Ointment

1 pound fresh green chickweed
1-½ pound lard (lanolin will also work)
2 ounces wax

Cut up the chickweed and place all the ingredients in a stainless steel pot. Cover the pot and place in oven under 200 F. for three hours. Strain through a fine strainer and cool. Leaf lard (found just above the kidney of pigs) has no salt and so is the best to use. The wax is used to stiffen the ointment. Use more or less to get the right consistency.

Chickweed has an amazing effect in soothing itchy skin. Make a strong tea and wash the area. It is especially suitable for babies and children. I have made strong decoctions of this herb and poured it into bath water for its soothing effect. Hives can also be treated this way.

Chickweed is the base of many weight loss formulas in both tea and capsulated form. As the common name suggests, chickens as well as other poultry, like chickweed seed. The greens have been used for centuries as a feed for pigs and rabbits.

Lily, Yellow Pond   *Nuphar variegatum*

Nuphar = new-far, Persian name for a water lily, *variegatum* = L. "irregularly coloured".

Identification: This pond lily rises from a thick rootstock which is attached to the bottom of the lake or pond. The leaves are broadly ovate, 10 - 25 cm long and deeply cordate. The large waxy flowers float on the surface of the water and are yellow with a reddish-tinge. The fruits are podlike, about the size of a hen's egg. They are leathery and contain large seeds.

Distribution & Habitat: The yellow pond lily is found in quiet ponds and shallow lakes in Canada and the United States.

Preparation & Uses: This plant was not often used because it was hard to gather. In the early spring the roots were useful additions to a meal. The skin of the root is first removed, revealing the glutinous, spongy, sweet insides. The seed pod contains seeds that make a poor popcorn substitute.

The rootstocks was used by the Montana Indians to cure venereal disease. It was boiled, the liquid drunk as a tea and a poultice made of the crushed roots, applying it to the affected area. The Sioux also used the rootstock as a poultice for styptic wounds. The Yukon Tagish used yellow pond lily as a remedy for gallstones.

Water Lily   *Nymphaea spp.*

Nymphaea = nimf-ie-a, from L. *Nymphe* (Theophrastus' name after one of the three water nymphs).

Identification: This aquatic perennial herb has a rootstock with erect rhizome. The flower is white with purplish lines. The leaf blades are 5-12 cm long and 3-7 cm wide and have green or purplish undersides.

Distribution & Habitat: White Water Lily is found in lakes and ponds mostly in northerly locations.

Preparation & Uses: The young leaves of water lily are said to be good in soups. The flower buds can be eaten raw or pickled. The roots are listed as antiseptic, astringent, demulcent and emollient. Water is a solvent. Its main use is as an antiseptic douche. The Indians have used this root for generations in all cases of leucorrhea, abrasions of the vagina, inflammation of the womb and ulceration of the womb. At one time this plant was known as "Breastweed", after its use for inflamed breasts. Grieve reports complete cure of uterine cancer by a decoction and a vaginal injection of white pond lily. It should be used as a douche as well as drunk.

A tea made of white lily roots is a good gargle for irritation and inflammation of the mouth or throat. As a chest medicine it has been used for asthma and tuberculosis. This same infusion has been effective as an eyewash and also makes a good skin lotion to heal sores. Anyone who has seen Waterhouse's painting "Water Nymphs" will deduce that this lotion is not only soothing but makes the skin soft and smooth. The leaves and roots are useful as a poultice for wounds, cuts and bruises.

The decoction is made by boiling one oz. of root for 20 minutes in one pint of water.

Mouse-eared Chickweed
Cerastium sp.

Yellow Pond Lily
Nuphar variegatum

Water Lily
Nymphaea sp.

Baneberry   *Actaea rubra*

Actaea = L. from the Gr. name for elder (the shape of the leaves), *rubra* = L. "red".

Identification: A perennial herb, standing 30 - 80 cm tall, having large 2 - 3 ternately compound leaves, leaflet ovate, lobed and sharply toothed and commonly pubescent on the beneath veins. The flowers are white, thin pedicel in a terminal raceme, sepal 3 - 5, obovate. Fruit are several-seeded berries, conspicuous being red or white.

Distribution & Habitat: Found in moist woods from Alaska, Yukon, east to Hudson Bay and Newfoundland, south into California, Arizona, New Mexico, Ohio and New Jersey.

Preparation & Uses: This poisonous plant (suppressing the vagus nerve, causing possible cardiac arrest) has been employed by various herbalists throughout history. It is not recommended for use except by very experienced professionals. Moore says the roots are like Black Cohosh in nature, but much stronger. I have interviewed medicine men that say it was used as a herbal tea, internally, when nothing else would work. It was very important to keep the patient inside, protected from the slightest breeze or they would die.

The powdered root has been made into tincture or mixed with water to be used as a good external counterirritant.

Crocus, Prairie   *Anemone patens*

Anemone = a-nem-o-nee, derived from the Semetic name for Adonis -Naamen (a name used by Theophrastus). His blood is said to produce the blood-red flower of *A. coronaria. patens* = L. spreading out from the stem.

Identification: Crocus is one of the first flowers to bloom in the early spring. It has a beautiful purple flower and numerous yellow stamens. The leaves are sessile, linear to lanceolate and the whole plant is covered in short hairs.

Distribution & Habitat: This plant is very common in dry open woods and prairie grasslands.

The First Crocus

There was once a Indian boy ready to go through his ceremony of manhood in the early spring. After the traditional sweats of purification he was sent up into the hills, with nothing but a buffalo robe, for three days of fasting and vision questing. The first night it became very cold, so he wrapped his robe tightly around himself and he heard a little voice say 'thank-you'. Surprised, looking around for the voice, he noticed a little white flower. It looked up at him and said, 'don't unwrap the robe it is cold out there'. The boy soon fell asleep, feeling just a little bit more secure, now that he wasn't all alone.

The next day he started talking to the flower and it kept him company as the long hours went by. The second night was just as cold and the flower was very grateful for the boy's warm robe. On the third day, the boy was starting to get a bit concerned because he had not as yet had a vision. If he didn't have a vision he would not become a man. The flower assured him that everything would be alright as they looked out together at the beautiful yellow sun, reflecting off the purple mountains. That night was the coldest of them all, they had to cuddle close in the robe to keep warm, but just before dawn, a great vision came to the boy. He saw himself as a great medicine man, taking care of many tribes of people. In the morning he was so happy with his newfound power, feeling grateful for the reassurance given to him by the flower, he told the flower it could have three wishes.

The crocus said, "I would like to have the warmth and beauty of the yellow sun at my heart, the grace of the purple mountains all around me and a heavy fur robe to keep me warm". To this very day the descendants of this little crocus have been given all three to keep them warm and happy in the early spring.

Preparation & Uses: Although this plant is poisonous, minute "homeopathic" doses have been used for eye ailments, skin eruptions, rheumatism, leucorrhea, obstruction of menses, bronchitis, asthma and coughs.

Columbine   *Aquilegia flavescens* & related species.

Aquilegia = ă-kwi-lee-gee-a, from Latin *aquila* (eagle), referring to the petal shape; others feel it comes from *aqua* (water) and *ligere* (collected) referring to the nectar that collects at the tips of the spurs or "claw-like nectaries", *flavescens* = L. pale yellow, turning yellow.

The common name, columbine, comes from the Latin *columba*–a dove or pigeon–the flower here resembling the flight of these birds.

Identification: This perennial herb stands 20-60 cm high with pale yellow, nodding flowers. The sepals of columbine are petal-like and the petals form long, slender, hollow spurs. The leaves are compound, divided into 3 leaflets. The fruit is a many-seeded, hairy pod.

Baneberry
Actaea rubra

Prairie Crocus
Anemone patens

Columbine
Aquilegia sp.

Marsh Marigold
Caltha leptosepala

Distribution & Habitat: Yellow columbine is commonly found in open woods, and on rocky slopes, acidic rock ledges and scree slopes from the foothills to slightly above the timber line.

Preparation & Uses: The young leaves of columbine make a good addition to any salad. When the leaves are young, they look quite similar to *Thalictrum occidentale* (Meadow rue) which are said to be quite bitter. I have made this mistake but have found both very tasty! Both columbine and meadow rue, when steamed, taste like snow peas. The flower contains nectar-laden tips which make great trail snacks.

Lust lists it as an astringent, diuretic and diaphoretic (the flowers promote perspiration). Amerindians boiled and ate the leaves in the spring. These leaves sometimes come out again in the fall when the weather is fair.

In 1640, Parkinson said that he used columbine leaves in lotions. He used it to treat sore mouths and throats and prescribed wine made from the seeds, mixed with saffron, to open obstructions of the liver. He also stated it was good for jaundice. The Spaniards ate pieces of the root on the morning of a fast.

A tea made from columbine stops diarrhea, the roots being the most effective. Ripe seeds can be vigorously rubbed into hair to discourage lice. The fresh root was mashed and rubbed on aching joints. A root tea has been used to stop excessive uterine bleeding.

Indians used to halt dizziness and biliousness by making a decoction of boiled leaves and roots. The dose was one and a half cupfuls several times a day. The seeds, when eaten or drunk in wine, were used by the Indians to speed childbirth.

A decoction was made of the whole plant and used to cure venereal disease. Several authors claim it does not work.

Caution: Large doses over long periods of time should not be taken.

Marsh Marigold   *Caltha leptosepala, C. palustris.*

Caltha = kǎl-tha, Latin for a yellow-flowered plant or old L. name prob. for marigold, *leptosepala* = lep-tō-se-pa-la, with slender sepals, *palustris* = pa-lus-tris, "of boggy or marshy ground".

Identification: This perennial herb stands 10–40 cm high and has white flowers, sometimes tinged with blue on the outside. The somewhat heart-shaped leaves arise from a pinkish naked stem. The fruit head is top-shaped and has several many-seeded pods. This plant is not actually a marigold. It is a buttercup.

Distribution & Habitat: Marsh marigold is found in wet alpine meadows throughout the Rocky Mountains.

Preparation & Uses: This plant is useful if only because it is locally abundant at higher elevations where it makes a good emergency food. Some people maintain that this plant is poisonous when raw. Kingsbury claims he used the flower buds and young leaves of this plant, mixed with lettuce as a salad, without any ill effects. It might be safer to cook it. The young leaves make excellent pot herbs – good until the flower emerges. The unopened bud of this plant can be pickled and used as a substitute for capers.

Marsh marigold's roots are diaphoretic, emetic and expectorant. The leaves are diuretic and laxative. A cough syrup was made by Ojibwas by mixing a leaf tea with maple syrup. This syrup was also used as an antidote to snake venom. It has also been reported to have mild anti-tumor activity.

Clematis   *Clematis verticellaris*

Clematis = klem-a-tis, from Greek meaning climbing plant, *verticellaris* = having whorls (several leaves of flowers all arising at the same level on the stem).

Identification: Clematis is a semi-woody climbing vine that often densely covers bushes, trees, fences or other support. It grows up to 2 m long and has opposite leaves, pinnate, ovate with a cordate base. The flowers have four purple or blue sepals and no petals. A white species *C. ligusticifolia*, and a fairly common yellow species, *C. tangutica*, are also present in the area.

Distribution & Habitat: Clematis is found in thickets and wooded areas throughout the West.

Preparation & Uses: Herbalists list clematis as a diaphoretic, diuretic and stimulant. The flowers and more specifically the sepals were used by the Indians as a relief from migraine headaches. It was taken internally as a tea but more often smoked as a smudge. This tea has a vasoconstrictory effect on the brain lining but a dilating effect on the veins. It has been used as a poultice for sores, itchy skin and leg ulcers. Some people have a skin sensitivity to this plant, while the tincture of the plant is sometimes used as a counterirritant.

Larkspur   *Delphinium bicolor, D. glaucum* & related species

Delphinium = del-fin-ee-um, from Greek *delphis* (a dolphin) referring to the shape of the flower, "Dolphin-head", a named used by Dioscorides, *glaucum* = "bluish-green, sea-green".

Identification: Larkspur is a herb with a somewhat woody rootstalk growing 15-50 cm high. The dark purplish-blue flowers are numerous in a terminal raceme. The leaves arise mostly from the stem and are palmately divided. The fruit is a many seeded follicle.

Distribution & Habitat: This common species is found in moist open woods, wet meadows, willow thickets, clearings, river flats, damp forest borders and avalanche slopes.

Preparation & Uses: *Delphinium bicolor* and *Delphinium consolida* (*consolida* = L. stable, firm) are the two types of larkspur used medicinally. *D. bicolor* is native to this area, while *D. consolida* is a European plant. Another species of Western North America is *D. glaucum*, also used by some herbalists. Caution should be applied in using all of these species as they are poisonous to cattle, and large doses must be avoided. The poison, which comes from the alkaloids (delphine and others), is most abundant in the early spring. Interestingly enough, though this plant affects cattle (often killing them) it does not affect sheep. In fact, some ranchers let sheep graze the area where larkspur grows before letting cows in. Larkspur is most poisonous in its early stages, decreasing in potency with age. The seeds are also supposed to be poisonous. Poisoning from mature plants usually requires consumption of at least three per cent of an animal's body weight.

I found an interesting Greek story about larkspur in A. Brown's book, *Old Man's Garden.*

> There was once a Greek fisherman who lost his life while trying to save a dolphin from being captured by pirates. The dolphin was so mournful that he carried the body of the fisherman on his back to the Greek God, Neptune. There he begged Neptune to restore life to the poor fisherman, who lost his life in such a gallant way. So Neptune transformed the fisherman's body into a beautiful flower, in the shape of a dolphin carrying a load on his back. The colour of the flower was the blue of the sea. *Delphion*, the root of the Latin *Delphinium*, is Greek for dolphin.

Clematis
Clematis verticellaris

BA

Tall Larkspur
*Delphinium
glaucum*

BA

Delphinium consolida is listed as being anthelmintic, purgative, emetic, cathartic, narcotic and a parasiticide. The plant is relatively ineffective internally and is seldom used this way because of its poisonous properties.

The flower and leaves have been used extensively to control body lice. Tincture of Green soap, found in many pharmacies, is made from *Delphinium*. A tincture of seeds has been used in the cure of asthma and dropsy, and as a specific for cholera morbus.

Delphinium bicolor was often used by the Blackfoot Indians. They would give an infusion of the plant to children who showed symptoms of diarrhea, frothing mouths and fainting spells. One dose was all that was usually needed. They would also use the flower mixed in water as a blue dye for quill work. Blackfoot women would sometimes shine their hair and straighten it with an infusion of larkspur.

Tall Larkspur
Delphinium glaucum

Meadow Rue
Thalictrum spp.

The internal dosage is 1 teaspoon of dried plant to 1 cup of water, steeped five minutes. Take 1 cup a day. The tincture is made from 1 oz. of seed to 1 quart of alcohol and taken in 10 drop-doses, once a day. Medicinal advice should be taken before using this plant. It is best picked before the seeds form, if the seeds are not needed.

Meadow Rue   *Thalictrum dasycarpum, T. occidentale*

Thalictrum = tha-lik-trum, from the Greek name of the plant.

Identification: This erect perennial herb rises 50 - 100 cm tall, from a yellowish root. Its basal and stem leaves are 2-3 ternate, the leaflet usually obovate-cuneate or orbicular, 3-lobed and coarsely crenate, the petioles dilated at the sheathing bases. The flowers are small, usually numerous in cluster, almost looking like chandeliers. Petal-like sepals are greenish.

Distribution & Habitat: In moist woods and meadows, from the Yukon to California and Saskatchewan to Utah and Colorado.

Preparation & Uses: The young leaves are quite tasty, almost like Chinese snow peas. Often mistaken for columbine, many references say that meadow rue doesn't taste good. I find both quite tasty.

Blackfoot Indian girls used to tie the flower or seed bunches in their hair. Girls felt it was a great love medicine, capturing the first male who saw them. There are several other tribes of Amerindians who also felt meadow rue was a love potion. It was given to a quarrelling couple. The Ojibwa and Potowatomi, for example, would secretly placed the seeds in the couple's food to overcome the quarrelling. The seeds were applied in poultices to stop cramps. The roots of purple meadow rue (*T. dasycarpum*) has been used as a purgative and diuretic, being listed in the U.S. Dispensatory of 1916. An infusion of the root was used to reduce fevers in many tribes, especially the Ojibwa. The roots contain berberine, and therefore have uses somewhat similar to barberry and goldenseal. The root was chewed and swallowed to reduce phlegm, improve blood circulation, for heart palpitations, to stop diarrhea, vomiting and occasionally as a panacea.

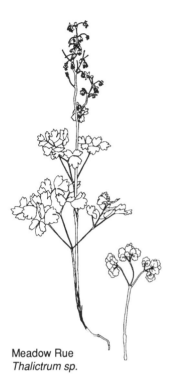

Meadow Rue
Thalictrum sp.

Barberry, Oregon Grape   *Berberis repens*

Berberis = ber-be-ris, L. for Barbary (from an Arabic name for North Africa); *repens* = L. for "creeping".

Identification: This creeping, evergreen shrub is usually less than 30 cm tall with rootlets along its length. The leaves are pinnate compound, somewhat holly-like, with spiny marginal teeth. The flowers are small, yellow and borne in clusters. The black or blue-black berries are 1/3 inch in diameter.

Distribution & Habitat: These plants like to grow in the shade, mostly on hill sides and slopes from the Pacific to the foothills throughout the whole area.

Preparation & Uses: The berries of this plant are quite juicy, with a pleasant acidy taste. They make good pies and jellies. To make this jelly all you have to do is boil berries with an equal part (or a little less if you don't have a sweet tooth), of sugar or honey, then strain them.

Barberry is one of our area's most valuable herbs. It is listed as a tonic, antiseptic, mild laxative, stimulant, bitter and refrigerant. It is also a famous and valuable Indian remedy. It is probably unequalled as a corrector of liver secretions. It is an excellent tonic for delicate and weakly people (especially children), building from anemia and general malnutrition to complete recovery in just a few weeks. It regulates the digestive system, lessens the size of the spleen, and removes obstructions in the intestinal tract. Even though the roots are usually used, the leaves are also considered efficient by some authors.

The Blackfoot Indians called it *Oti-to-gue* and steeped the peeled dried root. They used the herb to check rectal hemorrhage, dysentery and other stomach troubles.

The bark of the root contains several alkaloids (the main one being berberine) that promote the secretion of bile. When it is used in conjunction with cayenne as a carrier, it has a superior stimulant effect on the liver. The alkaloid in the root also tends to dilate the blood vessels and thereby lowers blood pressure. Berberine has wide spectrum antibiotic activity and has antibacterial and antifungal properties.

A tincture of the root is helpful in urinary complaints, as well as herpes simplex. It is advisable to use ginger with this tincture.

Blackfoot Indians would use either fresh berries or an infusion of the roots on open boils. The berries were also often used for kidney troubles.

Externally, the infused root was applied to wounds as an antiseptic. The root was also chewed and applied for the same purpose and to relieve itching.

As a horse medicine the berries were soaked in water and the juice was given to a coughing horse. Body sores were also treated with an infusion of the root as in humans.

Shepherd's Purse *Capsella bursa-pastoris*

Capsella = cap-sel-la, means little box, referring to the seed pod or the form of the fruit; *bursa-pastoris* = bur-sa-pas-tor-is, meaning pastoral purse - "shepherd's purse", referring to the seed pod.

Identification: Shepherd's purse is an annual herb 10 - 50 cm high. The flowers are small and white borne in terminal racemes. The basal leaves are deeply cleft, while the stem leaves are sessile, lanceolate to linear. The seed pods are triangular and flattened. The name, shepherd's purse, comes from the triangular or heart-shaped seed pod which looks similar to an old-fashioned European shepherd's bag.

Distribution & Habitat: This plant is commonly found as a weed in fields, gardens, lawns and pathways.

BA

BA

Barberry
Berberis sp.

Rue with Columbine
Thalictrum sp. & Aquilegia sp.

Barberry in berry stage
Berberis repens

TW

Shepherd's Purse
Capsella bursa-pastoris

BA

Preparation & Uses: The young leaves are prized as a pot herb by some people, rather than being condemned as weeds. The young leaves can be used in salads but are a bit strong and I prefer them blanched.

The ripened pods can be gathered and the seeds beaten out, as the Indians did, but this takes a lot of patience. The seeds can then be soaked, roasted, ground or parched. The whole pod can be added to salads or soups or dried for winter storage. The fresh or dried root has been reported as a substitute for ginger in flavour.

Shepherd's purse is listed as being astringent, diuretic, antiscorbutic, styptic and a vasoconstrictor. Water is a solvent. An extract of the herb or infusion of the dried leaf is an effective blood coagulant and is used internally and externally. Shepherd's purse also acts on the circulatory system to equalize blood pressure. It's been used to combat excess menstrual flow and other menstrual problems. This herb acts as a stimulant and moderate tonic for catarrh of the urinary tract and it is also helpful for both kidney and bladder.

Shepherd's
Purse
*Capsella
bursa-pastoris*

Shepherd's purse has been used to promote uterine contraction during childbirth and successfully employed in cases of hemorrhage after childbirth. It can also promote bowel movement through a similar action on the intestine.

The dose for an infusion is 1 cup a day. To make an infusion take 1 teaspoon of the fresh herb or 2 teaspoons of the dried herb and let it set in ½ cup of water. Take a teaspoon of the juice several times a day, or take 20-40 drops of the tincture two or three times a day.

The seeds of shepherd's purse have a germicidal action on several micro-organisms. The seed has also been employed to great effect against mosquitoes. In the early spring, sprinkle the seed on water where mosquitoes breed. The mucilage of the seed will kill the larvae and greatly reduce mosquitoes in the area. One pound of seeds destroys ten million larvae, though it may cause a proliferation of shepherd's purse!

Sundew   *Drosera rotundifolia*

Drosera = dro-se-ra, from Greek *droseros* (dewy), referring to the appearance of the leaves or the glistening glandular hairs, *rotundifolia* = L. "rounded-leaves".

Identification: Sundew is a small, insectivorous perennial herb with sticky leaves which grow from a basal rosette. These glandular leaves are often red and have long, reddish glandular hairs or tentacles which exude drops of sticky fluid. The fluid, in turn, attracts and catches insects. The white flowers number 3-10 on a leafless, flowering stalk.

Distribution & Habitat: Sundew is found in moist places, where it grows in sphagnum moss.

Preparation & Uses: Even though sundew has been used to curdle milk, its main use is medicinal.

Sundew is listed by Hutchens as a stimulant, expectorant, demulcent and antispasmodic. It is soluble in boiling water. Sundew is primarily known as an effective remedy for respiratory ailments and chest problems. It is useful in the treatment of coughs, asthma, whooping cough, bronchitis, tobacco cough, laryngitis and chronic catarrh. Sundew has a quenching effect for dryness and tickling in the respiratory organs. It is also useful to help counteract nausea and upset stomach.

Grieve suggests that it is beneficial for curing arteriosclerosis. Sundew contains an antibiotic (plumbagin) that has been effectively used against *Streptococcus*, *Staphylococcus* and *Pneumococcus*. It has also been used in Europe as an aphrodisiac.

The dosage is 10-20 drops of extract three times daily. To make a tea, steep 1 teaspoon in a cup of boiling water and take three times a day in tablespoon doses. Take 3-6 drops of tincture diluted in water. Sundew contains irritant substances and should be used in small quantities only.

External use has been known to cause water blisters. The irritating juice has been used for centuries to remove warts and corns, an effect attributed to a proteolytic enzyme and the antibiotic plumbagin. It is best applied with milk (ideally, buttermilk). It is also said to remove freckles.

Homeopathically, this plant has been used extensively, most prominently for cases of whooping cough.

Ancient lore indicates carrying some leaves of sundew will protect you from witchcraft and ensure that you have many friends.

Stonecrop *Sedum spp.*

Sedum = say-dum, from the classical Latin name for several succulent plants, *sedo* (to sit) or a name in Pliny (refers to the plant's "sitting" on rocks, etc. in the case of cushion species).

Identification: Stonecrop is a perennial herb with a leafy stem. The flowers are pink to purple, with superior ovaries. The leaves are alternate, succulent and without hair. The fruit is a group of pods which open along one side.

Distribution & Habitat: It is found on dry open rocky slopes from the foothills into the mountains, ranging up to the southern Yukon.

Preparation & Uses: The young leaves and shoots of stonecrop can be eaten, either raw or as a pot herb, whereas older leaves and shoots are bitter. Because of the high moisture content of the leaves, eating them will allay thirst. (I once went three days eating stonecrop instead of drinking the available polluted water.) *Sedum rosea* (roseroot) is one of the major edible plants of the northland. Stonecrop is a good emergency food. As mentioned, it can be eaten raw, is tasty, and allays thirst. The roots of roseroot were fermented in water by the Inupiat and eaten with walrus blubber or otter fat.

Stonecrop has also been reported as slightly astringent and mucilaginous. It is of value in the treatment of wounds, ulcers, lung disorders and diarrhea.

Roseroot leaves were infused, the root decocted, and used for colds, gargled for sore throats and used for irritated eyes by Dena'ina Athabascans.

Alum root *Heuchera spp.*

Heuchera = hoy-ka-ra, after Johann Heinrich van Heucher (1677-1747), German medical professor.

Identification: Alum root is a perennial herb with stout scaly rootstocks, growing from 20-50 cm tall. The small flowers are usually greenish, yellow or purplish and in clusters. The leaves are on long petioles rising from the base of the plant. They are rather round and irregularly lobed.

Stonecrop
Sedum sp.

Alum Root
Heuchera sp.

Wild Black Currant
Ribes sp.

Red Currant
Ribes sp.

Gooseberry
Ribes sp.

Distribution & Habitat: The plant is found on rocky places or poor soils in exposed places, usually in the more southerly mountains.

Preparation & Uses: The young shoots of alum root can be steamed or boiled to make an enjoyable pot herb.

The major use for alum root was its styptic and astringent properties (similar to alum). The raw root or wet pounded root was often eaten in small amounts to stop diarrhea. To stop fever and general debility, the root was decocted and drunk or gargled for sore throats. Because of alum root's powerful astringent properties, it is very effective in stopping hemorrhages from small, bleeding vessels such as the nose, mouth and surface capillary veins. The tea was also used for mouth and throat ulcers, and injected for bleeding piles and leucorrhea.

The Indians often chewed the root and applied it to wounds and sores as a styptic. The Blackfoot Indians would mix dried root with buffalo fat and rub it on saddle sores. The Nevada Indians made a decoction of *H. rubescens* roots and drank it to reduce high fevers and sometimes used it for heart problems. Pioneers herbalists would dip cloth into a weak solution of alum root tea and apply it to granulated or sore eyelids.

The recognized dosage is ½ teaspoon to 1 cup of water. Take 1/3 cupful 3 times daily. It is not good to use the root too extensively as it can dry out mucous membranes. The root is best dug before the plant flowers. Alum root was in the U.S. Dispensatory from 1820-1882.

Currant, Gooseberry   *Ribes spp.*

Ribes = Rie-beez, from Arabic or Persian, *ribas* (acid-tasting), referring to the taste of the fruit.

Identification: Shrubs with erect or procumbent branches. The flower colour varies from white, yellow, or green to red, depending on the species. The flowers are in racemes or are solitary and have 5 sepals, petals and stamens. The branches are usually prickly and the leaves are alternate palmately. The fruits are berries and sometimes bristly.

Distribution & Habitat: The genus *Ribes* usually grows in moist places, such as swamps, damp woods and moist run-off areas. Some species will be found on fairly dry river banks or in dry mountain forests.

Preparation & Uses: The berries of all species may be eaten although some taste better than others. They can be eaten raw, cooked or sun-dried. *Ribes* berries are excellent in pies and jellies. Of all the *Ribes* jams, I prefer gooseberry. Of course, the red currant jelly my mother made for us, as children, cannot be beaten. Black currant jelly is good, but not as pleasant-tasting as the red.

The Cree called black currants (*Ribes hudsonianas*) *A-mis-Ko-na-tik*, and used the stem, bark and chopped roots. They sometimes added skunk currants (*R. glandulosum*) to help a woman conceive.

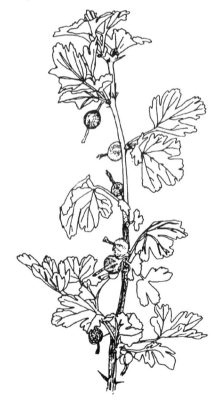

The Blackfoot call currants *Mon-to-na-na-tik* and used a liquid extract of the root for kidney ailments and women's uterine problems.

Black currant has been listed by Grieve as a diuretic, diaphoretic, and febrifuge. The juice of black currant can be boiled to form extracts with sugar, which is called rob. It is used for inflammation of the throat. Excellent lozenges can be made that way. An infusion of the leaves is cleansing and diuretic, while an infusion of the young roots is useful in eruptive fevers and dysenteric fever of cattle. The raw juice is also diuretic and diaphoretic, and it is an excellent beverage in febrile conditions (feverish diseases). A decoction of the bark has been found of value for calculi, to expel worms and in cases of dropsy.

Black currant jelly is deservedly prized for its usefulness in treating colds. It is both laxative and cooling. It should not be made with too much sugar or the medicinal properties will be impaired.

For sore throats take a tablespoon of jam or jelly and put it in a glass and fill with boiling water. This tea is soothing and has a demulcent effect. Take it several times a day and drink it while hot. Black currant wine is good and the following recipe is taken from an old cookbook.

To every 3 quarts of juice put an equal quantity of unboiled water. To this add 6 lbs. pure raw sugar. Put in cask, reserving a little for filling it up. Put the cask in a warm, dry place and it will ferment itself. Skim off the scum. When the fermentation is over, fill up with reserve liquid. When it has ceased working, pour in 3 quarts of brandy to the 40 quarts of wine. Bung it closed for 9 months in a bottle and drain the thick part through a jelly bag until it is clear, then bottle that, and keep it for 12 months.

Red currant is also listed by Grieve as a refrigerant, aperient and antiscorbutic. The jelly of red currant has an antiseptic effect, easing the pain of a burn and even preventing the formation of blisters if applied quickly enough. The plant also is a corrective of putrescent food, especially "high meat".

The juice of gooseberry was formerly said to be a cure-all for inflammations. The green berries have a sub-acid which makes them counteract the effects of putrescent food. Gooseberry is more valuable than rhubarb (even as a jam) as a spring medicine. According to Schofield, the Russians have done studies at the Institute of Biological Physics and have shown that unripe gooseberries can prevent degeneration of body cells, a factor which can cause illness and the aging process.

An infusion of leaves taken before monthly periods has been found a useful tonic for pubescent girls. (1 oz. of leaves to 1 pint of water taken in a tea cup, 3 times a day). In spring some Indians boiled young leaves of *Ribes* and ate them with uncooked fat. They also ate the flowers. One good secret to know is how the Indians removed the bristly spines on some *Ribes* fruits. They used to roll the berries on hot coals in a basket until the spines had been singed off.

It is not good to eat too many raw berries of this genus until you are accustomed to them. Too many will cause sickness or at least an upset stomach. This is due to their cleansing effect on the digestive system. The fruits are excellent for fasting as they remove toxins from the body.

The seeds of black currants have received a lot of attention from herbalists lately as they contain large quantities of both omega 3 and omega 6 essential fatty acids. The oil is used to treat skin conditions, asthma, arthritis and premenstrual syndrome.

Saskatoon, June-berry, Serviceberry   *Amelanchier alnifolia*

Amelanchier = ă-me-lan-kee-er, from the Provençal name of *A. ovalis* snowy-mespilus, *alnifolia* = "alder-like leaved".

Identification: This shrub or small tree grows from 1-4 m tall, often spreading by stolons to form colonies. It has pretty white flowers which appear in June. The bark is smooth and grey to brown in colour. The alternate leaves are simple, elliptic to obovate, with serrate margins at the tips. The sweet, juicy berries resemble blueberries in appearance.

Distribution & Habitat: It is quite common in open woods at low elevations and/or along river banks.

Preparation & Uses: The berries make good jellies, preserves, pies and sauces. They can be dried or canned for winter. The dried berries were substituted for currants by early settlers and were added to pemmican by the Indians.

An interesting method of preserving these berries in dried cakes. The Indians made a large spruce bark tub of about 30 gallon capacity. Into the bottom of these tubs they placed about a peck of berries, and on top of the berries they placed red-hot stones, then more berries and more rocks until the tub was full. This combination was left for about 6 hours, until the berries were completely cooked. They were then crushed between the hands, spread upon splinters of wood, tied together and placed on a slow fire. The juice running off from a collecting tube was rubbed over the body. After 2 or 3 days of drying, the berries were in good condition to last for several years. In this dried cake state, the berry is a good addition to soups, puddings or vegetables.

Blackfoot Indians would drink saskatoon berry juice for an upset stomach. It is also a mild laxative. These Indians also made eye drops from immature berries. If these were not available, they would use dried berries. The boiled juice was also used for eardrops. Other Indians made an eye wash from the green, inner bark of saskatoon. The Chippewa boiled the cambium as a disinfectant wash. They used the root bark of a related species, *A. canadensis*, as a women's tonic to stop excessive menstrual bleeding. Thompson Indians used saskatoon berry bark in a decoction and drank it to help pass afterbirth,

Serviceberry
Amelanchier alnifolia

Hawthorn
Crataegus sp.

Wild Strawberry
Fragaria sp.

sometimes in addition to sitting in a sitz bath. An infusion of roots was drunk to prevent miscarriages.

The Blackfoot Indians also made a purple dye of this plant, calling it *Oko-nok*, whereas the Cree called the plant *Saskatooniaktik*, and used the stems for arrows and pipestems. The wood is quite hard and can be used to make various tools. Saskatoon played a major role in native ceremonies, especially in the Sun Dance which was held when the berries were ripe.

Hawthorn   *Crataegus spp.*

Crataegus = Kra-tie-gus, from Greek *kratos* (strength), referring to the hard wood (the name used by Theophrastus).

Identification: The various species of hawthorn grow as shrubs and small trees. They usually have stout thorns on their branches and their leaves are alternate, simple, serrate and sometimes shallowly lobed. The flowers are white and the fruits are berry-like pomes.

Distribution & Habitat: Hawthorn is found in thickets, woods and along stream beds throughout the west.

Preparation & Uses: All species have an edible berry that can be used to make jam or jelly. The Indians ate the fruit fresh or dried in pemmican. The berries are a bit mealy and are therefore not considered prime food.

The fruit and flowers have been used by Amerindian, Chinese and European herbalists as a heart tonic, to normalize blood pressure, angina and for arteriosclerosis. Studies have confirmed its benefit in these areas. Use over long periods of time is necessary for the medicinal effects to be noticeable. It can also be used as a mild sedative and mild diuretic. Hawthorn berries are major ingredients in Chinese weight loss programs. I have known people to lose 10 - 25 pounds over a few months by consuming a diet high in hawthorn or drinking hawthorn tea.

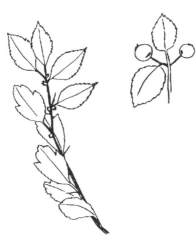

Strawberry   *Fragaria glauca*

Fragaria = fra-gah-ree-a, from Latin *fraga*, referring to the scent of the plant.

Identification: This common perennial herb is very similar to the cultivated strawberry but has smaller flowers and fruit. The flowers are white, usually with several on each stalk. The flowers have five bractlets, sepals and petals, with many stamens and carpels. This plant usually forms long stolons which root and form new plants. The leaflets are in threes, and are coarsely serrated, usually with silky hairs beneath. The roots are short and scaly. The juicy fruit is red, with numerous minute seed-like achenes, scattered over it.

Distribution & Habitat: Strawberries are often in open areas, along "cut lines", meadows or alpine areas.

Preparation & Uses:

> "Doubtless God could have made a better fruit than the strawberry, but doubtless God never did."
>
> Dr. William Butler

The berries of strawberry are small but sweet and very delicious. They may be used in the same ways as domestic varieties but I prefer the wild ones. My favourite way to eat them is to mix a large bowl of strawberries with whipped cream and then to pour the mixture into a thick, whole grain baked pieshell.

Chill and eat. Oh so good!

Strawberries can also be dried for future use. The leaves are extremely high in vitamin C and are also said to tone up one's appetite. The leaves make a pleasant tea to which other herbs can be added.

Lust states that the leaves and root are an astringent, diuretic, tonic and useful in checking dysentery. Extract of wild strawberry root is commonly found in drugstores across Canada to relieve diarrhea. Strawberry leaves are sometimes effective against eczema and acne. Fresh strawberry juice makes a good refrigerant for fevers. Hutchens lists it as a blood purifier and blood builder agent.

The strawberry leaves are also listed in many early pharmacopeias. Culpepper declares it to be "singly good for healing of many ills." Linnaeus (the father of botany) found the berries a good cure for rheumatic gout.

The fresh fruit of the strawberries removes discolouration from teeth. The juice should be allowed to remain on the teeth for about five minutes, then be cleaned off with warm water, to which a pinch of bicarbonate of soda has been added.

A cut strawberry, rubbed over the skin immediately after washing, will whiten it and help remove slight sunburn. For a badly sunburnt face, it is recommended to rub the juice well into the skin and to leave it on for about half an hour. Then wash it off with warm water to which a few drops of simple tincture of benzoin have been added. No soap should be used. The leaves have been used in baths for pain and aches in the hips and thighs. It would probably also be good to drink some tea of the leaves at the same time.

The Cree Indians call it *otehimika*. They made a tea of the root, combined with yarrow, and gave it in the form of a cooled tea to cure insanity. The Blackfoot used extract of the boiled roots to treat diarrhea, calling the plant *otsistini*. The boiled leaves can be applied as a poultice to take heat away from wounds. The herb, boiled and eaten, will strengthen gums, fasten teeth, soothe inflamed eyes, and will help hayfever if used enough.

Ocean Spray   *Holodiscus discolor*

Holodiscus = ho-lō-dis-kus, from Greek *holos* (entire) and *diskos* (a disk), referring to the unlobed disc; *discolor* = dis-ko-lor, two - coloured, the leaves are grey below.

Synonyms: iron-wood, arrow wood.

Identification: Growing up to 5 m, these bushes are covered with drooping clusters of small, cream-colored flowers in June and July, appearing a brown husk throughout the winter.

Distribution & Habitat: Very common along the B.C. coast and in at least one mountain range.

Preparation & Uses: This herb is listed as astringent, diuretic, tonic and emetic. The stem bark is decocted and drunk for hemorrhaging, diarrhea, upset stomach, colds and flus. As a tonic it is said to give endurance to athletes. It is applied to convalescent patients and to tone up uterine muscles after childbirth.

Silverweed
Potentilla anserina and related species

Potentilla = Po-ten-til-la, from Latin *potens* (powerful) referring to medicinal properties, *anserina* = 'of the goose, of the meadows'.

Identification: Silverweed is a perennial herb which produces runners that root and form leaf clusters at the nodes. The yellow flowers are borne singly on long flower stalks. The leaves are pinnate with 7-25 leaflets interspersed with smaller ones. The leaflets are serrated, silvery and hairy beneath, green above.

Silverweed
Potentilla anserina

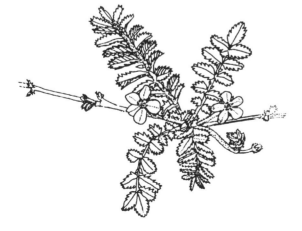

Distribution & Habitat: Silverweed is usually found in low meadows, lake shores and stream banks.

Preparation & Uses: The roots are good boiled or roasted and are quite tasty raw. They taste similar to parsnip but are a lot more woody. They are best collected in the spring and are an excellent emergency and general food source.

Lust lists silverweed as antispasmodic and astringent. A tea made in milk or water is good for diarrhea and dysentery. The antispasmodic qualities can relieve cramps, but it is best mixed with chamomile. It can be used for skin problems, throat and mouth sores.

The powdered root or bark and leaves of *P. canadensis* are also listed as an astringent, used as a gargle and mouth wash, as well as for diarrhea. The root bark has been recommended for nosebleeds and internal bleeding.

A decoction of *P. anserina* can be made by using 2 teaspoons of the plant in 1 cup of water or milk. An infusion of leaves of *P. canadensis* can also be used. The dosage is two or 3 teaspoons in 1 cup of water; 1 cup a day; or a decoction of 1 oz. of root bark in 1 ½ cups of water. Boil down to 1 cup. Take ¼ cup, 2 or 3 times a day.

Cinquefoil, Shrubby   *Potentilla fruticosa*

Potentilla = po-ten-til-la, from Latin *potens* (powerful) referring to medicinal properties; *fruticosa* = froo-ti-kō-sa, shrubby.

Identification: This free branching shrub stands 15-150 cm high. The outer bark often appears shredded. The leaves are 5-pinnate, numerous and the leaflets are linear-oblong, often revolute and lightly hairy on both sides. The yellow rose-like flowers are solitary with the petals longer than the sepals.

Distribution & Habitat: Found in open areas on the prairie in the foothills and mountains, often found in boggy areas or cultivated as an ornamental shrub.

Preparation & Uses: This plant is listed as being an astringent, tonic and vulnerary. The leaves were used for weak bowels, internal haemorrhaging, flu and profuse menstruation. It was extensively used for stomach problems. The tea was drunk 3 - 4 times a day for stomach and esophagus inflammation. The tea was also used to prevent saddle sores on horses. The tea was soaked over the animal.

Chokecherry, Pin cherry   *Prunus pensylvanica & virginiana*

Prunus = proo-nus, from the Latin name for plum tree, *pensylvanica & virginiana* = "of Pennsylvania, of Virginia".

Identification: These shrubs or small trees grow up to 8 m tall. White flowers are borne in racemes or umbel-like clusters. The leaves are alternate, simple and serrated. In *Prunus pensylvanica* (Pin cherry) the bark is reddish-brown. The leaves are lanceolate, and it has light red fruit. *Prunus virginiana* (choke cherry) has dark brown bark. The leaves are elliptic to obovate and the fruit is reddish-purple or black.

Distribution & Habitat: These cherries are common in dry woods, thickets and some open woods.

An Indian Girls' Game

> While out picking chokecherries, Blackfoot Indian girls would often play a little game. All of the girls would stand in a circle. Each one had to put a chokecherry in her mouth. The first one to giggle or make a sour face was disqualified, with her cherries being forfeited into the middle. Another round started with each remaining girl sticking another chokecherry in her mouth. This was repeated until one girl won all the cherries.

Preparation & Uses: The bitter astringent taste of chokecherry needs little commentary for those who've sampled the cherry as children. The fruit can be eaten raw as some Indians manage to do but it is not all that tasty. The dried fruit does taste quite good though, and can be stored for winter. Besides drying whole, the ripened fruit can be ground up, seed and all, then dried. This can later be soaked when needed and used as a sauce or an addition to soups. Ground, dried cherries were often stored in cakes.

Some Indians would mix the cherries with meat and dry it to make their pemmican. One shouldn't eat too many dried, uncooked cherries as they might cause nausea. Chokecherries make good jellies and wine. If making jelly, pectin should be added. Follow any jelly recipe. The juice of chokecherries is refreshing if mixed with water and sugar.

Chokecherry bark is classified by many Indians as one of their most valued herbs. The bark is listed as bitter, astringent, narcotic, stimulant, mild tonic, sedative and pectoral. Both hot and cold water are used as solvents. All the bark is useful, but the inner bark of the roots is reported to be the best. The bark was used to relieve headache and for "heart trouble" by the Bella Coola people. Herbalists have used it for intermittent fever, worms, dyspepsia, consumption, hectic fever, the congestion of phlegm and bronchitis. The Penobscot Indians used an infusion of the bark for coughs and lung troubles. The Potawatomis infused the bark and used it for an eyewash and the berries as a tonic. Blackfoot Indians infused the cambium of chokecherry and saskatoon berry and used the result as a purging agent. The berries were used to treat diarrhea and sore throats. Chokecherry contains small amounts of malic acid and hydrocyanic acid. The bark has been listed in the U.S. Dispensatory since 1820.

Chokecherry wood is very hard and not easily burned. It makes good forked sticks for carrying hot rocks to sweat lodges, lifting hot coals out of the fire for smudges and other such uses. It was used for digging sticks, tent pegs, back rests and household tools.

Shrubby Cinquefoil
Potentilla fruticosa

Chokecherry
Prunus virginiana

Pin Cherry
Prunus pensylvanica

Pin cherries (*Prunus virginiana*) are quite delicious cherries and can be eaten raw, cooked, made into jellies, jam and pies.

Caution: The leaves are considered poisonous because of the high quantities of hydrocyanic acid.

Wild Rose   *Rosa acicularis*

Rosa = ro-sa, from the classical name for various roses, *acicularis* = L. "needle-shaped".

Identification: This bushy shrub is the floral emblem of Alberta. It grows 30 - 120 cm high. The flowers are usually solitary with pink, or occasionally white petals. The leaves are pinnate with 5-7 leaflets which are coarsely serrated. The branches are densely covered with straight slender bristles. The pear-shaped fleshy hip is marble-sized, orange-to-red, containing many seeds.

Distribution & Habitat: This common plant is found in forested regions, along roadsides, and on open slopes.

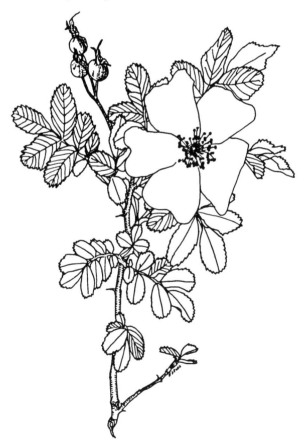

Preparation & Uses: The rose fruit ("rose hips") can be eaten raw, stewed, candied, or made into preserves or good tea. Sugar or honey improves the flavour.

Rose hip apple jam

I have found plain rose hip jam rather dull but if you mix it with other fruits such as saskatoons, apples or blueberries it has more flavor. For rose hip apple jam, remove the seeds and blossom and cut up both apples and hips. Add 1 cup rose hips to 2 cups cored, chopped apples. Add ¼ cup of water. Bring the sauce to a boil, adding ½ to 1 ½ cups of honey and 1 teaspoon cinnamon. Continue to cook until it thickens. Pour into sterilized jars and seal.

The fresh petals are a delight. I have often walked along wilderness paths chewing away on petals which almost melt in your mouth like a perfumed bubble gum. A great breakfast spread can be made by wrapping a stick of butter in rose petals. Place it in a cool place for a few days and spread its elegant taste on a cornmeal muffin. The petals can also be candied or used plain in salads (showing off their grace). The hips of this plant are extremely high in vitamin C and they also contain vitamin E, B, K and beta-carotene. The peeled spring shoots are great trail nibblers.

The seeds were sometimes cooked by Indians and eaten for muscular pains. The Blackfoot Indians called the roots *Kini*, from which they made a bitter drink for the treatment of diarrhea, flu, dysentery and worms. These Indians also called the fruit *apis-is-kifsu-wa* (tomato flower) and used it in pemmican.

The blossoms were used by some tribes for colic and "clogged stomach". The Ojibwa made a powder of dried blossoms into a tea for heartburn.

As a spring tonic, both roots and leaves were employed to cleanse the blood. The root has a mild analgesic property which was applied to headaches, rheumatism and such problems. A decoction of the blossom is astringent and can be used a gargle for sore throat and mouth sores. For eyes, a decoction of cambium or an infusion of the hip was used to soothe. An infusion of root cambium of both rose and red raspberry has been used to treat cataract.

Almost all parts of the plant have been made into a wash or dressing for cuts, sores and any situation indicating a need to coagulate blood. The petals make a good easy bandage. Rose is one of the Amerindian's most important wound herbs. The most common method of application is to sprinkle fine shavings of de-barked stems into a washed wound. Poultices were also used. Stems galls were particularly prized as a burn remedy. The growths were charred, crushed and dusted onto the burn.

A poultice of the leaves can be used to relieve insect stings.

The Chinese made a simple infusion of the flower to "regulate vital energy (Qi)".

A wine of rose petal can be used for uterine cramps and to ease labour pains. It also soothes after childbirth.

Blaine, the photographer for this book, developed an interesting drink – Wild Rose liqueur. First, you need to pick flower petals in partial or full bloom, with no wilted or dried ones. Let the blooms soak in alcohol (as pure as possible) for two weeks, or until the colour has all faded out of the plant material. You then decant off the liquid and dilute to forty percent alcohol, sweeten to taste and bottle. The resulting liqueur is said to be a cross between Grand Marnier and Chanel No. 5! No matter how long you sit up drinking this liqueur around the campfire, you'll always come home smelling like a rose.

Raspberry *Rubus sp.*

Rubus = rub-us, the Latin name for brambles or the blackberry.

Identification: This genus has many diverse forms. The common wild raspberry is an erect shrub that stands up to 2 m tall. The flowers are white and terminal. The stem has prickles and the leaves are pinnate, green above and white and hairy below. The leaf margins are doubly serrated. The fruit is red, falling intact from the dry receptacle.

Distribution & Habitat: Raspberry is commonly found along roadsides, river banks and in wooded regions.

Preparation & Uses: The flowers of all *Rubus* are delightful in salads. The young shoots can be peeled and eaten. As well as tasting delicious, the berries have many medicinal uses.

Raspberry is listed by Lust as an antiemetic, astringent and mild laxative. The leaves, and especially the root, made into an infusion (1 oz. in two cups of water, steeped for 15 minutes) are a good remedy for diarrhea. If this is mixed

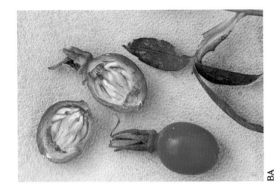

Rose Hips
Rosa acicularis

Wild Rose
*Rosa
acicularis*

Raspberry
Rubus sp.

Dwarf /Arctic Raspberry
Rubus arcticus

Dewberry
Rubus pubescens

Blackberry
Rubus sp.

Blackberry
Rubus sp.

with cream, it will relieve nausea and vomiting. This tea is also used to prevent miscarriage, increase milk flow and reduce labour pains. We suggest this herb regularly in the Wild Rose Clinic to stop nausea in pregnancy and produce safe, speedy and easy delivery. Pregnant women should drink this tea at least once a day for the duration of the pregnancy but especially in the last three months. The tea is also valuable for menstrual problems, decreasing the flow without stopping it too abruptly.

Raspberry leaves are soothing and toning to the stomach and bowels. If taken at the first signs of flu or a cold, raspberry leaf tea will often stop them short. It is a herb that has many qualities by itself. When combined with other herbs, its effects are almost miraculous.

The berries are mildly laxative.

Rubus ideaus (L. from Mount Ida, Crete or northwest Turkey) is the domestic red raspberry. It is as useful as the wild one for all the above treatments.

Rubus parviflorus (L. "small-flowered") was often eaten by Blackfoot Indians to treat chest disorders.

Cloudberries (*R. chamaemorus*) juice was used by the Yup'ik for treating hives.

Mountain Ash   *Sorbus aucuparia*

Sorbus = sor-bus, from the Latin name of *S. domestica* (the service tree); *aucuparia* = ow-kew-pah-ree-a, from L. *avis* (a bird) and *capere* (to catch), the fruits attract birds.

Identification: This European tree has naturalized in several areas and been planted along streets and in front yards. It has bright red berries.

Preparation & Uses: All parts of this tree are astringent. The bark is a detergent and tonic. This tree contains amygdalin and cyanogenic heterosides (found also in wild cherries) and is useful for throat inflammation. The berries are slightly cathartic when raw but not after being cooked. They are diuretic in both states. A decoction of the bark can be used for diarrhea, nausea, upset stomach and hemorrhoids. The decoction of the bark has also been used as a blood cleanser and spring tonic.

Hardhack   *Spiraea douglassii*

Spiraea = Theophrastus' name for a plant used to make garlands.

Identification: Looking similar to other *Spiraea*, this dense shrub grows up to 2 m. Its pink cluster of flowers blooms in May - June with a beautiful sweet smell.

Distribution & Habitat: Grows in wet swampy areas along the West coast from Alaska to California.

Preparation & Uses: The uses are similar to other *Spiraeas* (astringent and stomachic). It is felt that it also contains salicylic acid. It is specifically used as a poultice (made of leaves and bark) to treat ulcers, burns and tumors. The roots were peeled and boiled until soft, mashed and used as a prized poultice for burns.

White meadowsweet   *Spiraea lucida*

Spiraea = spee-rie-a, from Greek *speiraira*, Theophrastus' name for a plant used to make garlands, *lucida* = L. "shining, glittering, clear".

Identification: The wild species looks like the *Spiraea* you might find in your grandmother's garden. It is smaller, only 30 - 100 cm high with a flat-topped head of white flowers which turn brownish with age. The coarsely serrated leaves are oval, shiny green above and paler beneath. The stems and branches are erect, often dying down annually to near the base.

Distribution & Habitat: Meadowsweet can be found in open woods and on open slopes. It is often found in pine and aspen forests of the Rocky Mountains and foothills.

Preparation & Uses: The leaves and stems can be made into a decoction for stomach disorders. Meadowsweet is the major ingredient in the stomach formula I use a lot in my clinic (ST or stomach herb). The boiled stems are

Mountain Ash
Sorbus aucuparia

Hardhack
Spiraea douglasii

Meadowsweet
Spiraea betulifolia

Wild Licorice
Glycyrrhiza lepidota

Sweet Vetch
Hedysarum sp.

Sweet Vetch
(Bear root), with
root bark peeled
back.
Hedysarum sp.

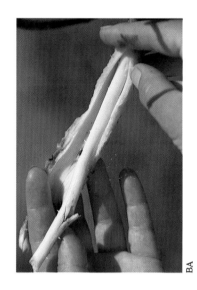

Sweet Vetch
Hedysarum sp.

Alfalfa
Medicago sativa

made into tea for the common cold. Boiled roots can be used for diarrhea. As with other *Spiraea* species, meadowsweet contains methyl salicylate (similar to aspirin).

There was widespread use of this plant by the Indians for venereal disease. They drank the tea 3 times a day over a long period of time and also used it as a douche.

The Blackfoot made an infusion of root and used the tea as an enema. This brew was also used as a tonic. They would save some of this tea and rub it into the affected parts.

The flower of the *Spiraea* makes a perfect paint brush with which to paint large surfaces.

Licorice   *Glycyrrhiza lepidota*

Glycyrrhiza = L. "sweet-root", *lepidota* = L. "scurfy, scaly".

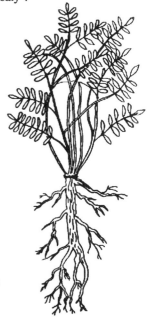

Identification: Wild licorice is a coarse perennial herb arising from a thick rootstock. The plant grows from 30 - 100 cm tall. The pinnate leaves have 11 - 19 lanceolate leaflets. The flowers are yellowish-white and formed in dense racemes. The seed pods are burr-like with hooked prickles.

Distribution & Habitat: Licorice can be found in moist meadows throughout the west.

Preparation & Uses: The North American variety is just as sweet and tasty as the old world variety (*G. glabra*). Chewed as a candy, or as a flavour additive for root beer and chewing tobacco, the taste is well known to us all. Roots were some-times roasted by the Indians to concentrate their flavour.

Both the American and European species have been employed for many medicinal uses. In China and India, licorice root is the number one medi-cine, quite likely making it the most commonly used medical substance (or drug) in the world.

Licorice soothes most mucous membranes in the body. The Cheyennes boiled the root (and sometimes the leaves) to make a tea for stomachaches and diarrhea. The root was chewed to soothe the throat by many nationali-ties, while the Indians felt it helped their singing voice. The Sioux used the chewed leaf as a poultice for the sore backs of their horses. An extract of licorice root has been used in many cough syrups to bring up phlegm – inter-esting when you consider it is also one of the most popular additives of chew-ing tobacco. The Chinese feel that licorice is the great antidote, adding it to a large number of herbal formulas. Since the major constituent is similar to the human adrenal hormone, it has often been used to support the adrenal gland in cases of stress. Licorice root is also useful as a mild laxative and for ulcers.

To regulate female hormones, especially in P.M.S. and menstrual cramps, I have found licorice very functional. Licorice has been shown to inhibit tumors, be antiinflammatory, antibacterial and useful against Addison's disease. In China licorice is often used as a first-aid remedy for cuts, burns and as an antidote. Licorice can cause high blood pressure in some, so it should not be consumed in large quantities by people at risk for hypertension.

No, you are not going to get all of these effects next time you go to the movies and decide to treat yourself to some black licorice from the candy counter. There is no licorice in those candies!

Milk vetch *Astragalus americanus*

Synonyms: Astragalus possibly Chinese Huang Qi

Identification: This perennial herb has taproots or a creeping rhizome with a single erect stem, 50 - 100 cm high, leaflets 7 -15 elliptic-oblong pinnates, 2-4 cm long, glabrous above, sparsely hairy beneath. The flowers are white, turning yellowish or sordid, 13 -15 mm long; pods drooping, inflated, ellipsoid, membranous, 1.5 -2cm long.

Distribution & Habitat: Found along stream banks and in moist wooded areas from Alaska and Yukon, east to Hudson Bay and south to B.C., Montana, Colorado and Manatoba.

Preparation & Uses: Caution should be exercised with this plant. Members of the genus are known to be poisonous. I'm including this plant for interest's sake because a strong possibility exists that this plant has the same properties, and maybe even the same species as the Chinese Huang Qi, a very important herb, that I use extensively in the clinic. Steven Foster, a well known herbal researcher initially suggested the similarity. Michael Moore picked up on this and passed on the comment during one of his herb walks. Robyn Klein decided to do more research and showed that the chemistry was very similar between the two species. I would say that the jury is still out, especially since toxicity tests have not been done. The subject does deserve further study. If it is truly Huang Qi, Milk vetch is a very safe plant indeed.

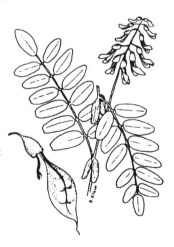

The Chinese Huang Qi is very important as Fu Zheng herb, i.e., one that builds up immunity, lowers blood pressure due to vasodilation, is diuretic, helps protect the liver from toxicity, increases endurance and has a tonic effect. From a Oriental Medicine point of view it tonifies Spleen and Qi, stabilizes the exterior and discharges pus.

Sweet vetch

Hedysarum boreale var. mackenzie

Hedysarum = hay-dis-a-rum, from Greek *hedys* "sweet" (a name used by Dioscorides), referring to flower, or perhaps the root.

Synonym: Bear Root.

Identification: This perennial herb has numerous stems and it grows 20-50 cm in height from a woody base and a thick fibrous root. There are 5-15 large, rose-purple flowers in showy, sweet-scented racemes. The leaves are made up of 5-7 pairs of silvery-grey pinnate leaflets. The fruit is a legume, which is flat and jointed.

Distribution & Habitat: This plant grows in damp places such as river banks and flood plains. It is seen as high as alpine meadows and extends eastward from the mountains in riverbeds.

Preparation & Uses: Even though it is a good general rule not to eat plants from the pea or legume family, sweet vetch is a nice change. The roots in the early spring are quite sweet and were often used as a licorice substitute by the Indians and early settlers. The roots are a bit hard to dig and taste best just after the shoots have started to come out (which makes it hard to identify). Mistaking this plant for another legume could make you quite sick so make sure you are right. Bears are also fond of the roots in the spring, and you can sometimes see where they have dug a hole for the roots.

Alfalfa   *Medicago sativa*

Medicago = Persian name for a grass; *sativa* = L. for "pleated, cultivated, sown, not wild".

Identification: Alfalfa is a deep-rooted perennial with a thick crown and decumbent or erect stems up to 8 cm long. The flowers are in racemes and are usually blue-violet to purple, occasionally whitish. The leaflets are obovate, toothed and slightly hairy. The deep and spreading root enables this plant to absorb its valuable nutrients.

Distribution & Habitat: This is an introduced forage plant that has often escaped the fields. It is commonly found in waste places and along roadsides.

Preparation & Uses: The seeds of alfalfa can be ground into flour, parched and eaten, or of course used as "sprouts". Besides being very tasty, the sprouts are very high in nutrients. Many health clinics put patients on alfalfa sprout diets. To sprout alfalfa seed, take a large jar and cover the bottom with seeds. Let them soak overnight. It is best to put a screen over the lid to make drainage easier. In the morning, drain off the water and rinse the seeds. This water is high in nutrients and can be used to water plants. The water is also good in stews. Rinse the seeds 2-3 times a day, making sure you drain them thoroughly each time. The sprouts grow best in the dark, although excellent sprouts can be grown in the light. After about 3 days the sprouts will have grown to fill the bottle. Expose them to sunlight for a few hours and the little cotyledons will turn green. They are now ready to eat.

The leaves of alfalfa can be eaten raw in salad, but are better dried and ground to obtain most of the nutrients. The word *alfalfa* comes from the Arabic word meaning "father of all food". Alfalfa is high in vitamins A, B, C, E, K and P. It contains potassium, phosphorus, iron, chlorine, sodium, silica, magnesium and many other trace elements because of its deep roots and preference for fairly rich soil. It has a fairly high protein content (18.9%) and also contains the antioxidant tricin.

Alfalfa is a very good tonic, both for gaining health or retaining it. The pleasant tea made from the leaves is very rejuvenating if taken every day. Alfalfa is listed as an appetizer, diuretic, tonic and nutrient.

The tea will improve appetite, relieve urinary and bowel problems, eliminate retained water and even help cure peptic ulcers, if taken regularly. Its action is slow but it will soon put the body in balance. In Europe and Russia the tea has been used as a dietary aid for celiac disease (along with a proper diet). Alfalfa is being used experimentally as an antifungal and estrogenic agent.

Alfalfa, especially the seed or alfalfa concentrate, has been found to be very effective in lowering high cholesterol conditions, by stopping excessive production of cholesterol in the body.

The authors of *Some Useful Plants* came up with a good way to make a natural tooth brush. Take the root, peel off the bark, dry it slowly, cut into 5-inch pieces then gently hit the end with a hammer.

Alfalfa
Medicago sativa

Red Clover   *Trifolium spp.*

Trifolium = tri-fo-lee-um, from Latin *tri* (three) and *folium* (leaf).

Identification: Clover is so familiar that one hardly needs a description of it. Suffice it to say that clover is found in waste places, escaping cultivation. It is often found in lawns, roadsides and disturbed soil.

Preparation & Uses: Clover is one of those plants that can be eaten in its entirety. It should be sparingly eaten when raw because it can cause bloating (though completely harmless) when cooked. The bloating effect is also decreased if the plant is first soaked in salt water. Clover is high in protein, making it a nutritious meal. As a tea, clover is excellent, especially the dried flowers and seeds.

Red Clover flowers are alterative, sedative, deobstructent, diuretic and expectorant. For stimulating the liver and gall bladder, an infusion of clover flowers is often used. Clover can also help in cases of constipation, sluggish appetite, skin problems, whooping cough, bronchial and renal conditions. A strong tea of clover flowers can assist as a gargle for sore mouths and throats, acting as a mild sedative. This tea can also be used both as a rectal and vaginal injection.

Red Clover
Trifolium pratense

Sticky Purple Geranium
Geranium viscosissimum

Externally, clover tea is used as a fomentation for rheumatic or gout pain and to soften hard milk glands. As a poultice, it is useful for athlete's foot and other skin problems. A good salve can be made from clover flowers for treating external cancer and indolent ulcers.

The recommended dosage is to take 2 tsp. of the flowers and steep them in ½ cup of water for 10 minutes. Take 1 to 1 ½ cups a day, in mouthful doses at any one time. The tincture dosage is 5-30 drops in water.

Cranesbill Geranium, Sticky Purple Geranium *Geranium viscosissimum*

Geranium = ge-ra-nee-um, from Greek (*geranos*) meaning crane, *viscosissimum* = from L. *viscosus*, sticky, clammy, viscid.

Identification: This perennial herb grows 30 - 60 cm tall and has reddish-purple flowers (sometimes white) with dark veins. The stem forms a woody base. The 3-5 palmately lobed leaves are coarsely toothed. The styles are united in a central pointed column, which resembles the bill of a crane or stork, giving it one of its common names. At maturity the column splits into 5 recoiling segments.

Distribution & Habitat: Cranesbill is distributed throughout the area. It extends from subalpine meadows to moist places in lower fescue grassland and thickets.

Preparation & Uses: The herb part of this plant is astringent and styptic, internally used for diarrhea, gastritis, enteritis, gout and hemorrhages. A hot poultice of boiled leaves is good for bladder pains, bruises and persistent skin problems. Tea of the leaf can be used as a douche. The green crushed herb can be applied to relieve pain and inflammation. The tea has been used as a wash for inflammation of the mouth or diluted and used as an eyewash. The powdered root, stops external bleeding and was used by the Blackfoot as one of the major first-aid remedies.

It can be used as an addition to a simple sweatbath, as a diaphoretic. Blackfoot Indians would drink an infusion of the leaves for a cold. Leaves were put in food storage bags to help stop the contents spoiling. As a cosmetic plant, Jeanne Rose says it wakes up the skin. It's astringent quality will at least tighten the skin.

Flax   *Linum sp.*

Linum = leen-um, from the classical Latin name for flax.

Identification: These annual or perennial herbs have stiff slender stems with simple, narrow, sessile leaves. The flowers are regular usually blue but yellow one also grow in the area; 5 sepals and petals.

Distribution & Habitat: In grasslands and dry open woods from Alaska, Yukon, James Bay south into California and west to Oklahoma, Wisconson and the Great Lake area.

Preparation & Uses: The crushed seed of flax have been used throughout the ages as a poultice for irritation, boils and pain. As a mild laxative it can be soaked for twenty minutes, drinking the mucilage. The oils obtained from flax seed contains both omega 3 and omega 6 essential fatty acids – oils that are very much needed in our modern day lives. They can help all kind over problems including lower cholesterol, give rise to prostaglandin (a local immune function), stop platelet aggregation and control a myriad of things from eczema, to breast lumps.

The stems are the source of linen, a fabric used for clothing since Biblical times.

Crowberry   *Empetrum nigrum*

Empetrum = em-pe-trum, from Greek *empetron, en* (on) and *petros* (a rock), referring to its habitat; *nigrum* = nig-rum, refers to the black colour of the berries.

Identification: A low, freely branching heath-like evergreen shrub. The leaves are linear, 3-6 mm long, covering the branches evenly. The small, bisexual crimson flowers are in groups of two or three. The fruits are shiny black berries.

Distribution & Habitat: Crowberry is found on muskeg and open coniferous forest. It is most common on north-facing slopes, where it sometimes forms thick mats.

Preparation & Uses: The juicy black berries can be eaten raw or cooked. The flavour of the berries is said to be an acquired taste, but after the first frost, it improves. Cooking and the addition of sugar and/or lemon also improves the flavour.

A type of beer can be made from the berries by crushing them and adding sugar, molasses or honey, then putting it into an air-tight container and allowing it to ferment for a few weeks. The liquid is then strained, cooled and is ready to drink.

The twigs and stem of crowberry have been used for colds, kidney trouble and tuberculosis, especially in the North country. The Dena'ina Athabasca made a tea for diarrhea. Some Eskimos used crowberry juice for sore eyes and to relieve snow-blindness. The roots have also been used for sore eyes and cataracts.

Sumac, Smooth   *Rhus glabra*

Rhus = rus, from the classical Latin name of *R. coriaria* or from an ancient Greek name for a sumach, *glabra* = L. "becoming smooth or glabrous".

Identification: This shrub stands 2 - 4 m tall. The leaves are pinnately divided. The flowers are greenish to white and are borne in dense clusters. The dry fruits are densely covered with hairs.

Distribution & Habitat: This shrub often grows in dense patches in the foot-hills, lower mountains, valleys and streamsides throughout North America.

Preparation & Uses: The Sioux Indians made a styptic wash of the boiled fruit to stop hemorrhaging after childbirth. They also boiled the root for a treatment of urinary pain and to stop urine retention. The berries were used to stop bedwetting. Rashes – especially those created by plants such as poison ivy – were treated with a poultice of the leaves. The Flathead Indians believed that a tea of the green twigs was a cure for tuberculosis. The twigs were reused, changing from green during the first boiling to red in the second. The patient drank several cups a day. Some species have berries with irritating "hairs". This can be overcome by wrapping the berries in a towel and squeezing out the juice. A wonderful "lemonade" can be extracted.

A leaf tea has been used for asthma, diarrhea and diseases of the mouth. Smoked, the leaves were again employed for asthma.

The root has been used by herbalists as an antiseptic dressing, especially for leg ulcers. The infusion of the bark has been used as an astringent for mouth sores, diarrhea, syphilis, gonorrhea and dysentery. The juice of the roots is known to cure warts. Moore suggests a glycerine tincture as excellent for all types of muco-epithelial sores (ie. lips, mouth, genital, nostril).

The Plains Indians also used the leaves in tobacco mixtures. This plant can be used as a dye and yields a yellow-tan, gray or black dye depending on the mordant and the part of the plant used.

Caution: Do not confuse this plant with Poison Sumac.

Snow Brush, Red Root   *Ceanothus velutinus*

Ceanothus = kee-a-no-thus, from Greek name of a spiny shrub, *velutinus* = L. with a soft, silky covering, velvety.

Identification: Snow brush is a shrub growing 1-3 m high, often in dense patches. It has olive-green twigs and the white flowers are small, borne in dense clusters. The glossy evergreen leaves are alternate, being ovate to elliptic with three prominent veins.

Distribution & Habitat: Snow brush is found along old roadsides and old paths.

Preparation & Uses: This genus has long been recognized as a substitute for commercial black tea. It tastes similar to it but is a little sweeter. *C. velutinus* is not prized as much as some species as a tea but is often used as a substitute for smoking tobacco, sometimes when it is mixed with bearberry. The flower of this plant make a nice soapy lather in warm water, and is gentle on the skin and hair. An infusion of the leaves is stimulating to the stomach and liver, and it relieves internal bleeding and nervous irritability. As a lymphatic remedy the root can be used to stimulate lymph and interstitial fluid circulation. Related to this usage, Moore points out its use to help reabsorb some ovarian cysts and testicular hydrocele. He suggests combining it with Dong Quai or Blue Cohosh and Helonias Root. For intermittent breast cysts, Moore combines this root with Cotton Root (*Gossypium thurberi*) and Milkweed (*Asclepius aperula*). It can also be used for tonsil inflammation, sore throats, enlarged lymph nodes, and chronic adenoid enlargements.

A related species' roots (*C. americanus*) were employed for lung ailments, stomachaches, snake bite and fevers. The alkaloids in the root have been shown to lower blood pressure.

Crowberry
Empetrum nigrum

TW

Smooth Sumac
Rhus glabra

BA

Buckthorn
Rhamnus alnifolia

BA

137

Buckthorn *Rhamnus alnifolia*

Rhamnus = ram-nus, from the Greek name for shrub.

Identification: This shrub is related to Cascara. It stands 50 - 200 cm high and has alternate, elliptic or ovate, serrated leaves. The flowers are greenish. The fruits are black berrylike drupes, which are poisonous.

Preparation & Uses: As in Cascara sagrada, the inner bark is cathartic but much faster acting and more griping than Cascara.

Cascara Sagrada *Rhamnus purshiana*

Rhamnus = ram-nus, from the Greek word for various prickly shrubs; *purshiana* = after Frederick Pursh, botanist.

Identification: This tall shrub or small tree stands from 3 - 12 m tall and has a trunk diameter of 10 - 40 cm. The leaves are dark green, oblong, 5 - 15 cm long and 6 cm wide. The flowers are quite small, greenish white and found in axillary clusters. The fruit is black and .5 - 1.5 cm in diameter.

Distribution & Habitat: Cascara can be found in relatively moist, low-lying, forested habitats from British Columbia to California and east to Montana.

Preparation & Uses: The bark of this herb has been found to be one of the most effective laxative cathartics. I would have to say that in my herbal practice I use more of this herb than any other (in the form of Laxaherb or LBT-3). The words "Cascara Sagrada" come from Spanish meaning "holy bark". This bark is a component in many of the commercial herbal laxative mixtures found in North America and Europe. The laxative effect of Cascara is not habit forming like some herb laxatives (e.g. senna) as it exercises the colon muscles. As a result, after six months of use, one can lower the dose or completely eliminate it, still maintaining active bowels. Indians also used this bark as a laxative.

The bark can be gathered from mid-April to the end of August. It should be stored for at least one year before use. The chemical structure changes during this time to make it less griping and more effective. About 3 million pounds of this bark are harvested annually.

Mallow, Common   *Malva neglecta* & related *spp.*

Malva = mal-va, from L. "soft" (the name in Pliny), *neglecta* = L. formerly over-looked, disregarded, neglected.

Identification: Common mallow is an annual herb with ascending or erect stems 20 - 30 cm long. The pale blue or whitish flowers are in axillary clusters. The leaves are alternate and nearly round and have long petioles.

Distribution & Habitat: Low mallow was introduced from Europe. It can be found on waste land, roadsides, backyards and disturbed areas.

Preparation & Uses: The young shoots and leaves of mallow have been prized for years as a good pot herb. This plant is very mucilaginous and will there-fore thicken soup. Salads can be made from the raw shoots and leaves.

The green, immature fruit, can be eaten raw, tasting a bit like cheese. The fruit is plentiful enough to be used in satisfying amounts. The fruit tastes good when added to soups, pickled in brine and vinegar, and mixed into salads.

A tea can be made from the leaves, which are prepared by pulling up the plant and hanging it upside down in the shade until dry.

One should not confuse *Malva spp.* with Marsh Mallow (*Althaea officinalis*) or *Hibiscus spp.*, which are both sometimes called Malva, or Marsh Mallow. Neither of these species grow in our area.

Medicinally, mallow is listed as an astringent, demulcent, emollient and ex-pectorant. Mallow's major herbal use is as a demulcent and it is used in the form of an infusion for respiratory and related ailments. These include colds, coughs, bronchitis, irritation of the air passages and many other related problems. Besides this, mallow is also used internally in cases of gastritis and enteritis.

Moore says that in New Mexico the tea is drunk to facilitate labor in child-birth and as a wash for skin irritation in infants. Externally, a decoction of mallow herb is helpful to wash wounds and sores. As a poultice, mallow can sooth irritation and inflammation. Intestinal inflammation can be treated by a warm leaf enema tea of mallow.

To make the decoction for external use, boil one tablespoon of leaves in ½ cup of water for a short period.

Cascara Sagrada
Rhamnus purshiana

Cascara Sagrada
Rhamnus purshiana

Evergreen Violet
Viola orbiculata

Early Blue Violet
Viola adunca

Western Canadian Violet
Viola canadensis

Pansy - Violet   *Viola tricolor & V. adunca*

Viola = vee-o-la, from the Latin name of scented plants, from the Greek nymph Io, who was turned into a cow. Zeus took pity on her and turned her tears into violets, to both console her and to sweeten her diet. To this day violets are said to represent modesty. *tricolor* = tri-ko-lor, three coloured, *adunca* = L. "hooked, having hooks".

Synonyms: Heart's ease, Johney-jump-up

Identification: Pansies are stout annuals needing no description and are seen commonly as border plants in many flower beds. They are native to Europe.

Preparation & Uses: Violet tastes tender and quite sweet. The flowers of *V. tricolor* taste almost like grape-flavoured bubble gum. Both the leaves and flowers are a good addition to any salad. Violet tea is great. Violets are high in vitamin C and beta-carotene (two fresh violet leaves fill the RDA for vitamin C).

Viola tricolor is listed as diuretic, expectorant, alterative, a mild laxative and a mild sedative. Violets are often used for their blood-purifying qualities. They are even reported to be useful in cases of cancer because they keep the blood so clean that cancer has "nothing to live on".

In the form of an infusion the leaves have been used to relieve bronchitis and fevers, to act as a mild laxative (the yellow ones are the most laxative ones). Leaf infusion has been used as a gargle for sore throats and coughing for

141

centuries. Viola extract has been put into some cough syrups, often combined with coltsfoot. Violets are said to have mild hormone regulating capa-
bility. In this regard, *Viola adunca* roots and leaves were used by Makah
women in Washington state during labour. Violet's diuretic properties have
been utilized in rheumatic diseases. These plants have been employed for
asthma, heart palpitations, skin eruptions, boils and eczema. Salve and poultice recipes can be found in many herbals.

The Athabascans made "incense" of mashed violet leaves and placed them on
coals or a woodstove. The Dena'ina believed that this incense will ward off
disease.

Prickly Pear cactus & Pin Cushion cactus *Mamillaria & Opuntia spp.*

Mamillaria = mam-i-lah-ree-a, from Latin *mammilla* (a nipple) referring to the
shape of the tubercle. *Opuntia* = o-pun-tee-a, from Greek because it grew near
Opus in ancient Greece or Tournefort's name for the succulent plants from a
Greek town of the same name.

Identification: These cacti are unmistakable. Prickly pear cactus is flat, and
pear-shaped. Pin cushion cactus literally looks like a pin cushion.

Preparation & Uses: The fruit of Pin cushion cactus is delicious and fleshy. I
will guarantee that if you enter a patch of pin cushion cactus while they are in
fruit and try just one, you will be in that patch for a long time, no matter what
you were supposed to be doing. The fruit of prickly pear can also be eaten
but should be peeled and it isn't quite as tasty as the pin cushion cactus.
Although the plant is abundant through most of the Rockies, it can be locally
rare. Please respect any regulations which govern plant picking in your area.

The pulp of the cacti can be eaten if you overcome the problem of the spines.
One solution is to remove the spines by burning them off, another way is to
split them in two, eating the insides.

West Coast Indians were said to drink a mash of *Opuntia* pulp, soaked in salt
water, to facilitate childbirth. Other Amerindians were known to make a
poultice of the pulp for wounds, bruises and warts. The pulp was drunk as a
lung remedy.

Moore says that in Mexico the juice of prickly pear was used as an anti-inflammatory diuretic and taken in 1 tsp. doses every 2 hours. He also stated that
the folkloric use of prickly pear has been verified for use in adult onset diabetes, to reduce or prevent insulin usage.

Green Ash   *Fraxinus pensylvanica*

Fraxinus = fraks-i-nus, L. name used by Virgil, *pensylvanica*, L. "of Pennsylvania".

Identification: This medium size tree stands up to 10 m tall. The pinnate leaf has five to seven leaflets, which are ovate to oblong-lanceolate in shape. The fruit is reddish-brown.

Preparation & Uses: The inner bark was scraped and made into an infusion to be drunk for depression and fatigue.

Ash is listed as a diuretic and diaphoretic. The inner bark tea was used by Amerindians as a emetic and strong laxative for worms, as an afterbirth tonic, to relieve stomach cramps, and to remove bile from the intestine. Externally a wash was made for sores, itching, lice and even snakebite. The inner bark was chewed and applied as a poultice on sores. The seeds were considered an aphrodisiac.

The wood is easy to work and was often used for pipe stems, bows, arrows, tipi pins, pegs, drums and racks for drying meat. The Sioux Indians used it for the center of their Sun Dance lodge.

Buffalo Berry *Shepherdia canadensis* and *argentea*

Argentea = L. for "silvery".

Synonyms: Soapberry

Identification: Canadian buffalo berry is a spreading shrub, standing 1-3 m tall. The unisexual flowers are yellowish, forming in clusters. The leathery leaves are lanceolate to elliptic, green above and silvery with brown dots on the bottom. The fruit is small, red or yellow.

Distribution & Habitat: Canadian buffalo berry is common on slopes and thinly wooded areas. Another species, *S. argentea* grows mostly from the Canadian border south.

Preparation & Uses: Buffalo berry berries are insipid and bitter, although sugar and cooking improve them. The insipid taste is due to high content of a saponin. They taste better when picked after the first few frosts of autumn. The berries can be made into a jelly that tastes good. The Indians used to mix these berries with buffalo meat to make pemmican. Reports say that this is also tasty. They also dried the berries (in cake form) to store them for the winter. These cakes were added to stews and puddings. The berries can be beaten with an egg beater and mixed with sugar. It becomes quite smooth and frothy and is called buffalo ice-cream. This mixture is quite tasty and I have even found it on the menu of a mountain restaurant. The frothing action (due to the saponin) gives it one of its common names - soapberry. The berries were eaten by some Indians to help relieve stomach troubles and constipation.

S. argentea has less saponin and is fairly tasty even before the first frost, but cannot be frothed as easily.

Prickly Pear
Opuntia sp.

Pin Cushion Cactus
Mamillaria sp.

Buffalo Berry
Shepherdia sp.

Young shoot of Fireweed
Epilobium angustifolium

Fireweed (flower stage)
Epilobium angustifolium

Fireweed   *Epilobium angustifolium*

Epilobium = e-pi-lo-bee-um, from Greek *epi* (upon) and *lobos* (a pod), Gerner's name indicating the positioning of the corolla on top of the ovary, *angustifolium* = L. "narrow-leaved".

Identification: This very common perennial herb has an erect stem that stands up to 150 cm tall. It has rose-purple flowers in an elongated raceme. The stems are leafy and the leaves being alternate, lanceolate, dark green above and paler and veined beneath. The seeds are in long silk-filled seed pods.

Distribution & Habitat: Fireweed is a very common fire successional plant colonizing any disturbed ground. It is found along roads, open woods and in recently burned-over areas. It is often in competition with *Arnica spp.*

An Indian Legend:

A young Indian maiden once set fire to the far end of an enemy's camp to cause a diversion to rescue her lover from torture. She untied him and fled with the enemy giving chase. The Great Spirit took pity on her. Wherever her moccasins touched the ground, great flames shot up. This soon turned her pursuers back. Eventually, the flames turned into brilliant fireweed flowers.

Preparation & Uses: The young leaves of fireweed make good greens in salads and can also be cooked. The whole of the young plant can be cooked like asparagus before it gets woody and I find it quite tasty. The more mature fireweed can be eaten if the outer pith is taken off, exposing a sweet glutinous substance. I find it hard to peel with disappointingly little inside. The petiole of the flower can be eaten and the flower buds and full flower add glamour and taste to a salad. The mature leaves can be used as a tea. The silky hair on the seed pod makes excellent tinder for fires. Fireweed has a very good survival food value because of a relatively high content of Beta-carotene and Vitamin C.

Some Europeans used the fireweed as an intestinal astringent in the form of a tea and as an antispasmodic, demulcent and emmenagogue. It is also said to have good effects on diseased mucous membranes, colon troubles, cholera and dysentery - it at least relieves the pain from these diseases. It is felt, by the Indians, that its veins carry an antiseptic which they use for healing sores and ulcers. They also use this herb for healing burns, which is interesting because it heals the burns of the earth too – the source of its common name. A poultice or ointment made of the roots can be used on skin inflammation, boils, ulcers and rashes.

Blackfoot Indians used an infusion of the root and inner cortex as an enema for children, to help them eliminate. The flowers were rubbed into rawhide as a waterproofing. The powdered inner cortex was put on the hands and face to protect them from the cold. I have tried this while working outdoors on cross country skis and found it very effective. The powder was used so that the hands would not be hurt when being warmed up again.

Evening Primrose   *Oenothera spp.*

Oenothera = oy-no-the-ra, from Gr. "Ass-catcher" - the name of another plant.

Identification: Evening primroses are very variable, some are tall and others small and prostrate. They are annual, biennial or perennial herbs with alternate or basal leaves. The flowers are pink, yellow or orange, and they open in the evening.

Distribution & Habitat: These plants can be found throughout the area.

Preparation & Uses: Cooked in the spring, the roots are fairly tasty. Cooked at other times, they taste peppery.

Both the leaves and the crushed seeds were used as a poultice to heal wounds and for bruises and piles. The plant was also recorded as being used for spasmodic asthma, whooping cough (especially when mixed with honey to make a syrup), gastric irritation, irritable bladder and chronic diarrhea. The roots have been rubbed on muscles to give athletic strength.

The seed oils are very high in essential oils, especially gamma-linoleic acid, which has been shown to heal a variety of malfunctions in the body. In clinical studies, it has been shown to be effective for heart disease, asthma, psoriasis, premenstrual syndrome, alcoholism, dry eye syndrome, and many other fatty acid problems. There have been over 250 scientific papers written about this herb from the late 1970's to the early 1990's.

Sarsaparilla, Wild   *Aralia nudicaulis*

Aralia = a-rah-lee-a, from the French Canadian name aralie, *nudicaulis* = L. "naked-stemmed, leafless".

Identification: Sarsaparilla is a perennial herb 20 - 60 cm high with a single compound leaf arising from a creeping rootstalk. Greenish or whitish flowers on an umbel are borne on a stalk. The leaves are bi-pinnate with ovate-oblong leaflets. The fruit is a greenish berry-like drupe which turns purplish at maturity. The long root is aromatic. Sarsaparilla is in the ginseng family. True ginseng does not grow wild in this area.

Distribution & Habitat: This plant is common in rich forest and woodland. It usually likes semi-open or open areas.

Preparation & Uses: The Miskwaki Indians made a poultice of the root to treat burns and sores. The Kwakiutl Indians mixed the pounded root with oil as a cough medicine (for spitting blood). The Ojibwa took the decoction for purification during pregnancy. The decoction of the root was also used as a wash for wounds and sores.

Wild sarsaparilla should not be confused with the Jamaican Sarsaparilla (*Smilax officinalis*). Though it has similar qualities, it is milder. A delicious tea can be made from the roots which are also used to make soft drinks.

Indians on long war and hunting excursions would often subsist on a bundle of sarsaparilla roots which gave them energy. Medicinally, sarsaparilla roots have been listed as a stimulant, diaphoretic, alterative, diuretic, demulcent and antiscorbutic. Dilute alcohol and water are used as solvents. The Indians also used it as a pectoral, vulnerary and cordial. Montagnais and Penobscot Indian women would cut up the roots, tie them in bundles, and then keep them in their lodges until needed. The Montagnais also fermented the berries in water which they then used as a tonic.

Wild Sarsaparilla
Aralia nudicaulis

Evening Primrose
Oenothera spp.

TW

Devil's Club
Oplopanax horridum

TW

BA

Devil's Club
Oplopanax horridum

149

The Penobscots dried the roots, crushed them to a powder and steeped them together with sweet flag (*Acorus calamus*) for use as a cough medicine. The decoction of the root was used to treat sore eyes, high blood pressure, as a blood purifier, for difficulty in passing urine, blood in urine, pain in the lower abdomen and back, and for pleurisy.

Hutchens also lists it as being valuable and dependable for treating rheumatism, gout, skin eruptions, ringworm, scrofula, internal inflammation, colds, catarrh, fever, stomach and intestinal gas. It has also been used as a very strong antidote for deadly poisons. As an antidote it is most effective when mixed with burdock – it should be drunk freely.

Sarsaparilla was a national phenomenon in the United States during the mid-1800's as a spring tonic. It was used in the U.S. Pharmacopeia from 1820 -1882 as a stimulant, alterative and diaphoretic.

Devil's Club   *Oplopanax horridum* (a.k.a. *Echinopanax horridum*)

Oplopanax = L. "prickly porcupine-ginseng".

Identification: This strongly aromatic shrub has a very coarse nature, being densely covered with spines and prickles. Standing 1 - 3 m (occasionally as high as 5 m), it has alternate leaves on long petioles, 5 - 7 lobed, palmate and 10 - 30 cm wide, with prickly ribs on the underside. The flowers are borne on umbels in large terminal clusters, 10 - 30 cm long, with greenish petals, 2 styles; fruits brightly scarlet, 4 - 5 mm long, 2 seeded.

Distribution & Habitat: Found from Alaska to Oregon and as far east as Lake Superior in moist rich soil, along stream banks, often in thick wooded areas such as cedar forest. It usually grows in dense thickets.

Preparation & Uses: When the young spring shoot first appears in the early spring (only for a few days) the green tender stalks can be eaten. The leaf clusters can be eaten raw or as Schofield suggests added to omelettes, casseroles or soups. As soon as the leaf spines stiffen, they are not edible.

Medicinally this plant has a multitude of uses. It belongs in the same family as ginseng. It is listed as being hypoglycemic, cathartic, emetic (in large doses), stomachic, analgesic and diaphoretic. Used heavily by West coast Indians for both medicinal and "strong magical powers", it was widely traded. One of the most famous applications amongst West coast Indians was for adult onset diabetes. It is reportedly capable of reducing the need for (and in some cases completely eliminate) injected insulin. The inner bark is boiled as a decoction. In our clinic we use a tincture of inner bark of the roots. The hypoglycemic effect was verified in 1938 in medical studies, after native people were found using it, but little subsequent attention has been paid to Devil's Club.

It has been suggested that hypoglycemics should not take this herb. Yet I've met hypoglycemic people who, ignorant of this fact, say it helps them get rid of "... the late afternoon hangover from reality". Modern practitioners have also employed this herb to curb sugar cravings. Many native groups used a root bark decoction, or simply chewed it. During fasts, it was felt to aid a person in curbing appetite and even to assist with visions.

Being a member of the ginseng family, some myths about this herb (deserved or not) claim it is a great body-balancer and strengthener. The southeast Alaskan Indians used the decoction to cure and prevent cancer. Both internally and externally the bark has been used for arthritis. Infusion, decoction, chewing the bark or simply laying the bark on the sore area were the application methods. As an analgesic, the tea was used by some and others burned the bark to a white ash and applied it topically both to wounds and to stop pain. For arthritis and rheumatism, sometimes the whole body was soaked in the tea (while the patient also drank it).

An ointment made of the root bark has been used for treatment of sore and stiff joints, swelling, as a liniment and for massage oils. A decoction was used as the water for sweat lodges or steams to treat rheumatism, digestive complaints and pneumonia. Both paste and poultices have been used to treat wounds, bites, stings and skin problems, including the festered sore that can be caused by this plant's prickles. Some have used a powdered root bark as a foot bath after long hikes.

Indigestion, constipation and general stomach complaints were treated with a decoction of the bark by Coast Indians. The Thompson Indians used its tonic, laxative and blood cleansing abilities as a spring tonic. In Alaska, the Tlingit and Haida tribes were reported to use a bark infusion for "general strength, colds, chest pain after colds, arthritis, black eyes, gall stones, stomach ulcers, and constipation." For chest complaints it was used for everything from colds, pneumonia, hoarse throats and even tuberculosis. A mixture of Devil's Club root, Labrador tea and clover roots, was used by native peoples during epidemics to ward off illness. It was also used in sweats and burned to ward off evil spirits associated with disease. It was used as protection from evil spirits – hung over doorways, on fishing boats or worn as amulets by shamans.

For toothaches, the root can be chewed or applied as a poultice to painful areas. It was sometimes chewed and spit on a wound as an emergency analgesic. Large amounts are said to cause a "drunkenness", maybe one of the reasons it has been used for vision seeking.

Several tribes used this herb for childbirth. The Bella Coola used it as a purgative before and after childbirth. The Skagit decocted it, with other herbs, after childbirth to establish regular menstrual flow. The Shuswap drank the decoction for several days after childbirth. The dethorned bark was laid on Skagit women to reduce milk flow when it was too heavy. The dried powdered bark was pulverized by the Cowlitz Indians and used as a perfumed talc for babies. This same mixture has been used as a deodorant by other groups.

The berries were used as a hair tonic, especially to kill lice and as a treatment for dandruff in small children.

The Lummi Indians of Washington State burnt the "sticks" and mixed the ash with grease to make a reddish - brown face paint.

Caution: The prickles produce a festering wound that can be treated by a poultice of the root bark but it is best to use extreme caution when hiking near the plant. The best time to harvest is in spring. It is felt that it is strongest then. One article suggests that if the root is harvested after a killing frost in the fall the sap contains some poisonous substances.

Cow Parsnip   *Heracleum lanatum*

Heracleum = hay-ra-klee-um, L. Hercules' healer (a name used by Theophrastus), *lanatum* = L. "woolly".

Identification: Cow parsnip is a herb 1-2 m high with leaves 30 cm broad and palmately-veined. The flowers are small, sweetly scented, in large compound umbels. The stems are stout and hollow. The fruit is flat and winged at the edges. Great care should be taken in selecting this plant as it looks like water hemlock which is deadly poisonous.

Distribution & Habitat: Cow parsnip is the commonest member of the carrot family in the Rocky Mountains. It is found growing in moist hollows along intermittent streams, among willow and other thickets, throughout the region.

Preparation & Uses: The cooked roots of the cow parsnip are said to taste much like rutabagas but I find them very distasteful. The very young leaves are delicious and are eaten in salads or cooked, but as they grow older they become too strong. The young stems of this common herb can be peeled and

Cow Parsnip
Heracleum lanatum

eaten raw but are best cooked. The hollow basal portion of the plant may be cut into short lengths, then dried and used as a substitute for salt. The leaves as well may be dried and the ashes used instead of salt. The flower stem, before the flower opens, may be peeled and the inner portion eaten raw like celery, or boiled until tender. The seeds, both ripe and unripe, can be sparingly added to salads for seasoning.

Blackfoot Indians cut up the stem into small pieces which were dipped in blood and stored for used in soups or broths. The Cree called it *pickquanahtick*. They put small pieces of the root onto a sore tooth and spat out the saliva. The Cree also used the root as a poultice for swellings, after fast boiling it.

The Blackfoot called it *po-kint-sam* and used the stem ritually in the Sun Dance. They used the fresh, young stems in a brew to treat diarrhea. An infusion of young stems was applied in the removal of warts. An infusion of the roots was used as a horse medicine and for respiratory trouble. The horse was held down and the solution administered through a blowing tube held to the nostril or the mouth.

The best use I have found for cow parsnip is as toilet paper. The leaves are large enough to be very convenient. This can be a very important use! A small percentage of people have skin sensitivity to this plant so they should check this out before getting a rash from "Nature's toilet paper".

The roots and seeds are considered antispasmodic, carminative and expectorant. The seeds are used in the same way as dill seeds for colic and flatulence. Dried roots (less acrid than fresh roots) can be made into a tea and drunk for nausea, used for gas and hiatus hernia. Tincture of the seed is also used for nausea, even just a few drops on the tongue. In the mid-19th century, a strong decoction of the root was drunk daily for several weeks and said to cure paralysis, epilepsy and to correct double vision. For paralysis, it mostly affects the spinal cord, though it is also known to be effective for sciatica. It can also be massaged into the area in the form of an oil or made into a poultice. These two preparations require the fresh, not dried, root. The fresh, green seed tincture of cow parsnip has an effective analgesic property when applied to a sore tooth, similar to clove oil. Moore, in fact, considers it stronger than the latter. Both roots and seed have been used for calming down a nervous spastic colon.

This plant was often found in the medicine bundles of hunters. It was said to attract deer to the initiate but was evil for the non-initiated. The leaves are known to work as a mild insect repellent. The seeds have been used for severe headache by the Meskwaki Indians.

Canby's Lovage, Osha   *Ligusticum canbyi, L. porteri, L. scorticum*

Ligusticum = L. from a plant named by Dioscorides, in Liguria, northeast Italy.

Identification: This delicate, tall perennial grows to a height of 120 cm. Its polypinnate leaves have a triangular appearance. Lovage is a member of the *Umbelliferae* family and flowers form in an umbel, like cow parsnip.

Distribution & Habitat: Canby's lovage can be found at high elevation in the Cascades in B.C. and Montana, Idaho, Washington and the Blue Mountains in Oregon.

Preparation & Uses: *L. scorticum* makes for a very delicious parsley substitute. The roots were chewed, or a decoction was made, to relieve colds, sore throats, toothaches, headaches, stomachache, fevers and heartburn. Shavings of the root were sometimes added to boiling water and used as an inhalation for sinus infections.

The Flathead Indians believed you should never wash the roots in the mountains, where they were found, because it would cause a rainstorm.

L. porteri was heavily used to treat viral infection, either chewed or in tincture form. It has been employed as a cough syrup (soothing and anaesthetizing) and as expectorant. In China (*L. wallichi*) has been used to lower blood pressure, for inducing uterine contractions and to slow down bleeding after birth.

Biscuit Root   *Lomatium dissectum (Tritenatum)*

(a.k.a. *Leptotaenia multiflora*)

dissectum = L. "cut into many deep lobes"; *lepto* = L. "slender";

Synonyms: Western Wild Parsley, Mountain Wild Parsley

Identification: This perennial herb is 30 - 60 cm tall, with leaves 5-10 cm long. The flower head is a compound umbel, with yellow flowers. The pinnate leaves are made up of 2 - 4 leaflets. The root is spindle-shaped. The fruits are oblong with lateral wings thick and corky.

Distribution & Habitat: This plant is found on the grassy slopes of the southern Rocky Mountains.

Preparation & Uses: All species in the genus are edible. The green stem may be eaten in the spring but it is quite tough in the summer. Tea can be made out of the leaves, stems and flowers. The root can be eaten raw and tastes like celery but the fresh root has a peppery-like aftertaste in the throat that causes some people to cough. Indians would peel and dry the insides of the root, then grind it into flour. The flour was mixed with water, kneaded until it was like a pie crust and flattened into cakes. It tastes a bit like stale biscuit and is quite enjoyable.

The Blackfoot Indians made it into loaves two feet long and one foot wide. A hole was made in the center so it could be fastened onto a pack for travelling. The tiny seeds are very nutritious eaten raw or roasted, or dried and made into flour. The Blackfoot Indians would take slices of the root and string them on buckskin. They were hung around a mare's neck in the belief that an exceptionally strong colt would be born in the spring.

Medicine men often would blow the fragments of a chewed piece of this root through a hollow eagle bone onto a patient's afflicted part. It was believed that the healing quality of the spray penetrated the body at the place it landed.

The fruit of this plant was sometimes stuffed into a pelt and used for a medicine bundle. The tanning process kept the skin from smelling. Good luck charms for young girls were made by stuffing the fruit of this herb into a porcupine foot. These were tied into the girl's hair. The fresh or dried root, made into a tea or tincture, is antiviral, being specific for sinus and chest infections. Moore says it is very effective in long-term "chronic" diseases like HIV, CFS and mononucleosis or lingering Echo virus.

The Nevada Indians used *L. multiflora* as a panacea, with common uses for coughs, colds, hayfever, bronchitis, influenza, pneumonia and tuberculosis. Decoction of the dried root was the most common preparation but the root was also smoked (often as a smudge) for lung problems. The roots were also used as an antiseptic in the form of a decocted wash, and were used on sores including gonorrheal infections. It was the most common plant used to treat severed umbilical cords. Poultices were made of the root for swellings, sprains or rheumatism.

It was thought to be a good remedy for distemper in horses. This was administered, by blowing the fumes of the root at the horse's nostrils after the horse was run hard enough to make it breathe heavily.

Sweet Cicely, Sweet Root   *Osmorhiza occidentalis*

Osmo = L. "scented, fragrant", *rhiza* = L. "root", *occidentalis* = L. "of the west".

Identification: Rising from a thick aromatic root, the stem is 30 - 100 cm tall, with hairy node; the leaves are ternate-pinnate, the lower one petioled, the upper one subsessile; leaflet ovate to lanceolate, 2 - 10 cm long, serrate and often incised; flower pale yellow in small umbels; fruit glabrous.

Distribution & Habitat: Found in montane woods from southern Alberta and B.C. south to Colorado and California.

Preparation & Uses: The root is probably the tastiest you'll ever eat in the wild. It tastes vaguely similar to root beer. A small amount of root goes a long way. The root is good for the mucous membranes, especially those of the intestinal tract. It stimulates mucous membranes and is a mild laxative.

Biscuit Root
Lomatium sp.

BA

Sweet Cicely
*Osmorhiza
occidentalis*

TW

Sweet Cicely root
*Osmorhiza
occidentalis*

TW

Yampa
Perideridia gairdneri

Yampa root
Perideridia gairdneri

Moore uses it to stabilize sugar metabolism, mixing it with equal part licorice and sassafras, to create a very pleasant tasting tea.

Other species in this genus have been used by various Amerindian tribes. The Swinomish chewed the root of *O. chilensis* as a very strong love charm.

O. longistylis was used by Amerindians as a general panacea for debility, a tonic for digestive disorder and an aid in childbirth. Externally the root was made into a poultice and applied on wounds.

O. claytonia root was used as a gargle for sore throats, a poultice for wounds and a wash for sore red eyes.

Yampa, Squaw Root   *Perideridia gairdneri*

Identification: Yampa is a perennial herb that grows 30 - 60 cm high and is usually not branched. The small flowers are white or pinkish and form in compound umbels. The leaves are pinnate and occasionally bi-pinnate with 3 - 7 linear leaflets. The root is tuberous. These herbs are now on the endangered species list in many areas.

Distribution & Habitat: Yampa is found on the edges of meadows and woodlands. It is abundant in southern Alberta.

Preparation & Uses: Yampa was one of the favourite edible plants of both Indian and white settlers of this area. The roots of the yampa are particularly prized and are best peeled before eating. The Indians used to place them in baskets in running water, then the women would tread on them with bare feet to remove the outer skin. Yampa roots can be eaten raw and are said to taste sweet and nutty. Harrington said that he usually did not remove the root peel and found it still good but I have not tried this. Yampa root can be boiled, fried and cooked in many other ways. They are best baked, either in an oven or a fireless pit.

The roots can be dried in the sun for future use and keep indefinitely. Dried root can then be softened in the mouth and eaten, fried or ground into a meal or flour.

The seeds of yampa plant can be used as seasoning and taste similar to caraway seeds, to which they are related.

The Blackfoot Indians used the root extensively. If large quantities of the root were eaten the effect was diuretic and mildly laxative. An infusion of the root was used as a diuretic, to wash the nostrils for catarrhal problems, applied to sores and wounds or massaged with a warm rock on a woman's sore breast. The root was chewed or brewed for coughs and sore throats, and also chewed to extend endurance to Blackfoot runners. The smoke from the smudge of the root was sometimes inhaled for relief from a nagging cough.

Blackfoot Indians used it as a horse medicine and would entice a lazy horse to chew some of the root to enliven it. The infusion was also poured down horses' nostrils to treat nasal problems.

Bunchberry *Cornus canadensis*

Cornus = kor-nus, from the Latin name for the carnelian cherry; *canadensis* = kan-a-den-sis, "of Canada".

Identification: Bunchberry is a low, erect perennial herb standing 5 - 20 cm high. The flower cluster is made up of small greenish flowers subtended by four white or cream coloured, petal-like bracts. The lower leaves are opposite whereas the upper leaves are in a whorl. The fruit is bright red, forming in a bunch.

Distribution & Habitat: Bunchberry is common in open and closed woodlands.

Preparation & Uses: Bunchberries are edible raw or cooked and are very good in puddings, although they are a little bland. Unripened berries can cause stomachaches. They are called *Musko mina* by the Crees, and *Metotsipis* by the Blackfoot. Taken internally or applied as a poultice, bunchberry reputedly can reduce the potency of poisons. I have had occasion to use this plant after becoming very sick from eating a incorrectly identified mushroom. I recovered soon after eating the bunchberries.

The infused berries were used by the Montagnais to treat paralysis, while the maritime Malecite Indians used the whole plant to treat fits. A root tea was used for infant colic. It is presently being examined for possible anti-cancer properties.

Externally, the chewed bunchberries have been used as a poultice to treat local burns. Combining and boiling the berries with high tannin containing plants (such as common tea or bearberry) creates a wash suitable for itching skin caused by poison ivy or bee stings.

Pacific Dogwood   *Cornus nuttali*

Identification: The flower head (a combination of bract and flower) looks similar to the other *Cornus sp.* but much larger. This dogwood forms into small trees but has been known to reach heights of 20 m. The red berries appear in the fall.

Distribution & Habitat: This plant forms the British Columbia floral emblem and is found along the coast. It grows in open woods and slopes.

Preparation & Uses: Pacific Dogwood is listed as a febrifuge, antipectoral, mild analgesic, anthelmintic, slightly antiseptic, cathartic (fresh) and bitter-tonic. The berries are stomachic, while the flowers are emmenagogic. The decoction of the bark was drunk as an effective tonic for stomach troubles, diarrhea and liver problems. An infusion of the flower heads was used to bring on menstruation when late.

An ointment or poultice of the bark was used for sores, skin inflammation and skin ulcers. The pounded twigs can be used as a toothbrush and are said to keep the gums healthy and the teeth white.

Red Osier Dogwood   *Cornus stolonifera*

Cornus = kor-nus, from the classical Latin name for *Cornus mas* or L. name for cornelian cherry, *stolonifera*, sto-lo-ni-fe-ra, bearing stolons (creeping stems which root at the nodes).

Identification: This shrub stands 1 - 3 m high and has an inflorescence of small white flowers. The twigs are deep red, sometimes greenish or purplish. The leaves are oval and hairy beneath. The fruit is white or tinged with blue. This plant is also sometimes called red willow or red osier willow, which is a misnomer, as the plant is not a willow.

Distribution & Habitat: It is common in moist woods, on river banks and in damp ravines amongst willow. It is found from the edge of the prairies to the timber line.

Preparation & Uses: Ripe berries of this plant are edible, although not very tasty.

Red osier dogwood was used in "kinnikinnick" smoking mixtures. The leaves were sometimes used, but more often the inner bark. The outer bark was first peeled away and the inner greenish bark scraped off. It is aromatic and a little pungent. It has a "narcotic" effect, so it should be used in moderation the first few times. The bark contains cornic acid which is similar to acetyl salicylic acid (ASA) but not quite as strong.

The roots of the plant were used by the Wisconsin Potawatomis as an effective remedy for diarrhea and as a mild astringent. The Blackfoot Indians would make an infusion of the inner bark to treat liver troubles and an infusion of the roots was given for chest disorders. The bark can be very laxative.

The wood of the red osier dogwood is very strong and makes good digging sticks, pipestems, arrows and pegs.

Bunchberry
Cornus canadensis

Bunchberry (in berry stage)
Cornus canadensis

Red Osier
Dogwood
Cornus stolonifera

Wintergreen
(very early spring)
Pyrola sp.

Bracted Wintergreen
Pyrola sp.

161

Wintergreen, Bracted   *Pyrola sp.*

Pyrola = pi-ro-la, L. "pear-like", compares the leaf with those of *Pyrus*.

Identification: This is low, perennial herb stands 2-8 cm tall, with greenish-white, yellow, pink, red or white flowers. The flowers are on terminal racemes. The leaves are basal, with petioles and usually close to an oval shape. The fruit is a dry capsule with many tiny seeds.

Distribution & Habitat: These plants are usually found in rich, moist soil often amongst sphagnum moss.

Preparation & Uses: Hutchens lists *Pyrola* as an astringent, diuretic, tonic and antispasmodic. The solvent is boiling water. Since it has a diuretic and astringent effect, it is a good internal treatment for gravel, ulceration of the bladder, blood in the urine and other urinary diseases. It contains the arbutin and ursolic acid also found in bearberry. Wintergreen's antispasmodic qualities make it useful for epilepsy and other nervous disorders. A strong decoction was used in Europe as a gargle for sore throats and mouths. The decoction is also useful for sore eyes.

The berries of many *Pyrola* species were esteemed as a diet drink and for cleansing the blood from scorbutic disorders. The leaves of *Pyrola* are good for rheumatism and a strong tea, called "mountain tea", is good for nephritic ailments.

Pyrola eliptica was used in a tea by the Mohicans as a gargle for sores and cankers in the mouth. Indians also boiled the root as drink for weakness and "black sickness".

Some Indians used *Pyrola rotundifolia* as an astringent and for coughs and diseases of the chest. The healing leaves of these plants were also used to heal wounds, hemorrhages and as a poultice for bruises and insect bites. It was widely accepted as a potent vaginal douche because of its astringent quality.

Blackfoot women often drank an infusion of the leaves and roots to expel afterbirth. This infusion was also used by them as a mild laxative. An infusion of the flowers was used by the Blackfoot to treat coughing in children.

The roots were cut up into pieces to make throat lozenges or applied to swollen neck glands as an infusion. The chewed root has also been applied for eye and ear disorders. Nevada Indians used *P. asarifolia* root as a decoction for liver complaints and jaundice.

I was once hiking in the woods with a friend who accidently kneeled on a hunting knife. The knife penetrated about two inches. There was some wintergreen growing nearby so I had him chew about five leaves and apply the chewed mass to his cut. The bleeding soon stopped and the pain disappeared.

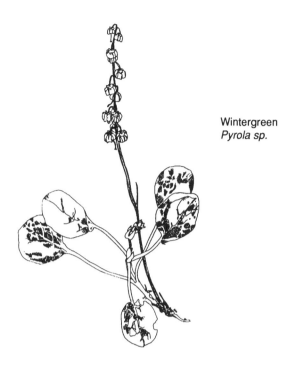

Wintergreen
Pyrola sp.

Arbutus   *Arbutus menziesii*

Arbutus = from the classical Latin name.

Identification: This distinctive tree is Canada's only native evergreen broad-leaf tree, growing up to 30 m tall. The glossy leaves are dark green. The peeling bark is reddish-brown. The flowers are cream-coloured, blooming in May, the red berries are seen in clusters in the fall.

Distribution & Habitat: Grows on dry rocky ground, especially rocky bluffs along the coast.

Preparation & Uses: An infusion of the bark can be used for colds. It is said that the Cowichan Indians decocted the bark as a treatment for diabetes. Other heaths have also been used to treat sugar metabolism problems. Salish Indians from Washington State decocted the bark as a wash for eye problems and minor wounds. The leaves were used as a poultice on burns and for rheumatic joints.

The bark's high tannic acid content was used by Salish Indians on Vancouver Island for tanning hides.

Bearberry   *Arctostaphylos uva-ursi*

Arctostaphylos = ark-to-sta-fil-os, from Gr. *arctos* (a bear) and *staphyles* (a bunch of grapes or "berries"); *uva-ursi* = oo-va-ur-see, L. for "berries-Bear's".

Identification: Bearberry is a trailing evergreen shrub often forming mats 50 - 100 cm wide. The flowers are pale pink to white, urn-shaped in terminal racemes. The leaves are oval, leathery and evergreen. The branches tend to lose their rusty red bark in shreds. It is quite similar to some *Vaccinium* species.

Distribution & Habitat: It is usually found in well-drained habitat, such as open woodland, bench land and gravel terraces.

Preparation & Uses: The berries are mealy and almost tasteless when raw, but quite palatable when cooked. Two related species (*A. alpina* and *A. rubra*) have better-tasting berries that are good raw and better cooked. Some people find them a little acidic or bitter. Because of its bitter taste, some people chew both berries and leaves to prevent thirst. It stimulates the flow of saliva.

A good cider can be made from these berries. First scald them for a few minutes until the seeds are soft and then crush them to pulp. To this, add equal parts of water, let settle one hour and strain. It really needs no sugar, but this can be added to taste.

Bearberry (also called uva-ursi by herbalists) is listed as diuretic, astringent, soothing, tonic and nephritic. Uva-ursi has a specific healing action upon the genitourinary organs. It is especially good in cases of gravel or ulceration of the kidneys or bladder. It will soothe, strengthen and tone the mucous membrane of the urinary passage. Uva-ursi has quite the reputation as a solvent for uronic calculi deposits. In chronic inflammation of the bladder and kidneys, it has no equal. It stimulates kidney activity and has an antiseptic effect on mucous membranes (due to arbutin 5-18%).

Bearberry is a mild vasoconstrictor to the endometrium of the uterus and is therefore useful to alleviate painful menstruation. Large quantities should therefore be avoided during pregnancy.

The leaves are powerfully astringent (due to 6 - 8% tannic acid) making a great sitz bath after childbirth. Because of the high tannin level it has often been used to tan hides. This can also be used to advantage when hiking, especially before the first hike of the season or with new boots. To toughen up the feet, simply soak your feet in a strong decoction for one hour the night before hiking. This will help you avoid blisters.

Another common name for bearberry is Kinnickinnick, which is a bit of a misnomer. Kinnickinnick means smoking mixture. Uva ursi, though often a major ingredient of smoking mixtures, is usually just one component of the mixture. Kinnickinnick components can vary from tribe to tribe. Here is a typical formula:

Equal parts:

Bearberry leaf
Labrador tea leaf (picked in spring when
    orange underneath)
Red osier dogwood inner bark
Wormwood leaf (*Artemisia frigida*)
Chokecherry inner bark
occasionally inner bark of alder (*Alnus
    crispa*)

Bearberry
Arctostaphylos uva-ursi

Bearberry
Arctostaphylos uva-ursi

165

Salal *Gaultheria shallon*

Gaultheria = gawl-the-ree-a, after Dr. Gaulthier (1708 - 58) a Canadian botanist and physician; *shallon* = sha-lon, from the Chinook Indian name "Sabal".

Identification: Salal is an erect, partly prostrate shrub with evergreen, leathery, ovate leaves. The pinkish-white flowers form in clusters. The fruit is black, hairy and berry-like.

Distribution & Habitat: Salal is found mostly in conifer thickets, on rocky cliffs, ravines and exposed shores along the coastal areas where it is locally quite abundant.

Preparation & Uses: The berries of this plant played an important role in the lives of the coastal Indians as it was locally abundant. The berries were made into syrup or dried into cakes and were reputed to taste very good, fresh, dried or cooked.

The plant is astringent, anti-inflammatory, carminative and used as a convalescent tonic. The leaves were chewed by Klallan Indians and spit onto burns. Swinomish and Samish Indians used the leaves in a tea form for coughs and tuberculosis. It has also been used for heartburn and colic. Salal has been used in some local kinnickinnick mixtures.

Labrador Tea *Ledum groenlandicum*

Ledum = lay-dum, from *ledon*, the Greek name for Cistus, from an old Gr. name for rock rose, *groenlandicum* = grun-land-i-kum, of Greenland.

Identification: Labrador tea is an erect shrub 30-80 cm high, with dense, rusty twigs. The white flowers are borne as a terminal, umbellike cluster. The leaves are oblong to elliptic, green above and densely rusty. The leaves are usually curled under at the margins.

Distribution & Habitat: This plant is common from the foothills to alpine areas, in muskegs and moist coniferous woods.

Preparation & Uses: The leaves are used more than any plant as a tea by the Amerindians. This tea is steeped for a dilute tea or prepared by boiling the leaves for 15-30 minutes for a spicy brew. Boiling releases large amount of ledol and therefore is not recommended. The pungent aromatic taste is reduced if the herb is steeped with lemon. This tea has a mild laxative effect. The tea has also been used for nervousness. A strong decoction of the leaves was used as a wash to get rid of lice. It was listed as an insect repellent, in 1874 in the Canadian Pharmaceutical Journal (effective against mosquitoes). It is also a remedy for insect bites, used as a tincture.

The leaves have a mild narcotic effect when smoked. It should therefore be used sparingly by the uninitiated. As a narcotic, it was picked in the spring. Leaves with an orange to reddish underside have the strongest effect. It is used in kinnickinnick mixture (see Bearberry *Arctostaphylos uva-ursi*) and gives a lighter effect than *Cannabis*. It contains a chemical called ledol, which is known to cause cramps, drowsiness, delirium, heart palpitations or temporary paralysis. I have drunk this tea many times and have known several foragers that drink the tea regularly but no one has seen these reported side effects.

The Cree called it *muskeko-pukwan* and used it in the form of a decoction for treating fevers, colds and other general ailments. Others used the tea as a blood cleanser, especially for rheumatism. This herb has been used as an abortive. That, plus its known toxicity, points to caution when consuming it if pregnant.

Ledum latifolium is listed in Hutchens as being pectoral, expectorant and diuretic. Boiling water is used as the solvent. It is useful as a nervine in coughs, colds, bronchial and pulmonary infections. The recommended dose is one teaspoon per cup of boiling water, which is steeped for half an hour.

Externally, a strong decoction is useful to treat itching and skin eruptions accompanying fever (exanthematous). This wash was also employed to rid the body of parasites, mites and to stop the itch of mosquito bites.

This plant should not to be kept in an enclosed area while drying because large amounts of the volatile oil can be poisonous.

Heaths, Blueberry, Bilberry, Huckleberry, Cranberry
Vaccinium spp.

Vaccinium = va-keen-ee-um, from its classical Latin name.

Identification: The genus *Vaccinium* contains many diverse dwarf shrubs. Most of them are 10 - 40 cm tall. They are deciduous except for bog cranberry. The flowers are solitary or in short clusters and are cup-shaped to urn-shaped. The fruits are many-seeded berries. These plants can be mistaken for bearberry which have more leathery evergreen leaves and mealier red berries.

Distribution & Habitat: The vacciniums enjoy a very diverse habitat. They are quite common from the foothills into the high mountains.

Preparation & Uses: All the berries of these plants are very palatable. They are quite sweet and were used widely by the Indians. Blueberries are particularity hard to pick in any quantity as the picker often confuses their mouth with the "basket". The only way around this, that I have found, is to give the picker a huge meal before they go out picking. The berries can be used in a variety of ways, eaten raw with honey and cream, cooked into a sauce or made into pies. They can very easily be mixed with dough for muffins, breads or pancakes.

Salal
Gaultheria shallon

Labrador Tea
*Ledum
groenlandicum*

Blueberry flowers
Vaccinium sp.

Blueberry
Vaccinium sp.

Bog Cranberry
Vaccinium sp.

They also make excellent jam and this is one recipe from Harrington:

    4 cups crushed berries
    1 package powdered pectin
    2 tablespoons lemon juice
    5 cups sugar or 2 3/4 cups honey

Mix berries, lemon juice and pectin. Place over high heat and stir until it comes to a fierce boil. Then add sugar and boil hard for one minute. Remove from heat and alternately, stir and skim for five minutes. Pour into scalded jelly glasses and seal with paraffin wax. It should make about nine glasses.

Indians dried the berries by the fire and used them as raisins. They are also good to put in stews. They were often kept for winter storage.

Medicinally heath leaves can be considered very similar to bearberry (*Arctostaphylos uva-ursi*), without the astringent quality, and roughly half as strong. Usually the dosage is just doubled. Skagit people decocted the bark of huckleberry (*V. parviflorum*) for colds.

Bilberry   *V. myrtillus*

myrtillus = mur-ti-lus, a small myrtle.

Hutchens lists bilberry as a diuretic and refrigerant. Dilute alcohol and boiling water are the solvents.

A good stock of bilberry tincture can be made by putting two or three handfuls of the berries into a bottle and covering this with a high quality brandy. Secure the bottle with a good-fitting cap or cork. This tincture improves with age.

Bilberry tincture can stop violent, continuous diarrhea, which might be accompanied by pain and some blood loss. Take 1 tablespoon of the tincture and add it to ¼ pint of water. Repeat this dose every 8-10 hours.

The dried berries are good astringents, which pass through the stomach unaffected and start their work in the small intestine.

A strong decoction of the berries is said to be helpful in typhoid fever. A tincture would probably be useful too. Both the fresh and well-preserved berry juice make a good mouthwash, helping many mouth infections. A gargle for respiratory catarrhal problems can also be made in the same way. The berries regulate bowel action, stimulate the appetite and, in general, tone up the body.

A decoction of the leaves can also have a positive effect in cases of slight diarrhea, along with cases of dysentery and derangement of the bowels. The decoction or infusion of the leaves stops diarrhea in some people and causes it in others. The herb has also been shown to rid the body of pin worms.

Many of the *Vaccinium*'s leaves have been shown to help diabetic and hypoglycemic individuals, lowering the need for insulin and helping them avoid it all together (if taken soon enough).

Lingon berry   *V. vitis-idaea*

vitis-idaea, vee-tis ee-die-a, = from vine of Mount Ida (Crete mountain, Idhi) or Idaea, Greece.

Synonyms: low bush cranberry, partridgeberry and foxberry.

Lingon berries are quite tangy when eaten raw, but as any Scandinavian knows they are delicious when cooked with a little sugar. They can be dried, frozen or canned easily. Lingon berries keep quite well due to a high benzoic acid content.

Medicinally lingon berry juice helps stimulate digestive enzymes and reduce heartburn. Inupiat Eskimos take mashed lingon berries, put them on a cloth and wrap it around their neck for sore throats. It can also be made into a poultice and applied for itchy skin eruptions, or measles.

The astringent and antiseptic quality of the herb has been used as a rinse for oily skin and hair. The leaves have been used as a disinfectant liniment.

As a dye, the berries produce a yellow to red colour with alum as a mordant.

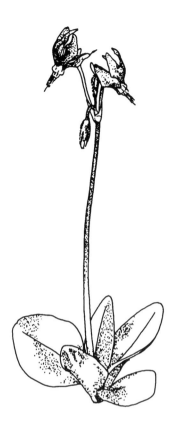

Shooting Star   *Dodecatheon spp.*

Dodecatheon = Do-dek-a-thee-on, from Greek, *dodeka* (twelve) and *thios* (god) from the twelve gods of Olympus. *Dodecatheon* has also been given the common name Indian Chief. If you look at a shooting star one can easily imagine it as a little Prairie Indian with a band of vermilion beads about his forehead and a long, plumed headdress on his head.

Identification: Shooting star is a perennial herb with pinkish to purple, nodding flowers. The flower stalk stands 10-40 cm tall with ovate basal leaves. The seeds are formed in a cylindrical capsule which becomes stiffly erect.

Distribution & Habitat: This is a widespread herb found in wet meadow or saline flats. It is often found amongst willows and in mossy places.

Preparation & Uses: The fresh leaves taste good, though some people do not like the texture. It makes a good pot herb and isn't bitter even when the leaves are mature. I use shooting star leaves as a major component of spring salads. The roots can be eaten roasted or raw.

The Blackfoot Indians made an infusion of the leaves (*D. radicatum*) and gargled it to heal cankers (especially for children). Eye drops were made from a cooled infusion of leaves, making the eye feel dry after application.

Shooting Star
Dodecatheon sp.

Buckbean
Menyanthes trifoliata

Buckbean (berries)
Menyanthes trifoliata

172

Indian hemp, Spreading dogbane, Canadian hemp
Apocynum androsaemifolium, A. cannabinum

androsaemifolium = L. "Man's blood-coloured flower", *cannabinum* = L. " resembling *Cannabis*".

Identification: Indian Hemp is a perennial herb with milky sap, standing 30-80 cm high with ascending branches. The greenish white flowers have tubular to urn-shaped petals. The opposite leaves are ovate to lanceolate. The seed pods are 8-12 cm long.

There has been much confusion about the naming of these plants. Indian Hemp is an official name in many floras, but it is also the name of *Jahorandi* and the source of pilocarpine. Care should be taken. Mixing up these herbs could have deleterious effects.

Distribution & Habitat: Indian Hemp is found in moist open areas and thickets from central Alberta south.

Preparation & Uses: This plant should not in anyway be confused with hashish or marijuana (*Cannabis spp.*) They do not have the same effect. Indian Hemp is listed as poisonous by many experts, due to the white milky juice found in the stems and leaves. It could be confused with other plants, but few poisonings have been reported either in humans or animals.

Medicinally, this plant was used extensively by the Indians. The roots are most often used, and are listed as an anodyne, hypnotic, antispasmodic, diuretic, diaphoretic, expectorant, cathartic and tonic, with water as a solvent. The dried root in the form of a decoction was used for kidney complaints, to stimulate the heart, rheumatism, dropsy, asthmatic complaints and whooping cough. The Ojibwa Indian ate the "sacred root" in medicine-lodge ceremonies, using it also for sore throats. The root was burned on a smudge and inhaled to treat headaches. The Meskwakis used Indian hemp root in a compound for an injured womb.

As a cure for threadworm or pinworm, it is supposedly infallible. One should take 20 drops of tincture 3 times a day for three successive days, then inject cold water as an enema and the worms will be dislodged. If this doesn't work, take this formula and a laxative tea the day before a full moon. The pinworms are most active at this time of month.

Indian hemp is stated as being a good cure for insomnia, producing sleep easily without side effects.

The rhizome and root of *A. cannabinum* were listed in the U.S. Dispensatory from 1820-82 and the National Formulary from 1942-50. The recognized dosage of Indian Hemp root is 1 teaspoon of root to 1 pint of boiling water, then take a tablespoon 3-8 times a day.

This plant has been shown to contain cardioactive glycosides which possess antitumor activity while raising blood pressure.

Moore points out the Dogbane (*A. androsaemifolium*) is safer to use than Canadian Hemp (*A. cannabinum*) and that Canadian hemp is not appropriate for herbal use as a crude herb. Dogbane has counterirritant effects and has been known to stimulate hair growth via mild irritation of follicles - 1 tsp. of root boiled in 1 cup water (apply as a final rinse).

This plant gets the name Indian Hemp is because Indians used it to make rope and twine, just as the whites made hemp into rope. It can be used for rope, mats, baskets, and general weaving.

Buckbean   *Menyanthes trifoliata*

Menyanthes = may-nee-anth-eez, from Greek *menanthos* "moon-flower" (Theophrastus' name for the flower), *trifoliata* = tri-fo-lee-ah-ta, having three leaves (leaflets).

Synonyms: bogbean, marsh clover.

Identification: Growing up to ½ m tall, with leaves on long petioles, with the petiole base sheathed, the leaflets are in threes as the name suggests. The flowers are white (somewhat pinkish), having 5 petals with fuzzy beards. The fruit consists of beanlike capsules.

Distribution & Habitat: Found in the Pacific North West, it grows in marshy areas and shallow ponds from Alaska to California. This plant is on some local endangered species lists.

Preparation & Uses: The fresh leaves are very emetic and should be dried if other uses are intended. The dried leaves are tonic, diuretic, stomachic and cathartic. As a tonic this herb is esteemed, due to high vitamin C, iron and iodine. Buckbeans stimulate stomach juices (due to a bitter glycoside) and can therefore stimulate appetite and aid in digestion. It can be used for water retention, gas pain, constipation and rheumatism.

A poultice of the leaves can be applied to skin sores, herpes, glandular swelling and for sore muscles.

Periwinkle   *Vinca minor*

Vinca = from Latin *vincio* (to bind) referring to the shoots of *V. pervinca*.

Identification: This low, trailing shrub has evergreen leaves that spread via rooting stems, producing a ground cover. The flowers bloom in the spring and are purple or occasionally white.

Distribution & Habitat: Found along dirt roads, escaped from gardens.

Preparation & Uses: This herb is astringent, tonic and sedative. The fresh flower is mildly laxative. As an intestinal astringent it can be used for diarrhea, bleeding ulcers and hemorrhoids. It can be calming, used specifically for excessive menstruation. Some periwinkles have been shown to inhibit cancerous tumour growth.

An ointment of the herb has been used on sores and bleeding hemorrhoids.

Milkweed   *Asclepias spp.*

Asclepias = a-sklay-pee-as, from Greek Asklepias, god of medicine, referring to its medicinal properties.

Identification: Milkweeds are perennial, stout, hairy herbs that stand 60 - 200 cm tall. The leaves are opposite or whorled, ovate to broadly lanceolate, on very short petioles. The flowers are in umbels and are purplish - pink, with one variety having greenish white flowers.

Distribution & Habitat: Milkweed can be found in moist waste areas, meadows, beside fences and stream beds, in loamy to sandy soil throughout North America.

Preparation & Uses: Check the poisonous plant section of this book. Indians ate the unopened flower buds, often boiling them with soups or meat (the flower buds acted as a meat tenderizer). The flowers are high in sugar content and were sometimes boiled down to produce a syrup. The Cheyenne peeled the immature fruit pods (up to the time the pods feel elastic) to eat the innards. It is not advisable to eat milkweed raw because it has been responsible for poisonings in livestock. Cooking neutralizes the poisons. The water should be changed at least once but it is tastier after the second water change. The young shoots (up to eight inches tall) can be cooked like asparagus. Eastern Indians baked and ate the tuberous root.

Medicinally, these plants were widely used. The milky latex was used to remove warts, moles, corns, calluses and ringworm. It was also used for treating sores, cuts and burns. It was accepted by the Canadian pharmaceutical industry as a good antiseptic barrier in the 1880's. A decoction of the root has been used to treat coughs, gonorrhea, syphilitic sores, asthma, indigestion, as a laxative and to induce urination. It was specifically used for kidney stones. It is also recorded as a folk remedy for cancer. Large amounts cause vomiting. The mashed root has been used as a poultice for swellings, especially rheumatic swelling. An infusion of the entire plant was used by some Indians to treat tender breasts and to mildly increase lactation. The root tea was also supposed to be used as a temporary contraceptive tea.

The silky hairs were burned off the ripe seeds which were then ground to form a salve for sores. The seeds were boiled by the Nevada Indians and the solution was used to draw the poison out of rattlesnake bites. They also boiled the root to bring out the rash associated with measles.

Some Indians and early settlers collected the silk from the pod to stuff pillows, beds and comforters. They even weaved it into a silky linen.

Periwinkle
Vinca minor

TW

Milkweed
Asclepias sp.

BA

Horsemint
Monarda fistulosa

BA

Wild Mint   *Mentha arvensis*

Mentha = men-tha, from the classical Latin name used by Pliny, *arvensis* = L. "of the field, of ploughed fields".

Identification: Wild mint is a strong smelling perennial herb standing 10-50 cm tall. The small pinkish, purple or white flowers are in dense axillary clusters. The stem, as in all mints, is square. The leaves are short, petioled, oblong, lanceolate with serrated edges.

Distribution & Habitat: This plant grows in wet places such as sloughs and boggy meadows.

Preparation & Uses: We all know that mints make refreshing teas, flavouring agents and scents. Indians used it to spice meat in the form of pemmican and in soups.

It is listed by herbalists as bitter, pungent, antispasmodic, antirheumatic, stimulant and having anodyne properties. A good remedy for children's teething pains consists of peppermint and skullcap infused together, strained and drunk cold.

This North American mint is not considered as medicinally useful as the European species, although the Indians throughout North America found

Wild Mint
Mentha arvensis

many uses for it. The Cheyenne ground the leaves and boiled them to prevent vomiting. This preparation was also used as a stomach tonic. The Missouri tribe used it as a carminative, and the Ojibwa as a blood purifier, to break fevers and as a stimulating tea. The Menominees combined catnip with wild mint and used it for pneumonia, by drinking it and applying it as a chest poultice.

Both rats and mice are said to have a strong dislike for peppermint. It might be possible to keep them out of camp with its liberal use.

Horsemint   *Monarda fistulosa*

Monarda = mo-nar-da, after Nicholas Monarde (1493-1588) a Spanish botanist/ physician; *fistulosa* = fist-ew-lo-sa, L. "tubular".

Synonyms: Wild Bergamot, Purple bee's-balm.

Identification: Horsemint is a perennial herb which grows 30-100 cm tall. It has rose or lilac-coloured flowers (rarely white). Those flowers are in densely aggregated terminal heads. The slender leaves grow opposite, and are toothed and aromatic. As in all mints, the stems are four-sided.

Distribution & Habitat: Horsemint is found in dry areas such as thickets, sunny slopes and open meadows.

Preparation & Uses: Horsemint is diaphoretic, carminative (expels wind from the bowel), diuretic and refrigerant. An infusion of leaves and flowers are good for fevers and colds. As a poultice it is useful for painful swelling joints. A tea of horsemint relieves nausea and vomiting.

Amerindian usage of a leaf tea includes flatulence, colic, colds, fevers, nose-bleeds, insomnia and heart trouble. It can be employed to induce fevers in measles and as a poultice for headaches.

The Blackfoot Indians used boiled leaves as a poultice, applying them directly to pimples to bring them out. The Winnebagos and Dakota Indians used the tea as a stimulant. Some Indians used to mash the leaves of horsemint, let them stand in cold water and drink the infusion to relieve backaches (prob-ably caused by poor kidneys).

This plant, placed in an infusion with pearly everlasting (*Anaphalis sp.*), was used by the Cree Indians as a diaphoretic and for delirium. It was also used to expel hookworm. Some Blackfoot Indians would chew the root as a cure for swollen neck glands. They also used to bind flower heads over a wound and remove them when the wound had healed.

The dried flower heads were sometimes used by Indian women to apply water to a green hide, making the hide easier to scrape.

Self Heal, Woundwort (Common), Heal All

Prunella vulgaris

Prunella = proo-nel-la, probably from Latin *prunum* (purple) referring to the flower colour or "Brunella" from the German name for quinsy "die Bräune" for which it was used as a cure, *vulgaris* = common, usual.

Identification: This small perennial herb stands 1 - 3 cm high with purplish-blue flowers (sometimes pink or white). The flowers are formed in a terminal spike, the corolla has an upper lip and a three part lower lip. The leaves are ovate to lanceolate.

Distribution & Habitat: Self heal is found in moist places, often by alpine brooks, damp thickets, open woods and fields.

Preparation & Uses: The leaves of this mint can be chopped up and soaked in cold water as a refreshing drink. It can also be dried and stored as a fine powder to make cold drinks.

Lust lists this herb as an antispasmodic, astringent, bitter, tonic, diuretic, styptic, vermifuge and vulnerary. Self Heal is claimed to cure laryngitis and is good for stomatitis and thrush. Its astringent effect makes it useful for hemorrhage and diarrhea. Its antispasmodic qualities led to use in controlling fits and convulsions. In the past it was believed to expel devils. Though I can't vouch for its effect on devils, it will certainly expel worms!

European herbalists have used this plant for many years. They claim it is able to heal any wound, internal or external, if mixed with a little water or wine. (Hence its common names).

Blackfoot Indians would raise boils with hot water then open the boil, cleansing the wound with an infusion of woundwort. They would also apply this infusion to neck sores. As an eyewash, the infusion is useful in keeping the eyes moist on cold or windy days. Horses were treated for saddle and back sores with an infusion of this plant. Some Indians used it as a gargle for throat irritations and as a drink for gas and stomach problems.

This plant contains the anti-tumor and diuretic compound, ursolic acid.

Skullcap   *Scutellaria galericulata*

Scutellaria = sku-te-lah-ree-a, from latin
scutella (a small disk), referring to the
appearance of the calyx on the fruit,
galericulata = L. 'helmet-shaped, like a
skullcap'.

Identification: Skullcap is a perennial herb
which grows from 10 - 80 cm tall. The
flowers are blue (rarely pink or completely white) with a white tube and
throat usually solitary or in racemes. The
leaves are mostly oblong, lanceolated,
becoming more rounded at the base with
serrated margins. The fruit is a nutlet.
The root is a rhizome.

Distribution & Habitat: This herb is commonly found in wet meadows and
along stream banks at low altitudes.

Preparation & Uses: *Scutellaria lateriflora* is considered by most herbalists to
be one of the best nervine agents that Nature provides. *Scutellaria galericulata*
has similar therapeutic properties. These herbs are listed as antispasmodic,
nervine, tonic, diuretic, sedative and slightly astringent. Dilute with alcohol
or hot water as solvents.

Skullcap is a most valuable remedy for controlling nervous irritation. Used as
an infusion, skullcap is good for spasms, insomnia and general restlessness. It
has been listed as a specific for hydrophobia or rabies by many herbalists,
and it is said to eventually render the patient free from this disturbance. In
fact, during the 1800's, skullcap was so famous for this application that one of
it's common names was "mad-dog's skullcap". There is some debate, however, over how effective it is. Effectiveness probably has something to do
with specific subspecies or the substrate the plant grows on.

Skullcap's tonic effect will not only help nervous irritations but support the
nerves, quietening and strengthening the whole system. For many years it has
been used successfully to alleviate cases of hysteria, cholera, delirium
tremens, fits, convulsions, epilepsy and related illness. It has had limited
success in the first stages of multiple sclerosis. A flavonoid, scutellarin, found
in the plant, has been proven to have a sedative and antispasmodic quality.

Skullcap has been used on morphine addicts to help break their drug habit. It
has also been effective in weaning individuals from barbiturates, Valium and
meprobamate abuse. Moore states that in combination with white (uncured)
American ginseng, skullcap is very effective in treating the D.T.'s of alcoholism (½ oz. skullcap and ¼ oz. ginseng, each day in frequent doses). It successfully quietens and promotes gentle natural sleep. In cases of cholera, it is also
classified as a specific, and usually mixed with other herbs.

Skullcap
Scutellaria galericulata

Heal All
Prunella vulgaris

Indian Paintbrush
Castilleja sp.

Dr. Shook in his *Advanced Treatise on Herbology* concluded "Skullcap is a slow-working but sure remedy for practically all afflictions but it must be taken regularly for a long period to be of permanent benefit".

The Ojibwa Indians used skullcap as a heart medicine. Other Indians used skullcap to promote menstruation and to cure rabies. Where skullcap was mixed with pennyroyal (*Hedeoma pulegioides*) as a tea, it was successfully used as a remedy for menstrual cramps and severe pain caused by colds. Poultices have been used for breast pains. Dosage for the infusion is 1 teaspoon of powdered herb steeped in 1 cup of boiled water for ½ hour. This is taken every 3/4 hour. For the tincture alone, 3 - 12 drops in water is good.

Caution: Skullcap should never be boiled. Overdoses of tincture cause giddiness, stupor, confusion of mind and twitching of the limbs.

Indian Paintbrush   *Castilleja spp.*

Identification: There are at least 6 species of Indian paintbrush found in the area and it is very hard to tell them apart. Indian paintbrush are perennial, biennial or annual herbs 15 - 60 cm high with alternate leaves. The flowers are borne in dense bracted spikes. The flowers are insignificant compared to the bracts which are brightly coloured red, yellow, pinkish, and sometimes white, depending on the species. In Glacier National Park there is a beautiful pink/violet variety. The leaves are usually cleft but often entire, close to lanceolate.

Distribution & Habitat: Various species of Indian paintbrush are found throughout the region in wooded or open slopes. Some, like *C. miniata*, prefer well drained south-facing slopes. Indian paintbrush is semi-parasitic. It can produce its own food but when times are rough it will parasitize other plant roots for nutrients.

Preparation & Uses: The flowers of Indian paintbrush can be eaten, and are tender and tasty. As a special treat, pull out the long white corolla tube and eat the sweet nectar at the bottom. Indian paintbrush tends to absorb selenium from the soil. Care should therefore be taken not to eat too much of it. In Alberta there is very little selenium in the soil, so there is no need to worry. In Colorado the level of selenium is very high and cases of toxicity related to this plant have been recorded.

There is a beautiful story about the origin of Indian paintbrush in Anora Brown's *Old Man's Garden* which she has taken from Mabel Burkholder's book "Before the White Man Came".

> Once upon a time, a Blackfoot maiden fell in love with a wounded prisoner she was attending. The maiden realised that the tribe was only nursing its captive in order to torture him later. She planned an escape of the prisoner, accompanying him for fear of the punishment for such a deed. After some time in her lover's camp she grew home-

sick for a glimpse of her old camp. She finally went to the site of her old camp, hid in the nearby bushes, and overheard two young braves discussing what would happen to the maiden who betrayed them, if only they could find her. Knowing she could never return, but nonetheless longing to return, she took a piece of bark and drew a picture of the camp upon it with her own blood, gashing her leg and painting with a stick. After drawing the picture, the maiden threw the stick away and returned to her lover's camp. Where the stick landed, a little plant grew with a brush-like end, dyed with the blood of this girl, which became the first Indian paintbrush.

The Chippewa Indians called it "Grandmother's Hair" and used it for women's diseases and rheumatism (this might be due to the selenium content). The Menomini used it as a love charm. The paintbrush was macerated in grease by Indians and used as a hair oil to invigorate the hair and make it glossy.

Small amounts of *C. linariafolia* root were decocted and used by the Nevada Indians as a remedy against venereal disease.

Lousewort   *Pedicularis lanata, P. artica, P. canadensis*

Pedicularis = L. "of lice", *lanata* = L. "woolly".

Synonyms: Elephant's Head, Betony, Wood Betony.

Identification: These showy annual perennial herbs stand 30 - 100 cm high and they have pink, rose, purple or yellow flowers. The flowers are borne on spike-like racemes. The leaves are pinnate and have several oblong leaflets. The plant has a strong yellow taproot and the numerous seeds in flattened, curved capsules. This species should not be confused with European Wood Betony (*Stachys betonica*).

Distribution & Habitat: These plants are common in moist places from the sub-alpine to the alpine zone.

Preparation & Uses: The sweet fleshy root can be eaten raw or cooked like carrots. The flowering stems, when young, are also good as a pot herb. Inuit children were known to suck the nectar from lousewort flowers. This sweet taste can lend a delightful addition to a salad.

Lousewort has been listed as a diaphoretic, sedative and antiseptic with water and alcohol as its solvents. The whole herb is useful in febrile and inflammatory diseases. A free and copious perspiration can be produced in a short period by a warm infusion of this herb. It is most valuable in treating ephemeral (short duration) fevers. As a sedative, the infusion of the flower stalks is mildly relaxing to the skeletal muscles and cerebrum, and is quite calming. The recommended dosage is 1 - 3 fluid ounces of standard infusion.

P. canadensis was infused and drunk for internal swelling. It was often used as a love charm, mostly to bring estranged married couples back together. The Ojibwa used it as an aphrodisiac. They chopped it finely and put it on their spouse's food to help spark their interest. It was also considered an evil medicine, regarded as black magic. The plant is known to contain small amounts of a poisonous alkaloid.

Moore states that it is an effective sedative for children and a tranquillizer for adults. It can cause "... befuddled lethargy and some interference with motor control, particularly in the legs". He goes on to say "... short term discomfort of minor consequence."

Caution: Because this plant is a parasite, one should pay close attention to plants growing in its vicinity. As Moore says, "it has two heads: one of itself and one of the host plant".

Lousewort
Pedicularis sp.

Elephant's Head
Pedicularis sp.

Common Mullein
Verbascum thapsus

185

Mullein

Verbascum blattaria, V. thapsus

Verbascum = ver-bas-kum, from its classical Latin name in Pliny, *thapsus* = thapsus, from a town in Sicily or from the isle of Thapsos, now Magnise; *blattaria* = bla-tah-ree-a, L. "cockroach-like".

Identification: Mullein is a biennial herb, producing a rosette of broad leaves in its first year. It has an erect stem 30-200 cm tall. The second year the leaves and stem are covered with dense, grey, felt-like hairs. The leaves are alternate, elliptical to oblanceolate, 10 - 40 cm long. The lower leaves have petioles while the upper leaves are sessile. The flowers are in spike-like racemes and are bright yellow.

Distribution & Habitat: Mullein grows in waste areas, along railroad tracks, dry meadows, pastures, gravely banks and around settlements. It can be found throughout North America and surprisingly, it is an introduced plant from Europe.

Preparation & Uses: Even though mullein has not been used as a food plant, it has many medicinal uses. The dried leaves were smoked by the Indians to relieve lung congestion, especially after the smoking of too much kinnickinnick. It was generally smoked in the form of a smudge. Herbalists throughout the world have found it useful for coughs, colds, lung congestion, hemorrhaging of the lung and for hemorrhoids (as a fomentation).

The Appalachian Indians used an infusion of the leaves for dysentery. Early settlers felt that if mullein leaves were tied to their feet and arms it would cure malaria. The leaves are very soft and soothing to the skin, and are used for diaper rash by simply using one of the big leaves, instead of a cloth diaper. The flowers have been used to treat chest and lung complaints. An oil of the flower is quite successful as a treatment for earaches and for removing warts. An infusion of the flowers as a tea is used for inducing sleep and relieving pain. The leaves also have an analgesic effect. Moore says the roots are diuretic, having an astringent effect on the urinary tract, making it good for incontinence and for toning up the bladder after childbirth. The leaves of mullein were in the National Formulary 1916-36.

The plant can be put to a variety of domestic uses. These include a good lamp wick, a torch if the whole plant is used, toilet paper and as a glove for picking stinging nettles.

Plantain, Common

Plantago major & related spp.

Plantago = plan-ta-go, sole of the foot. Some West coast Indians consider this plant "white-man-foot-print", as it came with the white man and could be found everywhere they went.

Identification: Common plantain has a flowering stalk 10 - 30 cm high, topped by a dense spike of greenish or sometimes white flowers. The leaves, all basal, are broad, oval to ovate. This common plant is easily recognized but has many variable features.

Distribution & Habitat: Common plantain is often found growing along roadsides and in waste areas and lawns. When mowing the lawn, people remove plantain's flower spike but do not damage the basal leaves.

Preparation & Uses: Plantain is high in vitamins C, A and K. The young leaves can be eaten raw like lettuce and are better cooked when older and tougher. Chopping plaintain leaves finely will often make it easier to eat.

Medicinally this plant is listed as alterative, astringent, diuretic and antiseptic. The seeds are high in mucilage. The bruised leaves were used as a poultice for wounds (a use which has been scientifically supported) and bruises. The Shoshone mixed plantain with an equal part of clematis bracts for this purpose, as well as to reduce swelling, rheumatic pains and boils. I have frequently used the chewed leaves as a poultice for bites and stings. Blaine, whose photographs grace much of this book, especially recommends the plant for wasp stings. Crush the leaves and place on stings. The pain will disappear in under ten minutes. Do not remove the leaves or the pain will return. This herb is even said to draw the poison out of snake bites.

Internally the infusion is an aid in normalizing stomach acids and secretions. Moore writes "the fresh juice of plantain can be almost miraculous in mild stomach ulcers. It can be preserved with 25% vodka or ten percent grain alcohol." The seeds of a related species *P. psyllium* are a very popular bulk laxative. Plantain's gentle diuretic effect works on dropsy, water retention and kidney and bladder infections. The seeds of all *Plantago sp.* have been shown to lower cholesterol. Plantain ointment has a soothing effect on hemorrhoids.

The roots were chewed by the Indians for toothaches.

Bedstraw, Northern *Galium boreale*

Galium = ga-lee-um, L. for "milk", *boreale* = bor-ee-al-ee, of the North.

Identification: Bedstraw is an erect perennial herb, 20 - 50 cm high, with small white flower heads. The faintly fragrant flowers form in clusters. The leaves are in whorls of four and are linear. The fruits are in pairs about 2 mm long and densely hairy.

Distribution & Habitat: Bedstraw is common in moist meadows and woodlands.

Common plantain
Plantago major

Common plantain leaves
Plantago major

Northern Bedstraw
Galium boreale

Cleaver
Galium aparine

Preparation & Uses: Bedstraw gets its name from its use as a stuffing for mattresses.The seed can be roasted, then ground for use as a coffee substitute. The bedstraws are actually in the coffee family. In early stages the sprouts are good eaten raw or steamed. *G. verum* (lady's bedstraw) is used for curdling milk for cheese preparation, thus the Latin genus name.

The Cree call it *keweti-ripe-wusleose*. They used it as a dye by combining it with cranberries to produce a red colour. Reports say that if this combination is boiled longer, the dye will turn yellow - red (it was used to dye porcupine quills). Medicinally it is similar to cleaver but milder.

Cleaver   *Galium aparine*

aparine = a name used by Theophrastus (Gr. "clinging, seizing").

Medicinally, the whole herb is diuretic, tonic, refrigerant and alterative. Hot water (but not boiling) is the solvent. Cleaver's high vitamin C content makes it antiscorbutic. It is reported to be very good for obstructions of urinary organs, especially if combined with broom, uva-ursi, buchu and marshmallow. It is particularly good for softening, reducing and eliminating stones and gravel. Due to its strong diuretic qualities it should not be given internally to people who have a tendency for diabetes.

Its refrigerant qualities are soothing in scarlet fever, measles and all acute diseases. A cold infusion is said to be able to remove freckles when it is drunk 2 - 3 times daily for 2 - 3 months, together with frequent washing of the freckled areas.

The crushed leaves are quite effective when applied to wounds and very soothing for burns. A poultice of oatmeal and bedstraw applied over an indolent tumour is said to be helpful. This treatment is carried out 3 times a day, in addition to taking spoonfuls of juice every morning and ensuring that the bowels are kept open.

For bad eczema, skin cancer, scrofula, ulcers and all skin troubles, an infusion made of 1 ½ ozs. of herb to 1 pint of warm water, steeped for 2 hours should be applied to the affected area. The juice of this herb is also good to apply directly to affected skin. Apply daily and allow to dry. Burn the cloth after each application. A skin salve can be made by mixing the fresh juice with leaf lard, lanolin or butter. The fresh leaves can be applied directly to skin irritations with good results. The herb is used in poultice form to retard bleeding and on spider bites. Experimentally the extract is being used to lower blood pressure.

A regular internal dose would be 2 - 4 fluid ounces, given 3 - 4 times daily, cold. This can be sweetened with honey. Twenty to forty drops of the tincture can be given 3 - 4 times daily.

Galium triflorum

The Cree called it *wehkinipews-shase* and used the flower as a perfume. The roots yield a fiery red-orange dye.

Honeysuckle, Bracted   *Lonicera involucrata*

Lonicera = lon-i-se-ra, after Adam Lonitzer (1528-86) a German naturalist;
involucrata = in-vo-loo-krah-ta, with involucre, the prominent bracts around
the flower, later enlarged in the fruit.

Identification: This erect or ascending shrub, grows 1 - 3 m high. It has yellow
flowers borne in pairs. The leaves are short-petioled, opposite and ovate to
obviate. The showy twin berries are purple-black and loosely enclosed in
petal-like dark red bracts.

Distribution & Habitat: Bracted Honeysuckle is common in damp thickets and
along streams. It is often found in association with Twin flower (*Linnaea
borealis*) and High bush Cranberry (*Viburnum edule*). It is sometimes found as
high as the tree line.

Preparation & Uses: The berries are said to be quite pleasant-tasting to most
people although I find them unpleasant. The addition of honey or sugar could
enhance their flavour. A few frosts also improve their taste. The leaves were
chewed by Mahah Indians during "confinement" and as an emetic for poison.

The Quileute Indians used the juice of the berries as a paint for doll faces.
This plant is often associated with the crow by many Amerindians.

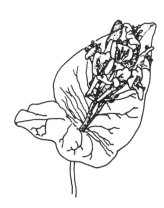

Elderberry, Black   *Sambucus melanocarpa*

Sambucus = sam-bew-kus, from its Latin name which in turn comes from Greek *sanbuke* (an instrument) referring to its use as a flute or from Gr. name for the elder tree, *melanocarpa* = L. "black-fruited".

Identification: This shrub grows 1 - 3 m high and often forms large clumps. The white flowers are small and numerous in large terminal compound cymes. The leaves are pinnate, usually with 5 - 7 leaflets which are serrated. The fruits are black.

Distribution & Habitat: Black elderberry forms clumps in moist thickets from the foothills into the low alpine regions.

Preparation & Uses: The fruit is sweet and juicy when mature and makes excellent pies, jellies and very good wine. Some people experience a little nausea if they eat too many berries raw, but cooking renders them safe for all.

Most parts of this plant are emetic, hydragogue and cathartic. The flowers are diaphoretic, diuretic, alterative, emollient, antiseptic and gently stimulant. An infusion of the plant is good for a headache due to a cold and is also helpful in jaundice and kidney complaints.

The inner bark of elderberry is said to be successful in treating epilepsy. This inner bark is taken from 1 or 2 year old branches. Steep 2 oz. of the bark in 5 oz. of boiling water for 48 hours. Keep the water quantity the same. Strain and give a wineglassful every 15 minutes when a fit is threatening. The patient should fast every seventh day. I have not employed this program and therefore cannot vouche for it personally.

A tea made from the flowers of elderberry is said to be quieting to twitching and good for inflammation of the eyes if taken internally. The berries are high in iron which makes them good for anemic conditions. The inner green bark is cathartic as an infusion in wine or expressed juice. It should be taken in doses from ½ fluid oz. to 1 fluid oz. It is a moderate purge, while large doses will produce vomiting. It is cleansing in small doses. It is used in dropsy to expel water. In children's diseases, it is quite good for liver derangement.

For tumors, swelling joints and similar problems, simmer any or all parts of elder and apply it as a poultice on broken skin. For burns and scalds it can be mixed with coconut oil to make a nice salve. Leaves can be made into a poultice and applied to bruises and on cuts to stop bleeding.

Many cosmetic uses have been claimed for elderberry. Every part of elderberry bush can aid in beauty complexion. It is claimed to remove spots, soothe irritation, remove freckles and preserve and soften skin if applied faithfully both internally and externally. As a wash it can be used for eczema, old ulcers and skin eruptions. An eyewash made from the flowers is very soothing.

Indians made flutes out of the branches, cutting them in the spring and letting them dry. They then bore holes in them with a hot poker or stick. Make sure that red elderberry is not used in this way as it is poisonous. The crushed leaves are also known as a fairly effective insect repellent.

I found this nice tale about how elderberry got its name. This is taken from Hutchens, who in turn found it in a 17th century Russian Botanic book:

> "There once was a king who was travelling in a hunting party. When it was getting late he realized that he was lost in thick woods. After a while he came upon a lonely farm-house and found an elderly gentleman crying on the porch. When the King asked why he was crying the man explained that he had slipped and fallen while carrying his grandfather from one room to another. His father was angry with him and had beaten him. This aroused the King's curiosity and he entered the house. To his surprise, he observed elders of advanced generations peacefully talking and going about their daily routine. After talking with them and observing them he asked how they kept in such good health to advancing years. They explained that as long as they could remember, their family had eaten only simple foods, salt, home-prepared bread, milk, cheese - with emphasis on elderberries."

Caution: *Sambucus pubens* (red elderberry) is said to be poisonous. Kingsbury says that the berries cause little more than nausea in humans, (especially if cooked with the seeds removed) but the root and stem can be dangerous. Children should be discouraged from using the stems to make blow-guns and flutes. The plant is distinguished by its red or yellowish berries.

Snowberry   *Symphoricarpos albus*

Symphoricarpos = sim-for-ee-kar-pos, from Greek *symphorium* (bear together) and *karpos* (a fruit) referring to the clustered fruit, ie. L. "clustered-berries", *albus* = "dead-white".

Identification: This shrub stands 60-150 cm tall and has white berries. The leaves are 1-4 cm long, oval, dull green and thick.

Distribution & Habitat: This shrub is found mostly on hill sides and montane slopes.

Preparation & Uses: The root and bark are listed as diuretic, stomachic and tonic. The berries are astringent, cathartic and emetic. For stomach problems, the root and sometimes the stems have been decocted for indigestion. It has been used as a remedy for morning sickness. The fresh leaves, fruit or bark can be used as a poultice for burns, sores, cuts, scrapes and wounds. Treated wounds heal with very little scabbing. The Nez Perce Indians made a decoction of the twigs for fever, female troubles and menstrual disorders.

Bracted Honeysuckle
Lonicera involucrata

Elderberry
Sambucus sp.

Snowberry
Symphoricarpos albus

High bush cranberry
Virburnum sp.

193

The Sioux used a decoction of the berries as a diuretic. Some Indian folk belief holds that snowberries were the "ghosts" of saskatoons and therefore part of the spirit world. As a result, those particular tribes wouldn't eat snowberries because they were the "sasktoons for the dead".

Cheholis Indians rubbed the berries into their hair as a soap. This group boils the bark and root to treat venereal disease.

Cranberry, High Bush   *Viburnum edule, opulus, trilobum & spp.*

Viburnum = vee-bur-num, for the Latin name of a species in this genus (the wayfaring tree), *edule* = "of food, edible", *opulus* = an old generic name for the guelder rose.

Identification: These shrubs grow 1 - 4 m high and have white flowers. The flowers are found on compound cymes. The leaves are simple, usually lobed and toothed. The juicy fruit is one-seeded and bright red. The winter-buds have 2 united outer scales which are usually reddish.

Distribution & Habitat: These cranberries are common in moist woodland and thickets. They venture up to timberline where they grow much shorter.

Preparation & Uses: The berries are tasty, especially when young, tasting similar to traditional cranberries even though it is not related to traditional cranberries (which are a heath). They have tough skins and a large seed but are quite palatable apart from that. The commonest use for these berries is to make a sauce as in the following recipe:

Cranberry Sauce

5 cups fully ripened fruit
¼ cup water
1 envelope unflavoured gelatin
1 cup sugar or honey

Wash and crush berries. Add water, heat to a boil and simmer 10 minutes. Cool and press through a colander until only the seeds and skin remain. Discard seeds and skin. Moisten gelatin with ½ cup of the cranberry juice. Add to remainder of pulp and heat. Add sugar or honey and stir until dissolved, then cool. The sauce should be thick but not jellied.

Hutchens lists the bark of *V. opulus* as being antispasmodic, nervine, tonic, astringent and diuretic. Water and diluted alcohol are the solvents.

With the common name, "Cramp bark", it is not surprising that it gives relief from cramps and spasms of an involuntary nature. These include asthma, hysteria and cramps during pregnancy. It can prevent the cramps entirely if it is used daily for the last two or three months of gestation. The recommended dose is to boil 1 tsp. of the bark in 1 cup of water for ½ hour. When this is cooled, drink 1 - 2 cups a day. It is highly esteemed as a female regulator and relaxant to ovaries and uterus. It is very effective in preventing abortion due to nervous afflictions.

Cramp bark is also very useful for intestinal cramps, while mildly effective on muscle cramps. In China the leaves and fruit are used as an emetic, laxative and antiscorbutic.

The Penobscot Indians used to steep and drink a tea of the berries for swollen glands and mumps. A related species *V. prunifolium* (Black Haw) is used as a tonic astringent for diarrhea and dysentery. A decoction of the bark and root was consumed for threatened abortions and was listed for such problems in the Canadian Pharmaceutical Journal – 1881 & 1883. Black haw has also been used to prevent miscarriages, relieving spasms during pregnancy and is successful against asthmatic spasms.

Valerian   *Valeriana septentrionalis* (and related species)

Valeriana = va-lee-ree-ah-na, from the Latin medieval name *valere* (to be healthy or "health") because of the medicinal qualities, *septentrionalis* = L. "of the north".

Identification: This slender stemmed perennial is 30 - 70 cm tall. The white flowers are small and sessile in compound cymes. The basal leaves are elliptical, lanceolate or spatulate. The stem leaves are opposite and pinnate, with 3 - 7 leaflets. The rootstock is scented.

Distribution & Habitat: Valerian is fairly widespread in moist meadows and boggy places.

Preparation & Uses: *Valeriana edulis*, a related species, is edible. The roots of this plant are large (over one foot long and two inches thick). It is said to be slightly poisonous raw but the poison is neutralized during cooking. Taste apparently improves after cooking yet the root remains quite nutritious. Indians used to cook it in pits or "fireless cookers". The roots are best collected in the spring or summer because they become fibrous in the fall.

Medicinally, *Valeriana officinalis* root has been used by herbalists as a major herb for many years. The related species of our area are thought to have the same effect as *Valeriana officinalis*. These herbs are listed as antispasmodic, calmative, stimulative tonic and nervine. Water is the solvent. Valerian is most popular as a nerve tonic and it is most effective when combined with skullcap (*Scutellaria*), blue vervain (*Verbena hastata*) and European mistletoe (*Viscum album*).

Valerian is useful in all sorts of nervous conditions, migraines and insomnia. It is useful in epileptic fits, St. Vitus dance, nervous derangement or irritations, debility and menstrual pain.

The Indians used valerian as a cure for distemper in horses. Cats love valerian (just like catnip) so you might have to keep your valerian "secure".

The correct dosage is 1 teaspoon of rootstock steeped in 1 pint of boiling water. Take 1 cupful in the course of a day. Of fluid extract, take 2 teaspoons in 1 cup of water. Let it stand 24 hours. Take ½ - 1 cup before bed. Of the tincture, take 20 drops, 3 times a day.

Valerian (white) with
yellow Arnica
Valeriana sp.

Caution: Valerian should never be boiled. Large doses of valerian causes poisoning. Symptoms such as headaches, mental excitement, visual illusions,
giddiness and even spasmodic movement can occur.

Bluebell, Harebell   *Campanula rotundifolia*

Campanula = Kăm-pahn-ew-la, L. for "little bell" referring to the shape of the
flower; *rotundifolia* = ro-tund-i-fo-lee-a, "rounded (basal) leaves".

Identification: Harebell is a perennial herb, 10 - 40 cm high, having purplish-
blue or occasionally white flowers. These nodding flowers are usually several
to a slender stock. The basal leaves are long-petioled but seldom present in
the flowering stage. The stem leaves are linear and without petioles.

Harebell
Campanula sp.

Distribution & Habitat: This common plant is fond of dry, well-lighted places. It will be found in dry meadows, hillsides, open woods and open gravelly and sandy places throughout the area.

Preparation & Uses: The Cree Indians call it *Mos-ho-se-u-tcha-pek*, using the leaves and shoots in salads or as a pot herb. The root can be boiled to give a nut-like taste although it does not give much bulk. After boiling they can be fried in butter or oil. Sometimes the larger roots are a little stringy. Even though they are small they can be utilized because they grow abundantly in large patches.

Campanula americana leaves were used by Eastern Amerindians as a tea for coughs and tuberculosis. Crushed roots were used for whooping cough.

Yarrow   *Achillea millefolium*

Achillea = a-kil-lee-a, after Achilles of Greek mythology; *millefolium* = meel-lee-fo-lee-um, "thousand-leaved", referring to its densely pinnated leaves.

Identification: Yarrow is an aromatic herb standing 30-70 cm high. Its composite flower heads are borne in a flat-topped inflorescence. The flowers are white or rarely pink. The alternate leaves are very finely pinnated or plume-like, with woolly hairs on them. It sun-dries, standing from fall till spring as a brown skeleton of its former self.

Distribution & Habitat: Yarrow likes open, sunny, well drained places. It is a pioneer species and tends to be found on disturbed soils. Because it prefers well drained areas, it is often found in slightly gravelly locales. It is also common in pastures.

Preparation & Uses: The legend behind the generic name "Achillea" goes back many years to when Achilles made an ointment from the yarrow to heal wounds of his soldiers after the Battle of Troy. The legend says he first learned of its uses from Chiron, the Centaur. Another version of the legend says that Achilles was dunked into yarrow tea at birth, making all but the heel he was held by invincible.

Yarrow is reported to be diaphoretic, diuretic, stimulant, astringent and tonic. It is a strong and soothing diaphoretic. When taken hot in an infusion, it will increase the body temperature, open skin pores, stimulate free perspiration, and equalize the circulation, making it one of the most valuable herbs for colds and fevers.

A famous remedy for colds/flus is made from equal parts yarrow, elder flower (or leaves) and mint, infused and drunk regularly. In opening the pores, yarrow purifies the blood by elimination of the morbid waste material produced in sickness. Yarrow regulates the function of the liver, and it is especially beneficial in its influence on secretion throughout the entire alimentary canal. As a stomach tonic it is quite effective when drunk as a fresh infusion. It is also said to be effective in treating anorexia (by stimulating digestive enzyme and bile flow) but I have yet to try this.

One of the most effective uses of yarrow that I know is its ability to stop bleeding. The leaves tied to a wound will stop bleeding fairly fast and aid in the healing process. The green leaves are best for this, although dried leaves work, as do the flower heads.

Indians also used dried leaves of yarrow in a tea with plantain to halt internal bleeding. The tea can slow excessive menstrual flow and aid in reducing mild hemorrhoids.

The juice of yarrow was used as an eye wash to reduce redness. Oil from this plant, obtained by distillation, reportedly stops hair falling out. As an enema for piles and hemorrhage of the bowel, inject 2 tablespoons, repeating several times after each stool. It is also good for leucorrhea. The root has an analgesic property and was sometimes used for toothaches.

The Ojibwa Indians used the florets as incense in ceremonies and also burned it to break up fevers. They also used the leaves as a poultice to cure spider bites.

It is used to stop nosebleeds in a odd way. If you have a nosebleed, stick a roll of yarrow up your nose and it will stop the bleeding. If you have a severe sinus-type headache, stick yarrow up your nose and it will make your nose bleed, thus releasing pressure on the head and alleviating your headache.

Yarrow tea was often used as a drink by Blackfoot Indians to speed up childbirth. It was also used to expel afterbirth. It also aids in bringing in a good supply of milk. It is effectively used in menopausal years, reducing the incidence of "hot flashs" and speeding up the transition. Yarrow was officially in the U.S.P. 1863-82.

Linnaeus says that in lieu of hops, the Swedish used yarrow to make a beer that was much stronger and quite tasty. Yarrow contains achillein, oil of achillea, and achillic acid.

Yarrow is the famous stalk chosen by the ancient Chinese sages for consulting the *I Ching* oracle.

Pearly Everlasting   *Anaphalis margaritacea*

Anaphalis = a-nah-fa-lis, from the Greek name (for an immortal) for a similar plant; *margaritacea* = mar-ga-ri-tah-kee-a, pearl-like, referring to the flower head.

Identification: This perennial herb stands 20 - 60 cm high and occasionally grows in clumps. The flower heads are numerous and pearly white to yellow in colour. Pearly Everlasting is very leafy. It has a white-walled appearance, with lanceolate to linear leaves. This herb forms rhizomes.

Distribution & Habitat: *Anaphalis* is found in the mountains and foothills on slopes and in open woods.

Preparation & Uses: Pearly Everlasting is listed as an astringent, diaphoretic, expectorant, febrifuge, anodyne, sedative and vulnerary. This plant is useful for colds, coughs, fevers and as a mouthwash or gargle for mouth and throat problems. The Bella Coola coastal Indians used Pearly Everlasting for tuberculosis and as an infusion for worms and leucorrhea. As a steam, this herb was used to treat rheumatism by both coastal Indians and the Chippewa. Some Indians would inhale the smudge smoke of this plant to relieve headaches. Others smoked it as a pleasing tobacco substitute. The Mohawks made a drink for asthma out of an infusion of the flowers, combined with the roots of mullein. The whole plant was sometimes used as a wash or poultice for external wounds. The juice from the fresh plant has been reported to act as an aphrodisiac.

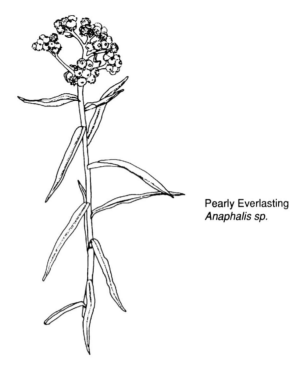

Pearly Everlasting
Anaphalis sp.

The Cheyenne used this plant as a ritual herb. They made a smudge and washed the body and any gifts in the smoke. The herb was also rubbed into the arms and legs before going into battle. The Chippewa combined it with wild mint, making a smudge of the two plants for paralysis. Medicine men of the Menomini tribe mixed a smudge of this plant with beaver gall bladders and blew the smoke into the nostrils of people who had fainted. They also used it to ward off troublesome ghosts after the death of a family member.

To make an infusion, steep 1 oz. of herb in 1 pint of boiled water, taking 3 - 4 tablespoons at a time.

Burdock   *Arctium minus & spp.*

Arctium = L. for "bear"; *minus* = L. for "smaller".

Identification: These large biennial herbs stand 1 - 2.5 m tall and have broad alternate leaves with several flower heads. The leaves are ovate to oblong, even cordate and up to 50 cm long. The flowers are tubular, pink or purplish. The seeds are borne in prickly burrs.

Distribution & Habitat: The plant was introduced from Europe and it now grows in waste lands throughout North America.

Preparation & Uses: I find the young shoots and leaves are quite tasty cooked as a pot herb, but some consider them too strong. The inner pithlike material

Yarrow
Achillea millefolium

Pearly Everlasting
Anaphalis margaritacea

Lesser Burdock
Arctium sp.

of the stems can be eaten raw. The roots are eaten both boiled and roasted and are often used as a coffee substitute.

An infusion of the roots is used as a cleansing tea, especially in the spring. It cleanses the liver by stimulating bile flow and has a mild laxative effect. The tea or a tincture of the roots has been used for stomach complaints and for a prolapsed uterus. A decoction of the roots is used for gout and rheumatism, to wash sores and as an antidote after eating poisonous food, especially mushrooms. The powdered seeds have been used as a diuretic. The leaves can be used as a poultice for poison ivy, poison oak, to soothe skin irritations, for impetigo, syphilis, gonorrhea and sunburn.

The seeds are an excellent diuretic. A tincture of the seed has been used as a folk remedy for joint inflammation.

Caution: Burdock seeds should not be used in pregnancy as it can cause spotting and even the rare case of miscarriage.

Burdock
Arctium sp.

Arnica
Arnica spp.

Arnica = ar-ni-ka, from Greek *arnakis* (lambskin) from the texture of the leaves; *montana* = mon-tah-na, "of the mountains".

Identification: Arnicas are perennial herbs growing from a rootstock 2 - 5 cm long. They have erect stems and stand 15 - 60 cm tall. The leaves are opposite, simple, entire or toothed. The composite flower head is yellow and flowering is from July - August.

Distribution & Habitat: It can be found in mountainous regions throughout the area. There are many species, all of which have similar properties, even though *Arnica montana* is usually considered the official herb.

Preparation & Uses: Arnica is well known to both herbalists and homeopaths as a stimulant and nervine. This herb is almost always used in the form of a tincture. Once you've had need to use it, you will never want to be far away from it. It is the best remedy I know for taking the pain out of sprains, bruises, and breaks. Used as an external liniment it will do wonders and everyone is always amazed at how fast it works. It should not be used if the skin is broken and the area is bleeding as it is toxic if it enters the bloodstream.

This herb should not be use internally, except under special conditions, because it can cause blistering of the intestinal tract. Homeopathic preparations can be taken internally and give similar sorts of results.

Wormwood
Artemisia spp.

Artemisia = ar-tay-mis-ee-a, after the Greek goddess Artemis or after Queen Artemisia of Caria, Asia Minor.

Identification: There are many species of *Artemisia* in the area and they vary in shape from herbs to small shrubs. They are usually quite aromatic, and have alternate leaves, entire or dissected with tubular flowers. These plants are mostly grey in colour. They vary from 20 - 200 cm tall, most being less than 40 cm.

Distribution & Habitat: Wormwoods are usually found in dry places or in well drained south-facing slopes throughout the area.

Preparation & Uses: *A. frigida.* As with all species of *Artemisia*, the fruit and seed may be dried and pounded into meal to make pinal or eaten raw. The Hopi Indians used to roast the leaf with corn as a flavouring. Crushed leaves can be mixed with stored meat to maintain a good odour.

Tea made from the leaves was a good cure for colds, sore eyes and used as a hair tonic. The taste is strongly bitter but some people like it. This herb tea stops lipid peroxidation, thereby protecting the liver from the "rancid fat syndrome" caused by continued donut and french fry consumption. It has also found use as a tea for frontal headache, especially if it is accompanied by indigestion. For headaches, a tea is drunk and a wash is applied to the area. The tincture (20 - 30 drops) lowers oversecretion of stomach acids. As its common name suggests, all wormwoods are excellent for ridding the body of worms, particularly pinworms and roundworms. An infusion of wormwood makes a refreshing bath to soak the feet in after a hard day on the trail.

Many Amerindian ladies used wormwood for controlling menstrual flow, and as a menstrual pad which would absorb and reduce skin irritation. The infusions of all *Artemisia* have a calming effect on the uterus, alleviating suppressed crampy menstruation, especially if associated with emotion difficulties. The foliage and flower were used as fumigant to revive a patient in a coma.

Leaves of wormwood were chewed by Blackfoot Indians and applied to wounds to lessen swelling. Bleeding nostrils were sometimes stuffed with soft leaves by these Indians. Vogel reports an Indian lady who cut off a finger as an offering and wrapped the bleeding stub in wormwood leaves.

This herb had the honour of being used as toilet paper, especially by children. It was also used as a foot deodorant.

One of the most important Amerindian uses of wormwood was for rituals. It is burned as an incense and the smoke is used to cleanse one's spirit. Wormwood is used as a flooring for sweatlodges and added to different smoking mixtures (e.g. kinnickinnick).

Even today, some people place this sage under their pillow to restore youth or help retain it.

The burning of wormwood as an incense was considered helpful by the Hopi Indians, as well as Tibetans, for "no-win situations."

A. absinthium, absinthe

This herb is good for internal bleeding, as a vermifuge and to get rid of bad breath. It was also used by some people as an antidote for poisonous mushrooms (when it was usually combined with vinegar). The oil of this and other sages is used to make absinthe. A somewhat "narcotic" drink, absinthe is banned in most of the world.

Hutchens lists this herb as a tonic, stomachic, febrifuge, anthelmintic and narcotic. It will tune digestion and correct debilities of the liver and gallbladder. It is often given to people who get travelling sickness (5-30 drops of

Heart-leaved Arnica
Arnica sp.

Wormwood Sage
Artemisia sp.

Wormwood Sage
Artemisia sp.

tincture; 3-4 times a day, an overdose causes stomach irritation). An infusion, 1 teaspoon in 1 cup of boiling water can also be used.

For external uses, the oil is good in liniments for sprains, bruises and lumbago. Fomentations are excellent applications for rheumatism, swellings, sprains and local inflammation.

A. vulgaris (mugwort, moxi)

A decoction can be made for colds, colic, bronchitis, rheumatism and fever. This decoction is also safe for suppressing menstruation.

The dosage is 1 teaspoon of herb to 1 cup boiling water, steeped for 20 minutes. Mugwort is used by acupuncturists for moxibustion.

A. campestris L. "of the pasture, from flat land".

Blackfoot women would make a decoction of leaves in order to abort difficult pregnancies. Others would chew the leaves for stomach troubles. An infusion of the herb was used for coughs. It was usually dried and stored in a rawhide bag until needed. An infusion of the leaves was sometimes applied for eczema.

The spittle of the chewed herb was applied to rheumatic parts of the body and as an infusion of the root applied to back sores. When running, people sometimes chewed the leaves for their mentholating properties. This herb was sometimes rubbed on hide while tanning.

A. ludoviciana L. "from Louisiana, USA".

The herb was a major ritual herb, and was often used to cleanse one's body. The smoke was rubbed over the body to "enliven" the aura. Sweat lodges were often lined with this herb, which was sometimes rubbed onto the body or chewed with a drink as an infusion to relieve chest and throat constriction.

The leaves can be applied to blisters and burst boils for their cooling effect.

Balsam Root   *Balsamorhiza sagittata*

Balsamorhiza = bal-sam-o-rhiza, L. "balsam-containing root"; *sagittata* = referring to the arrow shape of the leaves.

Identification: Balsam root is a perennial herb with large basal leaves and a taproot. The flower head is usually solitary with yellow rays and light yellow disc flowers. The leaves are triangular-oblong to cordate-sagittate.

Distribution & Habitat: This plant is found mostly in prairie grassland and open woods. It especially likes hillsides.

Preparation & Uses: Balsam root is one of those amazing plants in which all parts of the plant can be used the year round. Balsam root is quite tasty. The young shoots and leaves can be eaten as a salad herb or boiled as a pot herb.

The leaves get a little fibrous with age but boiling can overcome this. The roots can be collected all year round, eaten raw or prepared in any way imaginable. The seeds are good roasted or ground into flour.

The most active part is the root, especially the inner bark. It is a good expectorant, stimulates saliva, while softening dried mucus of the lungs, and stimulating the bronchioles. It contains an immune-stimulating factor similar to *Echinacea* but milder. The resin is specific for wound healing, being both disinfectant and topically counterirritant. It is known to be anti-fungal and antimicrobial.

Indians have been known to mash the root and apply this to swellings and insect bites. The boiled root was drunk as a remedy for rheumatism and headache. The decoction is said to produce profuse perspiration and stop venereal disease. The root was also chewed and applied to blisters and sores. The mashed roots were used by the Nevada Indians as a dressing for syphilitic sores.

The root was often burned as an incense for ceremonial occasions by the Blackfoot Indians. Hellson & Gadd said this incense was used to increase running ability in some ceremonies and for other rites. The smoke of the smudge was also inhaled as a treatment for headaches. Smoke of the balsam root was occasionally used to fumigate a room where a diseased person had stayed.

Ox-eye daisy   *Chrysanthemum leucanthemum*

Identification: A perennial herb with short rootstock, usually growing in patches on erect stems or simple forked tops, glabrous or sparsely hairy. Leaves somewhat hairy, basal oblanceolate to spatulate, 4 - 15 cm long, cauline leaves, petiolate – sessile, oblanceolate to linear, toothed to incised. Flower head solitary, 4 cm broad with white rays, yellow disc.

Distribution & Habitat: Grows in patches along roadsides, fields, waste lands throughout the continent.

Preparation & Uses: The cauline (stem) leaves are quite tasty and are added to fancy salads in gourmet restaurants.

Moore states that the tea made of this herb is diuretic, astringent and mildly hemostatic. It was used to stop occasional blood in the urine, piles and stomach ulcers. It is a specific for bleeding of the splenic or sigmoid flexure. As a douche, it can be used for cervical ulceration. It has many of the same effects as fleabane (*Erigeron*) but is a little stronger and more cooling to the urinary tract.

Chicory   *Cichorium intybus*

Cichorium = ki-ko-ree-um, derived from its Arabic name; *intybus* = in-tew-bus, derived from Latin and Egyptian name *tybi* representing January, the month it was usually eaten in (from a name in Virgil for wild chicory or endive).

Identification: Chicory is a perennial, growing 30 - 100 cm tall and branching widely. The flowers are usually purplish-blue but can be pink or white and look similar to dandelion flowers. The lower leaves are petioled and oblanceolated and toothed, while the upper leaves are sessile, clasping and lanceolate to oblong. The taproot is quite deep.

Distribution & Habitat: This plant is considered rare in native habitats, but is locally abundant. It is an introduced plant, native to Europe, and it likes roadsides and waste areas.

Preparation & Uses: The leaves of chicory can be eaten raw in salads or cooked as a pot herb and are especially good blanched. The roots can be eaten raw, (young ones tasting similar to carrots) boiled or roasted. The root of the chicory can be eaten any time of the year but some feel it is a little bitter in the fall immediately after the flowering period. The roots have long been used as a coffee substitute. It is prepared like dandelion roots and sometimes commercially mixed with dandelion root coffee. Take the cleaned root, slice and roast it, then grind into 'coffee'. Some people like to mix chicory root with real coffee to get a desirable bitterness.

Balsam Root
Balsamorhiza sagittata

BA

TW

Balsam Root
Balsamorhiza sagittata

BA

Ox-Eye Daisy
Chrysanthemum leucanthemum

BA

Chicory
Cichorium intybus

Medicinally, chicory is listed as an appetizer, cholagogue, digestive, diuretic, tonic, hepatic, for skin eruptions and as a laxative, with water as a solvent. Chicory is a herb that is often recommended for jaundice and spleen problems. The juice of the leaves and decoction of the flower promote the excretion of bile, the elimination of excessive internal mucus and the release of gallstones. This decoction is also useful for gastritis, lack of appetite and digestive difficulties. The root is decocted for upset stomachs, uric acid condition of gout, rheumatic and joint stiffness and is beneficial to glandular organs of the digestive system.

The decoction is made by putting one teaspoon of root or herb in 1½ cups of cold water, bringing it to a boil and straining. Take 1 - 1 ½ cups a day in mouthful amounts. Excessive amounts of chicory over a long period of time should be avoided as it causes loss of visual power in the retina. Experimentally, chicory extract has been shown to be antibacterial and to slow and weaken heat rate.

Chicory is very rich in vitamins A (beta-carotene) and C.

Thistle   *Cirsium spp.*

Cirsium = the ancient Gr. name for a thistle.

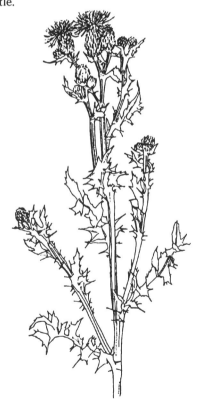

Identification: Thistles are biennial and perennial herbs, 10 - 120 cm tall, with flower heads of many flowers in a cup-shaped form. These flowers are usually purple, red, cream or white depending on the species. The leaves are sessile and alternate, often prickly. The seeds have many bristles on them.

Distribution & Habitat: Various species of thistles are found in various habitats throughout the region. There are six species listed for this area.

Preparation & Uses: The roots of this plant were eaten by the Indians raw, boiled or roasted. They are nutritious but quite flat-tasting when raw. Some species have roots that turn sugary when roasted. As an emergency food, thistles are useful because they are easy to identify and grow quite abundantly. You have to be careful to peel back the thistles, but this can be done easily with a sharp knife. When peeling the leaves, hold the plant upside down and peel from bottom to top. The resulting central stem is often a sweet and juicy stalk. The immature flower buds are also nice raw or steamed with lemon butter – better than artichoke hearts! The first few times you do this, it helps to recall that artichoke hearts are thistles also!

Thistle infusions are listed as a tonic, astringent and diuretic, are good for weak stomach conditions and are said to reduce fevers. Some claim the infusions kill worms and increase the supply of milk in nursing mothers. The root has been used as a astringent for dysentery and diarrhea. Externally the tea of the leaves has been used for eruptions, skin ulcers and poison ivy rash.

The Quinault Indians of Washington steeped the whole thistle plant and drank the resulting tea to inhibit fertilization. Houma Indians drank a decoction of roots, with whiskey, to clear phlegm from the lung and throat.

The downy seeds make good tinder.

Echinacea, Cone Flowers   *Echinacea spp.*

Echinacea = e-kee-nah-kee-a, from Gr. *echinos* (a hedgehog) referring to the prickly receptacles, scales.

Identification: Echinacea grows 30-100 cm tall from a taproot. It has bristly hairs on the stem and the leaves. The leaves are mostly basal and broadly lanceolate, 10 - 50 mm long. The solitary flower head appears from July to October and varies in colour from rose to purple. The taste of the root and the leaf is sweet at first, followed by a tingling feeling in the mouth.

Distribution & Habitat: This plant grows in dry, open areas and prairies throughout the United States.

Preparation & Uses: According to many authorities this plant was used medicinally by the Plains Indians more often than any other plant. It was considered the great antidote, especially in the case of snake bites, stings and poisoning. The herb was smoked to cure headaches and blown into horse's noses to treat distemper. The root can be used to treat toothache, and for swollen glands (as in mumps) by chewing. Medicine men used to bathe their hand in a decoction of the plant so they could do slight of hand with hot coals as a form of the ritual – pulling fire out of a patient. The juice of the plant was used to treat burns. The Sioux used the scraped root as a remedy for rabies, snakebites and septic sores. The Meskwakis Indians used the plant to cure fits and stomach cramps. The root was chewed by the Cheyenne as part of the Sun Dance ritual, after first going several days without food, water or sleep. These Indians also used the powdered root for mouth and gum sores, for rheumatism, arthritis, mumps and measles.

European and North American herbalists have long used this plant as a antidote and as a blood purifier. The most famous North American tradition of Western herbology comes from the Thomsonian line in which Echinacea was considered the greatest antioxidant, correcting the blood, liver and lymphatic systems of impurities. It was also used to increase the body's resistance to infection.

Orthodox medicine has never agreed with the concept of blood purifiers (alterative), but recent research has uncovered some remarkable information on cone flower. It can regulate and stimulate the immune system. It can stimulate the body to produce its own interferon, stimulate T-lymphocytes, and work as an antioxidant. It has been shown to work both as a prophylactic and curative in many cases of infectious diseases. In my clinical experience with this herb, I also find it one of the best builders of the immune system and feel it (or a brand name product containing it) will become a household word one day. There were over 200 pharmaceutical preparations containing echinacea in Germany by the early 1990's.

Echinacea sp.

Echinacea is a great herbal prophylactic, helping to prevent colds and flus, specifically during the first stage of an influenza. Echinacea is very functional in speeding up tissue repair, especially connective tissue, with a cortisone-like activity.

Fleabane   *Erigeron sp.* (25 species)

Erigeron = e-ri-ge-ron, from Greek *eri* (early) and *geron* (an old man) – Theophrastus' name, referring to the fluffy white seed heads.

Identification: This large and complex genus is closely related to other composites such as aster. These herbs are usually perennial with alternate leaves, rarely all basal. The flower heads are few or solitary. The ligules are white, pink, blue or purple, rarely yellow. These ligules are many in number and rather thin. The bloom occurs mostly in the early summer or spring.

Distribution & Habitat: These plants are found from low elevation to high alpine slopes.

Preparation & Uses: Samuel Stearn states, "the chief use of the fleabanes is for destroying fleas and gnats by burning the herb so the insects waste away in the smoke." Fleabanes are listed as astringent and diuretic, useful for cholera, diabetes, painful urination, dysentery and summer complaints, especially for children when all else fails. It is said to be good as an enema in cases of infection. Steep a teaspoonful in a quart of boiling water for 20 minutes. Use at 112 - 115 F. for the best results. It is also good for colon troubles.

Erigeron philadelphica - the flower is known as a "smoke". Blackfoot Indians used the entire plant to treat a variety of disease. It was most valuable in cases of chronic diarrhea or in childbirth hemorrhage.

White or
Hooker's
Thistle
Cirsium sp.

BA

BA

Bull Thistle
Cirsium sp.

TW

Echinacea *Echinacea sp.*

Smooth Fleabane
Erigeron sp.

BA

213

Erigeron canadensis - is listed by Lust as being astringent, diuretic and styptic. It is useful in cases of diarrhea, dysentery, internal hemorrhage and hemorrhoids. The root can be boiled to make tea for menstrual irregularities. As a diuretic it is recommended for bladder problems and rheumatism. An oil made from this plant was used in the early 19th century to stop uterine hemorrhaging (only two - three drops of the oil were needed). This plant was discussed often in the Canadian Pharmaceutical Journal during the last 100 years. Africans used this plant as a wash for eczema and ringworm. The essential oil of this herb can be used for cystitis and bronchial ailments.

To make an infusion, steep 1 teaspoon of leaves or plants in 1 cup of water for 30 minutes. Take 1 - 2 cups daily.

The roots of *E. caespitosis* (*caespitosis* = L. "growing in tufts") was used by the Nevada Indians as a cooled decoction eyewash. A strong tea made from the roots was used for diarrhea. The Nevada Indians used *E. concinnus* whole as a decoction for stomachaches.

Gaillardia, Brown Eyed Susan   *Gaillardia aristata*

Gaillardia = gay-lard-ee-a, after Gailard de Charenton-neau, 18th century French magistrate and botanical patron, *aristata* = L. "with a beard, awned".

Identification: Gaillardia is a perennial herb 30 - 60 cm tall with slender branching rootstocks. The showy flower head has yellow rays, sometimes tinged with red and orange radiating out from the centre. The disc of the flower head is brown, reddish-brown and sometimes even purplish. The leaves are lanceolate.

Distribution & Habitat: This herb is found quite commonly in small clumps on well-drained slopes in the foothills as well as in open grasslands and other dry places.

Preparation & Uses: The Blackfoot Indians found many uses for this plant. An infusion of the root was taken for gastroenteritis. It was rubbed on nursing mothers' sore nipples. Saddle sores and falling hair were treated with Gaillardia. The infusion of the root was used as eyedrops, administered in drops. Some Indians would chew the root and apply this to skin disorders. An infusion of the herb parts of this plant was also used as an eyewash and for nosedrops. The flower head was also infused to make a footbath.

To our ancestors, this plant represented the health, earthiness and wholesomeness of the common people. It also represented a gift of liveliness and sunshine from our Mother the Earth.

Gumweed
Grindelia integrifolia, G. squarrosa

Grindelia = after David Grindel (1717 - 83) German botanist, *integrifolia* = L. "with entire leaves", *squarrosa* = L. "rough".

Identification: These biennial and perennial herbs grow from tap roots, have glandular leaves and gummy heads. The widely branching stems are 30 - 60 cm tall, often purplish; alternate, narrowly oblong to oblanceolate, serrulate to coarsely toothed but can be entire. The flower head is yellow, 2 - 3 cm wide. The flower and buds are covered in a milky, thick, balsam-smelling resin.

Distribution & Habitat: Found in dry, often saline prairies from Manitoba through to California.

Preparation & Uses: The resin is listed as being antispasmodic, diuretic, expectorant and sedative. It has most specifically been used for treating spasmodic respiration problems such as asthma, dry hacking coughs or whooping cough. Moore says it was sometimes combined with Yerba Santa. As a mild stomach tonic, it has been used for indigestion and colic.

For kidney and bladder problems, both tincture and tea have been used. A little brandy is usually added to the tea to dissolve the resin. Moore says it is specific for cystitis caused by fungi or food but not so good for "honeymoon" cystitis. He also states it is a mild cardiac relaxant though not all that reliable.

The Blackfoot Indians made a decoction of the dried ground root for liver problems and as a spring purge. Nevada Indians used small doses of the decoction during measles and smallpox epidemics. Gumweed is known to increase excretions.

Externally, fresh gumweed or fresh plant tincture can be applied as a wash for poison ivy/oak. It has also been used as a wash for burns, rashes, sores, wounds and the like. A poultice can be made of the herb and used for rheumatic joints, breaks, and wounds.

Sunflower
Helianthus spp.

Helianthus = hay-lee-ănth-us, from Greek *helios* (sun) and *anthos* (a flower).

Identification: This well known genus contains both erect annual and perennial herbs, with opposite or alternate undivided leaves. The flower heads are large with yellow rays and yellow, purple or brown disks. The flower head follows the sun as it crosses the sky (heliotropic).

Distribution & Habitat: Sunflowers are found in sunny open places throughout southern Canada and the United States.

Preparation & Uses: Sunflower and maize were two of the plants that native people cultivated. The seeds of sunflower were eaten raw and roasted. Native peoples often made cakes out of sunflower seed flour for travelling. Some Indians even extracted the oil from the seeds as a hair tonic and on occasion oiled their bodies with it before going into battle.

Sunflower
Helianthus sp.

Brown-Eyed Susan
Gaillardia sp.

Gumweed
Grindelia sp.

The crushed roots of the sunflower have been applied to bruises, in a hot form for rheumatism and as a cold poultice for blisters or as a relief for headaches.

The seeds are diuretic and expectorant by nature. An infusion of the whole plant has been used by herbalists for coughs, bronchitis, and kidney weakness. Sunflower leaves are said to be helpful in the treatment of malaria.

The seed can produce a purple or black dye and the flowers produce a yellow dye. The oil has been used in soap making, candle making and as a lubricant for hair oil.

Jerusalem artichoke (*H. tuberosus*) grows in this area and has a very tasty tuber.

A leaf and stalk tea of Jerusalem artichoke was used for rheumatism. The flowers were also eaten for this ailment occasionally. The tubers are quite high in inulin, suggesting both antidiabetic and immuno-stimulatory action.

Rush Skeleton Weed   *Lygodesmia juncea*

Lygodesmia = L. "willow-lily", *juncea* = L. "rush-like".

Identification: This perennial herb is a rush-like plant, 10 - 40 cm high. It has a tough, rigid and sparsely leaved stem containing milky sap. The lower leaves are linear, up to 5 cm long and the upper leaves are scale-like. The solitary flower head is pink.

Distribution & Habitat: This plant can be commonly found in the sandy, dry parts of the Great Plains.

Preparation & Uses: Cheyenne, Omoka, Ponca and Hopi Indian women drank a tea of this plant to increase milk flow. It was also reputed to give women a feeling of contentment and one of inner power. The infusion has also been used to treat sore eyes.

Rush Skeleton Weed
Lygodesmia spp.

Pineapple Weed, False Chamomile   *Matricaria matricaioides*

Matricaria = may-tri-care-ee-a, from Latin *matrix* (mother) and *caria* (dear), referring to its medicinal use for the female area and colic.

Identification: This plant is often mistaken for chamomile. In fact, it is a close sister plant to chamomile (*M. chamomile*). Chamomile is quite rare on the east side of the Rocky mountains (where pineapple weed is quite common). Pineapple weed is an annual, 10 - 40 cm tall with a non-rayed composite flower head. Chamomile can be distinguished from this plant by its white rays. Pineapple looks more like commercial chamomile in a package when all of its white rays have dried up and fallen off. It actually does have a pineapple scent. Its leaves are pinnate.

Distribution & Habitat: Pineapple weed is found in almost all waste areas. It can be seen growing in cracks in the sidewalk in the centre of most towns and along many a backwood's dirt road.

Preparation & Uses: Pineapple weed is tasty as finger food or in salads. As with chamomile, pineapple weed is very good as a tea. In fact, I prefer it because it is sweeter. The Blackfoot Indians called it *mat-o-at-sin*, using the dried plant as a perfume. They often put it in buckskin bags for this very purpose. It was also used as an insect repellent. As a treatment for diarrhea, the whole plant was decocted. It is similar to chamomile in many of its medicinal qualities but much milder. It is used for stomachaches, flatulence, as a mild relaxant and for colds and menstrual problems. Externally it can be used for itching and sores.

The Dena'ina K'et'una boiled pineapple weed and gave it to a mother after birth, believing it helped to bring in good healthy milk.

Coltsfoot   *Petasites spp.* (a.k.a. *Tussilago spp.*)

Petasites = pe-ta-see-teez, from Greek *petasos* (a hat), "Sun-hat." Dioscorides used the name referring to the large leaves.

Identification: This perennial herb rises from a thick creeping rhizome, with large basal leaves. The flower stalk grows up to 30 cm tall in early spring, fruiting and dying usually before the leaves show. The flowers are purple, white or yellow, the stem reddish. The leaves are from thumb size to 30 cm.

Distribution & Habitat: Coltsfoot can be found on stream banks, in swamps and wet tundra. It ranges from Alaska to Washington and into Alberta.

Preparation & Uses: The young flowering stem is a tasty spring vegetable, steamed, or stir fried. The young leaves are edible but feel a little cottony in the mouth. The rootstock of *P. frigidus* was roasted by Siberian Eskimos and eaten.

The most common use for this herb is cough suppression. It is applied to cases of whooping cough, asthma, bronchial congestion and shortness of breath. It was a specific used (in the form of a smudge) by many Amerindian groups to cure problems caused by smoking too much. It has also been used for menstrual cramps.

Externally, a decoction or poultice was used for sores, insect bites and arthritic pain.

Prairie Cone Flower   *Ratibida columnifera*

Identification: This perennial herb rises from a tap root in a stiff stem 30 - 50 cm tall, leaves are alternate, pinnately divided into 5 - 9 linear or oblong lobes, the yellow (rarely purple) rays coming from a greyish-yellow disc that turns purple brown. Not to be confused with *Echinacea* (also called cone flower).

Distribution & Habitat: Found in open places, along roadsides from Manitoba to B.C., south to California, Texas and Arkansas.

Preparation & Uses: The disc flower in a semi-dried to dried state is edible, tasting similar to corn, tasting better the longer you eat it. It is kind of chewy, and takes a long time to eat. If nothing else it makes you feel you have eaten a lot! The Dakota Indians used the disc and leaves as a tea beverage.

The roots are mildly diuretic. The whole plant probably has similar attributes to *Echinacea*.

Goldenrod   *Solidago spp.*

Solidago = So-li-dah-gō, from L. *solido*, "uniter", meaning to make whole or strengthen, referring to the medicinal qualities.

Identification: There are some eleven species of this genus in our mountains. This perennial herb has numerous clusters of yellow flower heads. The leaves are alternate, entire or toothed. The stems are usually slender and erect. It blooms mainly in late summer and autumn. Many of the species hybridize. The roots are fibrous.

Distribution & Habitat: Common in waste ground, gardens and dry to moist places throughout North America.

Preparation & Uses: The young leaves are used as a herb. Tea can be made from the dried leaves and from the dried, fully-expanded flowers.

This herb is listed as a moderate stimulant that is aromatic and can be used to cover the repellent taste of other herbs. It is good for weak bowels and used when the bladder has lost its muscular energies. An infusion of leaves and stems serves to ease colic pain. It is mixed with fat to make a poultice for sore throats.

Pineapple Weed
Matricaria matricaioides

Arrow-leaved coltsfoot
(flower stage)
Petasites sp.

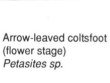

Arrow-leaved coltsfoot
Petasites sp.

Goldenrod
Solidago sp.

Goldenrod
Solidago sp.

An antiseptic lotion can be made from any of these species by boiling the stem and leaves, or by using dry, powdered mature leaves. A tea wash is said to be good for rheumatism, neuralgia and headaches. The sap is quite rubbery.

The Alabamas used the roots to make tea which was drunk for colds. Pieces of the root were sometimes put into the cavity of a tooth if it ached. Pioneers also used it for kidney stones, ulcer pain and diuretic properties.

The herb is also diuretic when warm and carminative when cold. It is often used to dissolve kidney stones. The dosage is 1 teaspoon of leaves in 1 cup of boiling water, steeped for 10 minutes.

A nice, yellowish-tan or golden dye can be made from these plants. The flowers are picked when coming into bloom. The mordant for yellow tan is alum; chrome for old gold. Put 1 to 1-½ pecks of goldenrod flowers in enough cold water to cover them and bring them to a boil. Boil for 1 hour or longer to extract the colour. Then strain the liquid into a bath for dye. For yellow-tan; put the alum mordant and wetted wool into lukewarm dye bath. Continue heating and simmer for 1 hour. Without rinsing then put the wool into a second bath containing 1/6 ounce of potassium dichromate and 1/6 ounce of acetic acid. Keep the wool moving while simmering for a further 15 minutes.

Rinse and dry. For old gold; put the wet wool into a lukewarm dye bath as soon as the chrome mordant has finished reacting. Simmer for 1 hour after boiling point is reached. Rinse well and dry in the shade.

Ragwort & Groundsel   *Senecio vulgaris* (and related species)

Senecio = se-ne-kee-ō, from Latin *senex* (an old man), referring to the fluffy white seed heads, *vulgaris* = L. "usual, common, vulgar".

Identification: The genus contains annual and perennial species. They grow 10 - 80 cm tall and are composites with yellow rays and yellow flower heads. This large and taxonomically complex genus usually has alternate and variously-toothed leaves.

Distribution & Habitat: Due to the large number of species and types, these plants enjoy considerable range in habitat. There are some 20 species in the mountains and foothills.

Preparation & Uses: The name groundsel is derived from Anglo-Saxon, meaning "ground swallow", referring to the rapid way it spreads or swallows the ground. Grieve lists *S. vulgaris* as diaphoretic, antiscorbutic, purgative, diuretic, anthelmintic and emollient. The herb has been used as a poultice and as a stomach soother. The weak infusion can be used as a simple, gentle and easy purgative whereas a strong infusion is used as an emetic. A decoction made with wine is said to be helpful for the stomach and bile flow and also in expelling gravel from the kidneys.

The "down" of the flower, mixed with apple cider vinegar is said to be a good dressing for wounds. Some old herbalists believed that if a root was smelt immediately upon digging it up, it would get rid of many types of headaches. No metal parts could be used in the digging of the root. It was also claimed to be especially good applied to wounds caused by iron.

S. aureus root and leaf tea was used by Amerindian women to regulate menses, vaginal discharge and for childbirth complications. It was also used for lung ailments, as a diuretic and as a mild astringent.

Chapped hands were often rubbed in a hot infusion of ragwort, successfully removing much of the roughness.

The recognized dosage is a dram of the juice or infusion taken internally.

Dandelion   *Taraxacum officinale*

Taraxacum = tair-axe-a-cum, G. *taraxos* means disorder, while *akos* means remedy, thus "Disturber" (from a Persian name for a bitter herb), *officinale* L. "sold in shops".

Identification: This common plant hardly needs identification. It is a perennial composite with a solitary yellow flower head, made up of many flowers. The stems are hollow with a milky juice. The leaves are in rosettes and are deeply pinnately toothed, arising from a fleshy tap root. The seeds are achenes with white pappus.

Distribution & Habitat: There is barely a lawn in the city that is void of this common herb. It is so plentiful that it is usually not considered a God-sent "gift".

> Dear common flower that grow'st beside the way
> Fringing the dusty road with harmless gold
> 'Tis the spring's largess which she scatters now
> To rich and poor alike with lavish hand
> Though most hearts never understand
> To take it at God's value, but pass by
> The offered wealth with unrewarded eye.
>
>   James Russell Lowell

Groundsel
Senecio vulgaris

Dandelion
Taraxacum officinale

Goat's Beard
Tragopogon sp.

Preparation & Uses: The young leaves of dandelion can be used for salads or cooked as greens if collected before the flowers appear. The best place to look for dandelion leaves is in deep shady areas covered with sand or leaf litter. The leaves of plants growing in such places are naturally blanched. These yellow or whitish leaves, which haven't had enough sunlight, are the tenderest and the best tasting. You can dig up a bunch of dandelion roots, plant them in boxes and store them in the basement. This is best done in the fall and will give you a natural, tasty "green" all winter.

A good salad can be made from blanched dandelion leaves, onions, radishes, parsley and a little sugar. The blanched leaves also taste good with diced eggs, vinegar and oil.

The leaves of dandelion are extremely high in Vitamin A. (Beta Carotene, pro-vitamin A, 7,000 I.U./oz). They are also an excellent source of B complex and Vitamin C.

The leaves of dandelion can also be cooked like spinach. If they are slightly bitter, because of age, the water should be changed once or twice. Cooked leaves can be dressed with crisp bacon, and hard boiled eggs. They can also be creamed into soups, scalloped or baked with meat.

I once found this interesting recipe for dandelion pancakes. Take young blossoms and drop the heads onto the pancake batter while it is cooking in a frying pan. When the pancakes are turned over, the heads will cook. This will add variety and colour to any camp breakfast.

The roots can be sliced and cooked like carrots or as a delicious addition to stew. Dandelion root can also be roasted slowly until dark brown inside, ground up and then brewed like coffee. For making coffee, it is best to dig up the roots in the autumn. This coffee has none of the side effects that caffeinated coffee has. In fact, it is very healthy and can be found commercially in many health food stores.

Both the leaves and roots were listed officially for several years in the British Pharmaceutical Codex and in the U.S. Dispensatory from 1831 - 1926 and the National Formulary until 1965. It has been listed as a medicinal plant since the tenth century.

The Mohegan Indians steeped the leaves for physic uses, whilst the Ojibwas Indians made a tea from the root for heartburn. Meskwaki Indians used the root for pains in the chest when other remedies failed. Kloss, in his famous book "Back to Eden", says dandelion has 28 parts sodium, making it a natural nutritive salt for purifying the blood and destroying acid in the blood. He usually used the roots. The roots of dandelion are also said to increase urine flow, while being slightly laxative. The roots are reported to be good for jaundice, skin diseases, scurvy, eczema, and useful for all kinds of kidney and liver troubles. Diabetics can use the dandelion as a very tasty coffee substitute. Lust says that dandelion can strengthen female organs.

This amazing plant can increase the activity of the liver, pancreas and spleen, and is especially good as a treatment for the enlargement of these organs. For bladder trouble, a tea is best made with cider vinegar.

It has also been reported that dandelion roots can lower blood sugar, have an antimicrobial effect (especially against *Candida albicans*) and be useful for weight loss. One of dandelion's major constituents, inulin, is known to be immunostimulatory. Dandelion has been shown to work against two tumor systems, stimulating macrophage action, thus substantiating the Chinese use of dandelion for breast cancer during the last 1,000 years.

The white latex of fresh dandelions is the best thing I have ever found for treating warts. Apply topically 3 times a day for 7 - 10 days. The warts will turn black and fall off. The seeds are used in China as a strong antibiotic, specific to the lungs.

Hobbs reports that dandelion can lower cholesterol and high blood pressure, while giving support for emotional problems, skin problems and P.M.S. After seeing all of these uses, one wonders why we want to destroy this wonderful "free health food pharmacy" that grows everywhere.

When you want to use dandelion, make sure you get it from an unsprayed area. Of course no description of dandelion would be complete without a recipe for dandelion wine. I found this one in Harrington's *Edible Plants Native to the Rocky Mountains*.

Dandelion Wine

1 gallon dandelion petals	4 lb. sugar
1 gallon boiling water	1 yeast cake(compressed)
4 oranges	1 lb. chopped raisins
1 lemon	1 slice toast

Pick the flower from the heads, throwing away the hollow stalk and the denuded heads. Place them in a crock or jar and pour the boiling water over them. Cover and leave for about five days, stirring several times during that period.

Strain off the liquid and add the sugar to it. Peel the orange and lemon and drop in peel, then add juices of these fruits and the chopped raisins. Boil for 20 minutes in a preserving kettle and return it to a crock.

Cool the liquid, place the yeast on the toast and put it in. Cover and leave for about 3 days. Then decant the liquid into jars or bottles. Some say that the wine should be aged for at least a year before using.

This wine has been claimed to have good tonic effects on the blood. If you would prefer a non-alcoholic drink of dandelion, try one developed by the University of Alaska Cooperative Extension Service:

100 small, washed dandelion leaves
1 ½ cups tomato juice
2 tablespoon Worcestershire sauce
Dash of tabasco

Place all ingredients in a blender, blend for 3 - 5 minutes.

Salsify   *Tragopogon porrifolius*

Tragopogon = trǎ-go-pō-gon, from Greek *tragos* (a goat) and *poson* (a beard) referring to the pappus of the fruit, *porrifolius* = po-ri-fo-lee-us, with leaves like *Allium porrum* or "leek-leaved".

Identification: This perennial or biennial has a large taproot 30 - 80 cm long from which the leaves and stem arise. The leaves are grass-like. The flower head is 5 - 10 cm across and is purple with the bract exceeding the floret. Related species (*T. dubius* and *T. pratensis*) have yellow flowers.

Distribution & Habitat: These garden plants are found growing wild in open areas throughout the West.

Preparation & Uses: The roots of both salsify and the goat's-beards are edible but those of the salsify are much larger and tastier. Salsify roots are cultivated and can be found in some gourmet shops and on the menu of some restaurants. Salsify is also called oyster plant and tastes something like a cross between parsnip and oyster. Goat's beard tastes more like parsnips.

The milky juice of salsify was sometimes used as a chewing gum by Indians and was considered a remedy for indigestion by the Greeks.

Arrowhead
Sagitarria cuneata

Pipsissewa
Chimaphila sp.

Bear Grass
Xerophyllum tenax

Yellow Puccoon
Lithospermum sp.

Hazelnut
Corylus sp.

229

Other Useful Plants

1. *Sagittaria latifolia*   Arrowhead or Wapato

Wapato tuber can be roasted, baked, boiled or ground into flour. The cooked stems are tasty but unpleasant when raw.

2. *Orobanche fasciculata*   Broom Rape

This entire plant is edible in salads or roasted. The decocted blanched or powdered seed eases joint and hip pain. It is also used as a toothache remedy.

3. *Mimulus guttatus*   Monkey Flower

The leaves were a source of salt for the Indians. The young leaves, shoots and stems are eaten cooked or raw, although they are bitter when raw. The stem and leaves can be used as a poultice for burns and wounds. It is also astringent.

4. *Atriplex spp.*   Orach

The young leaves are tender and taste pleasant raw or cooked throughout the summer. Orach is high in vitamins and minerals.

5. *Chimaphila umbellata*   Pipsissewa

The leaves can be eaten raw. The leaves and roots can be boiled for a tonic, high in Vitamin C. Pipsissewa produces a natural antibiotic that can be used by humans. Pipsissewa is used as an ingredient in commercial root beer.

6. *Veronica spp.*   Speedwell

The leaves and stems can be eaten raw or cooked, though a little bitter in older plants if eaten raw. Speedwell is rich in Vitamin C. Speedwell is listed as a cathartic, removing mucus and is used for colds, coughs, catarrh and asthma. It was in the U.S. Pharmacopeia from 1820 - 1916, off and on, under a variety of names and in the National Formulary from 1916 to 1955.

7. *Oenothera caespitosa*   Rock Rose

The leaves can be eaten and are best if blanched. They should be cooked in at least one change of water due to the plant's bitterness. The root can also be cooked. First year roots are preferred although they too are bitter. The Blackfoot Indians pounded the root, wet it and applied it to sores and wounds to reduce inflammation.

8. *Xerophyllum tenax*   Bear Grass

The roots are fibrous but can be eaten either boiled or roasted. The leaves were once used to make clothing and to decorate baskets.

9. *Lithospermum spp.*   Puccoon, Stoneseed

This plant was heavily used by many tribes throughout North America as a form of birth control in the form of a root tea. Degree of effect was said to vary from temporary sterility to permanent. Lithospermum has been shown to prevent gonadotrophin from stimulating ovaries in lab mice. Other endocrine glands also shrunk in size. Some tribes of Amerindians felt it should not be used, feeling if the blood flow stopped in the female area, it would start later in another area, such as the lungs. These herbs have also been burned as incense in ceremonies, as a skin and eye wash, for sores and for rheumatism.

10. *Corylus sp.*   Hazelnuts, Beaked

Just remove the husk and shell, and proceed to eat the nut. It can also be ground into a flour and used to make very delicious cakes (tortes).

Appendices

A. Glossary of botanical terms

B. Summary of herbal therapeutic groupings

C. Herbal preparations

D. Sources & Recommended Reading

Appendix A
Glossary of botanical terms

Achene - a small, 1 - seeded dry fruit differing from a nut in having thin walls.

Adventitous roots grow from a plant stem or leaf rather than from a true root system. (eg. strawberry or spider plants)

Alternate leaf - one leaf growing from a node.

Annuals plants complete their life cycle in a season. They live through the winter as a seed and come up each year as a seedling, flower, fruit, and then die (eg. strawberry blite). A special type of annual is an **ephemeral** which completes its entire life cycle in a month, weeks or even days. Many of the common weeds are this type.

Anthers - small compartments at the top of the stamen that produce the pollen and harbour the pollen sacks.

Apetalous - a flower that is missing the petal and may or may not be missing the sepals.

Axillary - located in or arising from the upper angle formed by a leaf or branch with the stem.

Basal leaf - a leaf that grows at the base of the plant. Also known as **rosettes**.

Biennials have a two year cycle, producing leaves and stems the first year, with flower and fruit in the second year, e.g. burdock.

Bisexual plants contain both sexes in the same flower.

Bract - special leaves that grow right at the base of the flower or inflorescences.

Bulb is a short thickening of an underground stem with many fleshy or scale-like leaves, appearing like a root, e.g. onions.

Calyx the name given to the collective of sepals, growing at the base of many flowers.

Carpel - the structure formed by more than one pistil in a flower (female sexual part of a flower).

Catkin - a scaly, spike or raceme bearing many small apetalous flowers (e.g. willow).

Cauline Leaf - grows above the base on the stem and below the bracts.

Coalescent - when part of the structure, particlarly the series of the flower parts, are united, eg. bluebell.

Composite - flower head made up of many flowers.

Compound leaves are leaves made up of several leaflets. (See pinnate and palmate.)

Cordate - heart-shaped.

Corm - an enlarged fleshy base of a stem, bulb-like.

Corolla the collective name for the petals of a flower.

Corymb is an inflorescenee of the raceme type (see raceme) that has a rounded or flat top.

Cyme is a determinate inflorescence.

Dicot (dicotyledons) flowering plants with two seed leaves in the embryo of the seed. Broad leaves with netted veins with tap or fibrous roots. Vascular bundles organized in concentric rings.

Dioecious - having distinct female and male plants in the species.

Drupe - a fleshy or pulpy fruit with a stone (e.g. plum).

Fibrous root - formed from a mass of thin spreading roots of fairly uniform size (e.g. grasses).

Floret - a small flower such as in grasses.

Follicle - a pod-like fuit opening on one side.

Glabrous - without hairs.

Herbacious - describing a plant with soft-tissued stems, which does not live from year to year.

Inflorescence - a grouping of flowers. There are two types: indeterminate and determinate. The indeterminate inflorescences have the terminal flower on the stem and grow last. In the determinate variety, the terminal flower grows first.

Internode - the space between nodes. (See nodes)

Leaflet - a structure appearing to be a leaf but really a part of a compound leaf. (See pinnate and palmate.)

Leaf blade - the main body of a leaf, whether a blade of grass or the body of a maple leaf.

Leaf margins If the margin is smooth and normal it is said to be entire. If the the margin is more or less regular with shallow indentations, the leaf is said to be toothed. If the indentations are numerous and deep they are said to be lobed. The following diagam shows some of the most common margins (edges) of leaves.

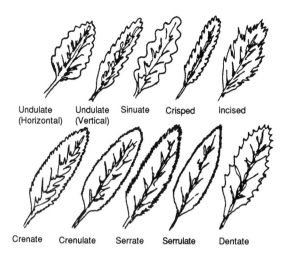

Undulate (Horizontal) Undulate (Vertical) Sinuate Crisped Incised

Crenate Crenulate Serrate Serrulate Dentate

Leaf Shape the following are the most common leaf shapes. We often find shapes that appear "in between" one form or another.

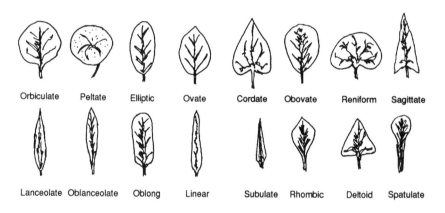

Orbiculate Peltate Elliptic Ovate Cordate Obovate Reniform Sagittate

Lanceolate Oblanceolate Oblong Linear Subulate Rhombic Deltoid Spatulate

Ligules - the elongated ray flowers in Compositae; a small thin projection from the top of the leaf-sheath, as in some grasses.

Midrib - the main or middle vein in a leaf which is usually larger than the rest of the veins.

Monocots (monocotyledons) A type of flowering plant that has one seed leaf, parallel veins in the leaves and fibrous roots. The vascular bundles are randomly organized.

Monoecious - describing a plant that is bisexual but each flower on the plant is either female or male.

Node a junction on a stem where the leaf grows from.

Ovary - a reproductive structure located at the base of the pistil which produces the seeds.

Ovules are parts of the ovary in the base of the female sexual parts of a plant.

Opposite leaves two leaves growing out of the same node.

Palmate is a leaf made up of several leaflets resembling the shape of a hand or palm (e.g. geranium).

Panicle - a compound raceme, spike or corymb inflorescence.

Pedicel - the first internode in the recepticle of a flower.

Peduncle - the second internode in the recepticle of a single flower.

Perianth - sepals and petals which are indistinguishable.

Perennials - plants that last for many years, surviving the dry or winter season, not only as a seed but as a root system. You can usually find dead stems from previous year's growth at ground level, eg. ginseng.

Petals - are usually the coloured part of the flower that attacts the insects. Collectively they are called the **corolla**.

Petiole the "stem" of a leaf.

Phloem - part of the plant's vascular distribution system, consisting of tubes that transport food nutrients.

Photosynthesis - the process of making carbohydrates, in chlorophyll-containing plants, in the presence of sunlight.

Pinnate - a leaf made up of many leaflets, resembling a feather, with the leaflet forming along the midrib, eg. rose.

Pistil - the female sexual part of a flower. If there is more than one they are known as carpels.

Prickle - a sharp, pointed growth on the side of the stem, e.g. roses.

Prostrate - flat on the ground.

Raceme - an inflorescence consisting of a main stem axis bearing single flowers alterately or spirally on the stalk.

Recepticles are found at the base of the flowering part and are made up of a series of crowded internodes.

Rhizome is a horizontal underground stem which serves as a means of food storage and asexual reproduction.

Runners - horizontal shoots of stems that produce adventitious roots (e.g. strawberries).

Sepals The outermost part of a flower. They often look like small leaves at the base of a flower but can be coloured and petal-like. Collectively, sepals are called the **calyx**.

Sessile - a leaf which appears to be attached directly to the stem.

Sheath - a sessile leaf appears to surround or sheath the stem.

Shrub a woody stemed plant with no main trunk but many major branches of similar size rising from the ground level.

Spike - raceme-like inflorescence with sessile flowers.

Spine is a sharp specialized stem that emerges from the ground, e.g. yucca.

Stamens are the male sexual parts of the flower. Collectively they are called the **androecium**.

Stem direction

Erect	- standing upright.
Creeping	- stem climbs, using other structures.
Diffuse	- spreading in all directions.
Declining	- stem bending towards vertical.
Decumbent	- stem resting on the ground with slightly raised tips.
Procumbent	- stem lies on the ground.
Prostrate	- same as procumbent.

Stigma is the top of the pistil (female sexual part of a flower) that receives the pollen from the male part.

Stolon a long stem that produces an adventitious root, e.g. black berries.

Styles - part connecting the ovary and stigma.

Taproot a single enlarged primary root, such as a carrot.

Terminal (raceme) - located at the end.

Ternate - divided into three parts.

Thorn specialized sharp pointed woody branch, eg. buckthorn.

Tree a woody stemmed plant with a main trunk rising from ground level. A tree is usually over 3 m tall when mature.

Tuber a thickening of a portion of a rhizome for food storage, eg. a potato.

Umbel - a flower cluster on pedicels all rising to the same level, similar to an upside-down umbrella.

Veins (leaf) a network of tubes on the blade of a leaf. The main vein is a midrib.

Whorled leaves three or more leaves growing from a node.

Xylem part of the plant's vascular distribution system, consisting of tubes of water-conducting cells. The xylem transport water up the stems.

Appendix B
Summary of Herbal Therapeutic Groups

Alteratives - cleaners of the blood system, tonic for the blood, gradually alter and correct impure blood conditions. Modify nutrition, clean lymphatic glands, overcome morbid processes.

Analgesics - relieves pain.

Anodynes - allay pain by reducing the sensitivity of the nerves. Can be used locally or on the whole body.

Antacids - neutralize acid in the stomach and intestines.

Anthelmintics -

(a) - cause the expulsion of worms from the stomach and intestines.

(b) - vermicides - destroy or kill intestinal worms without necessarily causing evacuation.

Antiarthritics - relieve problems of gout and other arthritic conditions.

Antiemetics - prevent or relieve vomiting.

Antihydropics - give relief from dropsy, also aid in voiding or evacuating urine.

Antilithics - relieve calculus problems (e.g. kidney stones, gall stones and deposits in joints and muscles).

Antioxidants - stops oxidation, especially from singlet O^*.

Antiscorbutics - prevent or cure scurvy. These are sometimes classified as alteratives.

Antiseptics - prevent putrification, cell decay, formation of pus or gangrene. They inhibit the growth of intruding organisms. Herbal antiseptics don't destroy tissue.

Antispasmodics - reduce or prevent involuntary muscle contraction (spasm) and relieve nervous irritation.

Antisyphilitics - relieve and cure venereal disease.

Aperients - mildy purgative to the bowels.

Aphrodisiacs - increase sexual power or excitement.

Aromatics - usually fragrant or spicy tasting herbs that stimulate the gastro-intestinal mucous membranes. They are also used to cover strong, bitter and unpleasant-tasting herbs.

Astringents - draws together, checks hemorrhage, stops diarrhea.

Bitters, simple - stimulate the gastro-intestinal mucous membrane without affecting the general system.

Calmatives - sedative, soothing.

Carminatives - contain a volatile oil which excites intestinal peristalsis and promotes the expulsion of gases. Prevent griping pains while using cathartics.

Cathartics - purgatives, cleaning waste material from liver, gall ducts and alimentary canal; excreting waste through the bowels.

Cholagogues - stimulate the secretion and flow of bile.

Convulsants - cause convulsions. Stimulants should always be used before convulsants (i.e. cayenne or peppermint).

Cordial - dilates the pupil of the eye.

Correctives (corrigents) - render more pleasant the strong action of other remedies, especially purgatives.

Counter-irritants - cause irritation or inflammation of the skin to relieve a deeper-seated problem.

Demulcents - soothe, soften and allay irritation of mucous membranes through mucilaginous and slippery properties. In poultices, they retain warmth and moisture while absorbing the pus discharge from the skin.

Deobstructants - overcome obstruction in the alimentary canal.

Deodorants - cover or destroy foul odours.

Depressants - sedatives.

Detergents - used for cleaning wounds, ulcers, boils, etc. Different from commercial detergents.

Diaphoretics - promote sweating.

Digestive - aids digestion.

Disinfectants - destroy noxious properties of decaying organic matter.

Diuretics - general increase of urine flow (see special classification).

Ecbolics - induce abortions.

Emetics - evacuate stomach contents by inducing vomiting.

Emmenagogues - promote menstrual flow and discharge; regulate menstruation to normal minimum instead of excess or lack.

Emollients - used to soften and protect tissue.

Evacuants - chiefly purgatives.

Expectorants - acting on the lungs to promotes discharge of mucous.

Febrifuges - dissipate fever by enhancing evaporation of perspiration (also known as antipyretics).

Galactagogues - increase secretion of milk.

Hemostatics - stop or prevent bleeding.

Hepatics - increase flow of bile and influence liver.

Hydragogues - promotes a water evacuation of the bowel.

Hypnotics - relax and promote sleep.

Hypoglycemics - lowers blood sugar.

Laxatives - mild purgatives.

Local anaesthetics - locally stop sensation.

Narcotics - powerful anodynes and/or hypnotics.

Nephritics - influence nephritia tubes of kidneys.

Nervines - nerve tonics.

Nutritives - substances which nourish the body and assist in assimilating food.

Palliative - to relieve or alleviate symptoms without curing.

Parasiticide - kills parasites.

Pectorals - relieve problems of the chest or lungs.

Peristaltics - increase peristalsis (the wave-like muscular contraction in the bowels).

Prophylactics - prevent disease.

Purgatives - cause powerful discharge from the bowels. Stronger than cathartics.

Rubefacients - to cause reddening of the skin by means of counter-irritation, e.g., mustard pack.

Refrigerants - cool the body temperature by promoting free perspiration. Also known as febrifuges and antipyretics.

Sedatives - calm or tranquilize by lowering functional activity.

Sialogogues - excite the salivary glands to secretion.

Soperifics - cause sleep. Also known as somnifacients.

Sorbefacients - cause absorption.

Specifics - direct curing powers to certain tissues, thereby aiding in certain diseases.

Stimulants - increase functional activity (see special classification).

Stomachics - stimulate and tone action of the stomach.

Styptics - externally astringent, causing contraction of the blood vessels, thereby stopping bleeding.

Sudorifics - produce profuse and visible sweating when taken hot. Act as tonic when taken cold.

Taenicides - kill tapeworms.

Tonics - permanently increase systematic tone by stimulating nutrition.

Vermicides - kill intestinal worms.

Vermifuges - cause expulsion of intestinal worms.

Vulneraries - promote healing of cuts and wounds.

Appendix C - Herbal Preparations

This appendix briefly reviews the basic methods of herbal preparation. Many of the old herbals and herb texts will have methods which vary slightly. Working with herbs is the first and best method of developing effective preparation methods.

Herbs are medicinal plants and the preparations made from herbs can be taken internally or they can be used externally. In the case of internal application, you have the choice between infusions, decoctions, macerations, juices, tinctures, extracts, powders, etc. External use requires poultices, lotions, compresses, dressings, eyebaths, gargles, enemas, boluses, etc.

An alphabetical list of preparations follows:

Bolus

A bolus is a suppository - shaped poultice intended for internal use. It is used internally in the rectum or vagina either to draw out toxic poisons or as a carrier for healing agents. A bolus for the vagina is usually about the thickness of the middle finger and about one inch in length. They are usually used in a series of three (which is more comfortable for the patient than the single three-inch bolus). Boluses are typically prepared warm, and then allowed to cool to the point where they can be easily shaped. They generally contain a powdered herbal agent(s) mixed with a base. A base of slippery elm and cocoa butter is one of the oldest forms and best.

Boluses consisting of a herbal mixture of slippery elm and cocoa butter oil are prepared as follows:

Heat cocoa butter over hot water (and not over direct heat, as it burns so rapidly) and then stir in the slippery elm and other desired herbs. Allow the preparation to cool and then roll it into several boluses about the width of your middle finger, cutting into one inch pieces. Set them aside and allow to harden. They are now ready for vaginal insertion, one after the other. Because the boluses will melt at body temperature, it is advisable to introduce a tampon after their insertion. The boluses should be inserted fresh every day. After 6 days a cleansing douche or rectal wash is used to cleanse the area.

Capsules

Herb capsules are easy to make. Simply take ground herbs and insert them into soluble hard gelatin capsules. Capsules come in various sizes - "000" to "5" - to permit easy swallowing; "5" is the smallest size while "000" is the largest. And why do we encapsulate herbs? Because they would otherwise be difficult to take- i.e. they may be very offensive to the taste. Or simply because of convenience.

Compound

A compound is a herbal formula. It is a preparation made up of two or more herbal agents which are organically compatible. Not all compounds are effective. We cannot always say that because one herb has property A and another has property B that the two of them together will give us properties A+B. Some of the ingredients contained in one may negate the value of some of the ingredients contained in the other. "Special Combinations" are often the result of many years of painstaking research and development.

Concentrate

Concentrates are fluid extracts that are strengthened through evaporation of their fluid. Alcohol concentrates are produced by allowing the alcohol to evaporate without in any way decreasing the strength of the herb. Water concentrates are usually made by slowly simmering the herbs until the volume of the extractive agent is reduced.

Decoction

A decoction is a water solution of plants extracts. They are prepared at a boiling temperature and differ from infusions in that coarse and brittle plant structures - i.e. the roots, bark and chips - comprise the decoction substances. Because of their volatile nature, decoctions are intended for immediate use, and should typically be put to use within twenty-four hours. Some authorities state that they should not be kept longer then six hours before application. The longevity of decoctions may be increased by the use of certain preserving agents, such as glycerin, or refrigeration. A standard decoction consists of fifty grams of closely ground plant material in 1000 cc. of cold water. The procedure of preparation is as follows:

The ground plant (approximately 50 gms.) should be placed into a vessel which has a lid cover (Never use aluminum or iron cookware - stainless steel, porcelain or pyrex cookware is suitable), and then one quart (1000 cc.) of cold water should be added. Mix, and then place the vessel over heat and bring to a boil and simmer for fifteen to twenty minutes. Remove from the heat and cool to about body temperature. Then, pour the decoction into a jar through a suitable strainer. Since some of the fluid will have evaporated during boiling, you will end up with less than one quart of fluid.

Enema

An enema is the introduction of a large amount (three to eight cups) of liquid into the bowel via an enema tube. An enema is carried out to disencumber an obstructed bowel, to cleanse it, or to serve as a means of introducing nutrition into the body when an individual is unable to take nourishment otherwise. A good cleansing enema consists of warm (not hot) water and nothing else, although herbs (like coffee) can be used for special purposes.

Extract

An extract is a solution of the essential constituents of a herbal agent. It is prepared by boiling the plant material in water and then evaporating the strained decoction to a desired concentration. Extracts harbor the more active principles of the medicinal plants., Various solvents may be used, including alcohol, water, glycerine, etc. Extracts should always be prepared at the lowest temperature possible that is compatible with good extraction of the healing principles. If care is not taken, some of the lighter and more volatile oils and other important ingredients may be lost. In addition, the vessel in which the extract is prepared should always be tightly covered until such time as the extract has reached a sufficiently cool temperature (ie. body temperature).

Fluid Extracts

A fluid extract is an alcohol or glycerin preparation of herbal extract containing the active constituents in a definite ratio of plant material to solvent. There are several types of fluid extracts.

Heated Extracts are prepared by boiling (but preferably simmering) a herbal agent in water and then evaporating the strained decoction to a desired concentration - this yields a more concentrated herbal remedy.

A **Fluid extract** is made by evaporating an already prepared fluid (such as an infusion or decoction) to the desired concentration.

A **Cold Extract** is similiar to an infusion. It is prepared by taking twice as much herb as is desired for an infusion and then letting it sit in an enamel or non-metallic pot for eight to twelve hours. It is then strained and taken as one would take an infusion.

Glycerin is often used as a preserving agent in extracts. Glycerin can be derived from a vegetable or petroleum base. Preferably, use only the glycerine which has come from a vegetable base.

Fomentation

A fomentation is a herbal preparation used to draw out poison, allay irritation, reduced inflammation, or relieve pain. To make a fomentation, prepare the herb as a tea (as either an infusion or decoction), strain, and then absorb it into a piece of muslin, cotton wool, turkish towel, flannel or gauze (natural fibre material). Wring out the cloth sufficiently so that it is not dripping and then place it on the affected area. Fomentations are usually applied as hot as can be tolerated and then reapplied as they cool or dry. The fomented area is often covered with a sheet of plastic and then a towel to keep it moist and hot. A hot apple cider vinegar fomentation is excellent for arthritis, rheumatism and other types of aches.

Infusion

Infusions are prepared by steeping a herbal agent in liquid, usually water. Domestic teas are usually prepared this way - herbs are submerged in hot or boiling water and allowed to steep for a certain length of time. Cold infusions are made in a similar manner, the only difference being that cold water is used, often dripping the water slowly over the herb. Generally, infusions are made from the more delicate parts of the plant, such as the buds, leaves, or flowers (you will recall that decoctions are prepared from the coarser parts, such as the roots, bark or chips).

Injection

An injection is a small 1 - 2 cup enema or vaginal douche (obviously, the term is not synonymous with the hypodermic needle injection of allopathic medicine).

Juice

Juices, also called "expresses", are prepared by juicing a fresh herb, with great emphasis on the word "fresh". The juicing can be done with either an electric juicer, or hand juicer, or a press. Juices are typically the best embodiment of the active ingredients of a herb. Juices may also be extracted by placing the herbs, wrapped in muslin cloth, in a mortar and then crushing them with a pestle.

Liniment

A liniment is a liquid or semi-liquid preparation of a herb. Liniments are applied to relieve skin irritation and muscle pain and include herbal oils, tinctures, or liquids and are intended for application to the skin by gentle friction or massage. Liniments are thinner than ointments and have application primarily as anodynes (pain relievers) or counter - irritants.

Maceration

Maceration is a term synonymous with cold infusion. The herb (approximately 50 gms.) is placed in a 1000 cc. menstruum (usually alcohol but potentially water.)

Oils

Oils are prepared by taking a specified amount of herbs and mixing them, crushed or whole (depending on the herbs), with a botanical oil. The amount of oil used depends on the herb and the desired strength of the final preparation, but two parts of oil for each part of herb is regarded as an ideal ratio. Some oils, such as Balm of Gilead, are best heated (but not boiled) for a given length of time (e.g. 20 minutes), while others, such as garlic oil, are best steeped for several days, and then strained. Always use an oil of high quality, such as a cold-pressed olive or almond oil.

Essential oils differ from oil preparations as these are the volatile oils present in the herb (e.g. clove oil, cinnamon oil.)

Ointment

Sometimes called salves, ointments are soft, semi-solid herbal preparations, prepared as follows:

A herbal preparation (i.e. an infusion or decoction) is placed in an oil and the water is evaporated. The result is then mixed with heated lanolin or lard. Melted beeswax is subsequently mixed in until the desired consistency is obtained. And there is your ointment! A little gum benzoin or a drip of tincture of benzoin is a helpful preservative. In hotter climates, more beeswax is necessary to maintain stiffness. In general, salves tend to have less beeswax than ointments.

Paste

A paste is a mixture of herbs and water (or sometimesoil) with a muddy consistency.

Poultice

A poultice is a soft, usually heated, semi-liquid herbal mass which is spread on a cloth and then applied to an area of the body. A bruised herb is mixed with water, heated, applied to a cloth, and placed on the appropiate area. The poultice is easily applied if heaped onto a cloth and then wrapped or placed on the desired area. The cloth should be moistened frequently to keep it wet and heated. Non-irritating herbs come in direct contact with the skin. While most poultices can be left in contact with skin for a long time, those that can act as irritants should be applied for short periods only (a mustard plaster or this type of poultice needs a layer of wax paper between the poultice and skin). After removing the poultice, it is advisable to wash the treated area, using water or a herbal tea (such as chamomile or mugwort). Covering the area with plastic will keep the water from evaporating and permit its absorption into the skin. The area may also be covered with a towel to keep the heat in.

Salve

A salve is similar to an ointment but is thinner and uses less bee's wax.

Smudge

A smudge is a dried herb, mixed with water and then placed on hot coals. The steam which results is inhaled, or used as a "wash" for one's spirit or aura. This method of herbal application was widely used by many tribes of Amerindians.

Syrup

A syrup is a thick, sticky, liquid-like preparation. A herbal syrup is made by taking a herbal agent and boiling, simmering, or heating it in honey and/or glycerin, and then straining it through cheese cloth. Often a tea is made first then strained, concentrated and then the syrup or glycerine or honey is added. Syrups are especially useful for administering medicines to children or fussy adults. Some syrups are made in a vegetable base.

Tincture

Technically, tinctures are fluid extracts, but here the medicinal virtues are withdrawn into an alcohol, glycerin, or vinegar solution (acid tincture) since water alone, in this instance, will not retrieve some of the medicinal principles. The menstruum (the alcohol, glycerine, etc.) also acts as a preservative. A typical tincture is prepared by steeping one part herb in two parts of alcohol for ten to fourteen days (maceration.) The resulting mixture is then strained, poured into a sealed jar, stored in a dark place, and shaken twice daily. It has been found that tinctures increase in potency during the first ten to fourteen days after macerating and then decrease slightly in strength subsequently. A herb prepared in tincture form will last virtually forever.

Astrologers and alchemists have discovered that commencing the preparation of the tincture at the time of the new moon and carrying it through to the full moon will result in a stronger tincture.

Appendix D - Sources & Recommended Reading

Angier, Bradford, Field Guide to Edible Wild Plants, Stackpole Books, Harrisburg, PA, 1974.

Beasley, Henry, The Druggist's General Receipt Book(7th ed.), Lindsay & Blakiston, 1871.

Brown, Tom, Tom Brown's Guide to Wild Edible and Medicinal Plants, Berkeley Books, NY, 1985.

Brown, Annora, Old Man's Garden, Gray's Publishing Ltd., Sydney, B.C., 1970.

Christopher, Dr. John R., School of Natural Healing, Biworld Publ., Provo, Utah, 1976.

Coombes, Allen J., Dictionary of Plant Names, Timber Press, Inc., Portland, OR, 1985.

Craighead, J.J., Craighead, F.C. and Davis, R.J., A Field Guide to Rocky Mountain Wildflowers, Houghton-Mifflin Co., Boston, 1963.

Culpeper's Complete Herbal, W. Foulsham & Co., London, U.K., n.d..

Erichsen-Brown, Charlotte, Medicinal and Other Uses of North American Plants, Dover Publications, Inc., New York, 1989.

Foster, S. and Duke, J.A., Eastern/Central Medicinal Plants, Houghton-Mifflin Co., Boston, 1990.

Gledhill, D., The Names of Plants (2nd edition), Cambridge University Press, Cambridge, U.K., 1989.

Grieve, M., A Modern Herbal, Jonathan Cape, London, U.K.,1985 reprint.

Gunther, Erna, Ethnobotany of Western Washington, University of Washington Press, Seattle, WA, 5th printing (paper), 1988.

Harrington, H.D., Edible Native Plants of the Rocky Mountains, University of New Mexico Press, Albuquerque, NM, 1967.

Hart, J., Montana – Native Plants and Early Peoples, Montana Historical Society, Helena, MT, 1976.

Hellson, John, C. (& Gadd, B.), Ethnobotany of the Blackfoot Indians, National Museums of Canada, Ottawa, ON, 1974.

Hobbs, Christopher, Taraxacum officinale in Elstat, E.K., Eclectic Dispensatory of Botanical Therapeutics, Vol. 1, Eclectic Medical Publ., Portland, OR, 1989.

Hutchens, A.R., Indian Herbalogy of North America, Merco Press, Windsor, Ont. 1973.

Jason, D. & N, et al., Some Useful Wild Plants, Talonbooks, Vancouver, B.C., 1975.

Johnston, A., Plants and the Blackfoot, Lethbridge Historical Society, Lethbridge, Alta., 1987.

Kephart, H., Camping and Woodcraft (Vol.1), Macmillan Publishing Co., Inc., New York, 29th printing, 1973.

Kingsbury, John, M., Poisonous Plants of the United States and Canada, Prentice-Hall, Inc., Englewood Cliffs, NJ, 1964.

Kirk, Donald R., Wild Edible Plants of the Western United States, Naturegraph Publishers, Healdsburg, CA, 1970.

Kloss, J., Back to Eden, Woodbridge Press, Santa Barbara, CA, 1972.

Lampe, K.F. and McCann, M.A., AMA Handbook of Poisonous and Injurious Plants, American Medical Association, Chicago, IL, 1985.

Lust, John B., The Herb Book, Bantam Books, NY, 1974.

Medsger, O.P., Edible Wild Plants, Collier-Macmillan Publ., New York, 1974.

Moerman, D., Medicinal Plants of Native America, Univ. of Michigan Museum of Anthropology, Technical Reports, Number 19, Ann Arbor, MI, 1986.

Moore, Michael, Medicinal Plants of the Mountain West, Museum of New Mexico Press, Sante Fe, NM, 1979.

Moore, Michael, Medicinal Plants of the Desert and Canyon West, Museum of New Mexico Press, Santa Fe, NM, 1989.

Moss, E.H., Flora of Alberta (2nd edition), University of Toronto Press, Toronto, ON, 1983.

Nowell, Dr., Dominion Herbal College course on herbology, Vancouver, BC, 1962.

Porslid, A.E., Rocky Mountain Wild Flowers, National Museums of Canada, Ottawa, Canada, K1A 0M8, 1979.

Rose, Jeanne, Herbs & Things, 1974.

Schofield, Janice J., Discovering Wild Plants, Alaska Northwest Books, Anchorage, AK, 1989.

Scully, Virginia, A Treasury of American Indian Herbs, Crown Publishers, Inc., 1970.

Shook, Edward E., Advanced treatise on herbology, mimeograph, n.p.

Stearns, Samuel, The American Herbal or Materia Medica, Thomas & Thomas, N.H., 1801.

Sweet, Muriel, Common Edible & Useful Plants of the East and Midwest, Naturegraph Publishers, Inc., Happy Camp, CA, 1975.

Train, P., et al., Medicinal Uses of Plants by Indian Tribes of Nevada, Quarterman Publications, Inc., Lawrence, MA, 1978.

Treben, Maria, Health through God's Pharmacy, Wilhelm Ennsthaler, Steyr, Austria, 1982.

Turner, Nancy, & Kuhnlein, Harriet V., Traditional Plant Foods of Canadian Indigenous Peoples, Gordon and Breach Science Publishers, Phila., PA, 1991.

Vogel, Virgil J., American Indian Medicine, Ballatine Books, New York, 1973.

Willard, T. L., Textbook of Modern Herbology, c.w. Progressive Publishing Co., Calgary, Alberta, 1988.

Willard, T.L., Wild Rose Scientific Herbal, Wild Rose College of Natural Healing, Ltd., Calgary, Alberta, 1991.

Willard, T.L., Textbook of Advanced Herbology, Wild Rose College of Natural Healing, Ltd., Calgary, Alberta, 1992.

Index

Boldface page numbers indicate a photograph.

Colds
  arbutus 163
  aspen 66
  biscuit root 155
  cedar, red 34
  cranesbill geranium 134
  crowberry 135
  currants 107
  devil's club 151
  echinacea 212
  elderberry 191
  fir 35
  goldenrod 221
  horsemint 178
  juniper 33
  Labrador Tea 167
  lovage 154
  mallow 139
  meadowsweet 126
  ocean spray 113
  onion, nodding 46
  pearly everlasting 199
  pineapple weed 218
  raspberry 122
  sarsaparilla, wild 150
  skullcap 182
  spruce 38
  stonecrop 103
  vacciniums 169
  wormwood 203, 206
  yarrow 198
Colic
  bitter root 84
  bunch berry 159
  cow parsnip 153
  goldenrod 219
  gumweed 215
  horsemint 178
  rose, wild 118
  salal 166
  wormwood 206
Colon problems
  fireweed 146
  fleabane 212
Coltsfoot 218, **220**
  pansy formula 142
Columbine 91, **92**
Cone Flowers 211
Constipation
  alder 69
  buckbean 174
  clover, red 131
  devil's club 151
  larch 37
Consumption
  chokecherry 115

tiger lily 51
Convalescent
  salal 166
Convulsion
  false hellebore 55
  self-heal 179
  skullcap 180
Cordial
  sarsaparilla, wild 148
Corns
  milkweed 175
  sundew 102
Cornus canadensis 158, **160**
Cornus nuttali 159
Cornus stolonifera 159, **161**
Corylus sp. **229**, 231
Cosmetic
  elderberry 191
Cotton Root
  snow brush formula 136
Cough syrup
  lovage 154
  marsh marigold 94
Coughs
  balsam poplar 62
  biscuit root 155
  bluebell 197
  cedar, red 34
  chokecherry 115
  coltsfoot 219
  homeopathic prairie crocus 91
  Labrador Tea 167
  mallow 139
  milkweed 175
  mullein 186
  nettle 74
  pansy 141
  pearly everlasting 199
  purslane 85
  salal 166
  sarsaparilla, wild 148, 150
  speedwell 230
  sundew 102
  sunflower 217
  tiger lily 51
  wintergreen 162
  wormwood 206
  yampa 158
Coughs, dry hacking
  gumweed 215
Counterirritant
  balsam poplar 63
  baneberry 89
  clematis 95
  dogbane 174
  nettle 74

Muscular pains
  rose, wild 118
Mushrooms, poisonous
  wormwood 204
Narcotic
  chokecherry 115
  dogwood, red-osier 160
  Labrador Tea 166
  larkspur 96
  wormwood 204
Nausea
  chokecherry 115
  cow parsnip 153
  false hellebore 57
  horsemint 178
  mountain ash 122
  raspberry 122
  red elderberry 192
  sundew 102
Neck sores
  self-heal 179
Nephritic
  balsam poplar 63
  bearberry 164
Nephritic problems
  wintergreen 162
Nettles **72**
Nerve root 59
Nerve tonic
  valerian 195
Nervine
  arnica 203
  cranberry 194
  false hellebore 57
  Labrador Tea 167
  skullcap 180
  valerian 195
Nervous conditions
  valerian 195
Nervous irritability
  snow brush 136
Nervous irritation
  skullcap 180
Nervousness
  Labrador Tea 166
Neuralgia
  goldenrod 221
  nettle 73
Nosebleeds
  horsemint 178
  silverweed 114
  yarrow 199
Nuphar variegatum 87, **88**
Nutrient
  alfalfa 129
Nutritive
  balsam poplar 63

Nymphaea spp. 87, **88**
Nymphomania
  false hellebore 57
Ocean Spray 112
Oenothera caespitosa 230
Oenothera spp. 147, **148**
Omega 6 essential fatty acids 108
Onion, Nodding **45**, 46
Oplopanax horridum 27, **149**, 150
Opuntia sp. 142, **144**
Orach 230
Oregon Grape 98
Orobanche fasciculata 230
Osha 154
Osmorhiza occidentalis 155, **156**
Ovarian cysts
  snow brush 136
Ox-eye daisy 208, **209**
Oxalate poisoning
  sorrel, mountain 75
Oxyria digyna 75
Oxytropis sp. 23, **24**
P.M.S
  licorice 127
Pacific Dogwood 159
Pain
  flax seed 134
  mullein 186
Pain, abdominal
  sarsaparilla, wild 150
Panacea
  biscuit root 155
Pancakes
  vacciniums 167
Pansy 141
Paper Birch 70
Paralysis
  bunch berry 159
  pearly everlasting 200
Parasites
  Labrador Tea 167
Parasiticide
  larkspur 96
Partridgeberry 170
Pearly everlasting 178, 199, **201**
Peas 23
Pectoral
  chokecherry 115
  Labrador Tea 167
  sarsaparilla, wild 148
Pectoral antispasmodic
  nettle 73
Pedicularis lanata 184, **185**
Pegs
  green ash 143

Pemmican
  hawthorn 110
  rose, wild 118
Pennyroyal
  skullcap use 182
Peptic ulcers
  alfalfa 129
Perfume
  bedstraw 189
  pineapple weed 218
Perideridia gairdneri 157
Periwinkle 174, **176**
Perspiration
  lousewort 184
Petasites spp. 218, **220**
Phacelia spp. 27
Phosphorus
  nettle 71
Physic
  dandelion 225
Picea spp. 38, **40**
Pickle
  solomon's seal, false 53
Pies
  barberry 98
Pigweed 78, 79, **80**
Piles
  alum root 105
  cedar, red 34
  evening primrose 147
  nettle 73
  ox-eye daisy 208
  yarrow enema 198
Pilocarpine 173
Pimples
  balsam poplar 65
  bistort 76
  horsemint 178
Pin cherry 114, **116**
Pin Cushion cactus 142, **144**
Pin worms
  bilberry 170
Pineapple Weed 218, **220**
Pinus contorta 39, **40**
Pinworm
  indian hemp 173
Pinworms
  wormwood 204
Pipe 9
Pipe stems
  green ash 143
Pipsissewa **228**, 230
Placenta
  tiger lily 51
Plantago major 186, **188**
Plantain **188**
  yarrow formula 198

Plantain, Common 186
Platelet aggregation
  flax seed 134
Pleurisy
  sarsaparilla, wild 150
Pneumonia
  biscuit root 155
  devil's club 151
  false hellebore 55
  mint, wild 178
  nettle 74
Poison
  echinacea 211
  prairie crocus 91
  red elderberry 192
Poison Ivy 22, **24**
  alder 69
  bunch berry 159
Poison ivy rash
  thistle 211
Poison ivy/oak
  gumweed 215
Poison Oak 22
Poison Sumac 22
Poisonous Plants 21
Polygonum spp. 75
Pond Lily **88**
Popcorn substitute 87
Poplar 33, **64**
Populin
  paper birch 70
Populus tremuloides **64**, 65
Portulaca oleracea 84
Potassium
  nettle 71
Potentilla anserina **113**
Potentilla fruticosa 114, **116**
Poultices
  larch 37
Prairie Cone Flower 219
Prairie Crocus **92**
Prana 16
Pre-menstrual syndrome
  currants 108
Pregnancy
  raspberry 122
  sarsaparilla, wild 148
Pregnancy cramps
  cranberry 194
Pregnancy warning
  bearberry 164
  burdock 202
  lodgepole pine 41
Premenstrual syndrome
  dandelion 226
  evening primrose 147

Prickly Pear cactus 142, **144**
Prophylactic
    echinacea 212
Prostate inflammation
    yucca 58
Prostatitis
    aspen 66
Protoveratrine 57
Prunella vulgaris 179, **181**
Prunus pennsylvanica 114, **116**
Psoriasis
    evening primrose 147
    larch 37
    sphagnum moss dressings 28
Puccoon **229**, 231
Pulmonary complaints
    chickweed 86
Pulmonary infections
    Labrador Tea 167
Pulmonary problems
    fir 35
Pungent
    mint, wild 177
Purgative
    camas 49
    devil's club 151
    larkspur 96
    ragwort 222
    solomon's seal, false 53
Purple bee's-balm 178
Purslane 84
Pyrola sp. **161**, 162
Qi 16
Rabies
    echinacea 211
    skullcap 180
Racks
    green ash 143
Ragwort 27, 222
Raisins
    vacciniums 169
Ranunculus spp. 22, **24**
Rashes
    balsam poplar 65
    fireweed 146
    gumweed 215
    sumac 135
Raspberry 119, **120**
Raspberry, red
    rose, wild formula 118
Ratibida columnifera 219
Rauwolfia 57
Rectal hemorrhage
    barberry 99
Red Cedar, Western 34, **36**
Red Clover 131

Red elderberry 26
Red Osier Dogwood 159, **161**
Red Root 136
Refrigerant
    barberry 98
    bilberry 170
    cleaver 189
    currants 107
    horsemint 178
Relaxant
    pineapple weed 218
Renal conditions
    clover, red 131
Respiratory ailments
    mallow 139
    sundew 102
Respiratory catarrh
    bilberry 170
Respiratory problems
    cow parsnip 153
    juniper 33
    lodgepole pine 41
Restlessness
    skullcap 180
Retinal damage
    chicory 210
Rhamnus alnifolia **137**, 138
Rhamnus purshiana 138, **140**
Rheum spp. 22
Rheumatic disease
    pansy 142
Rheumatic gout
    strawberry 112
Rheumatic joints
    arbutus 163
    fir 35
    gumweed 215
Rheumatic pain
    clover, red 131
    nettle 74
    plantain 187
    spring beauty 82, 83
Rheumatic problems
    larch 37
Rheumatic stiffness
    chicory 210
Rheumatic swelling
    milkweed 175
Rheumatism
    alder 69
    aspen 66
    balsam root 207
    biscuit root 155
    buckbean 174
    burdock 202
    devil's club 151

Other Books written by Terry Willard, Ph.D.

Helping Yourself with Natural Remedies

A general guide to natural health care organized by ailment and extensively illustrated and indexed. Perfect for the interested layperson. *Helping Yourself* includes practical programs for the most common health problems using herbs, minerals, vitamins and behavioural changes. (126 pp.)

Textbook of Modern Herbology

A first year text for the aspiring herbalist, *The Textbook of Modern Herbology* is the basis for the Introductory Herbology course at the Wild Rose College of Natural Healing. The *Textbook* integrates human physiology, botany, biology and herbal lore to provide a solid foundation for future study. (411 pp., hard cover)

Reishi Mushroom: Herb of Spiritual Potency and Medical Wonder

An exciting account of Dr. Willard's search for the elusive truth about Reishi mushroom, long a revered herb in the Orient. The reader follows Terry from mainland China to the coastal rain forest of British Colombia and finally into the modern clinics of North America. Fully referenced with both modern biochemical research and ancient folklore – the new standard on this herb in the English language. (167 pp.)

Wild Rose Scientific Herbal

For the practicing herbalist or the serious student, the *Wild Rose Scientific Herbal* integrates the information of a entire herbal library under a single cover. Over 125 herbs are described, illustrated and discussed. Information from modern phytochemistry is thoughtfully blended with the energetic descriptions of traditional Chinese and Ayurvedic medicine. (416 pp., hard cover)

The Textbook of Advanced Herbology

The culmination of a decade of research, the Textbook is a brand new kind of reference – a review of the biochemical families of herbal constituents from the herbalist's perspective. The reader is introduced to basic chemistry and then to the families or groups of active chemical constituents found in plants. Each chapter contains a "mini materia medica" which ties medicinal plants to the particular chemical family. Extensively illustrated and indexed. A required text at herbal colleges in several parts of the world. (436 pp., hard cover)

The Wild Rose College of Natural Healing

The College was established in 1975 and provides classroom courses in Calgary, Alberta and Vancouver, British Columbia. A correspondence option offers diplomas in herbology and wholistic health therapy to students around the world. Accreditation is through the Canadian Association of Herbal Practitioners. Please contact the College for further information.

FAX / Mail Order Form

FAX to: (403) 283-0799
Mail to: Wild Rose College of Natural Healing
400-1228 Kensington Rd. N.W.
Calgary, Alberta
T2N 4P9
Voice: (403) 270-0936

Helping Yourself With Natural Remedies	$17.50	———
Textbook of Modern Herbology	$55.00	———
Reishi Mushroom: Herb of Spiritual Potency and Medical Wonder	$17.50	———
Wild Rose Scientific Herbal	$65.00	———
Textbook of Advanced Herbology	$65.00	———
Edible and Medicinal Plants of the Rocky Mountains	$25.00	———
Wild Rose College Calendar	$3.00	———
Shipping and Handling ($3.00 for first item, plus $1.00 for each additional item except calendar)		———
Canadian customers: add 7% G.S.T.		———
Total value of order		

PLEASE PRINT

Name: _____

Street Address: _____

City: _____   State or Province: _____

Country: _____   Postal or ZIP Code: _____

METHOD OF PAYMENT   Money Order ☐   Personal Cheque ☐

VISA/MC # _____   Exp. Date: _____

Signature: _____